PET SENSE

PET SENSE

CARING FOR PETS AND NATIVE FAUNA

JENNIE CHURCHILL B.V.Sc.

illustrated by John Readhead

ANGUS
& ROBERTSON

AN ANGUS & ROBERTSON BOOK

First published in Australia in 1990 by
Collins/Angus & Robertson Publishers Australia

Collins/Angus & Robertson Publishers Australia
Unit 4, Eden Park, 31 Waterloo Road, North Ryde
NSW 2113, Australia
William Collins Publishers Ltd
31 View Road, Glenfield, Auckland 10, New Zealand
Angus & Robertson (UK)
16 Golden Square, London W1R 4BN, United Kingdom

National Library of Australia
Cataloguing-in-Publication data:

   Churchill, Jennie, 1951–
   Pet sense: caring for pets and native fauna.

   Includes index.
   ISBN 0 207 16211 5.

   1. Pets. 2. Wildlife rescue–Australia. I. Readhead,
   John, 1933–   . II. Title.

Typeset in 10.5pt New Baskerville
Printed by Griffin Press

 5 4 3 2 1
95 94 93 92 91 90

Contents

Preface

Animals and people can mean a great deal to one another. Pets are totally reliant on their owners for sustenance and shelter, and in return give pleasure, enjoyment and, above all, companionship.

Research has shown that humans may benefit in other ways from the development of a close rapport with an animal friend. Stress levels decrease significantly when humans have a faithful pet to communicate with and to touch. Pets are suddenly taking on an important therapeutic role as dogs, cats and other furred and feathered creatures invade homes for the aged, prisons and hospitals. Animals have been the means to a communication breakthrough with introverted children, the depressed elderly, and aggressive delinquents. Vets and animal lovers, of course, have known about these special qualities for a very long time.

So that we may enjoy and care for the animals that surround us, we must first learn about their needs and habits. Too few pet owners take the time to acquire even the most basic knowledge about the new addition to their family, and become tied to their pet by necessity rather than by desire. This book will hopefully provide the starting point to a better understanding of the animals we keep as pets, and to our responsibilities as pet owners. It is not a veterinary textbook but rather a guide to pet care, with advice on routine health care, behaviour, feeding, housing and possible emergency situations. Descriptions of diseases are included as references and to increase the pet owner's awareness of symptoms of illness.

The inclusion of Australian native animals, birds and reptiles is geared to helping those many people amongst the Australian public who are at last becoming aware of our heritage, and who are willing to devote so much time and energy towards its preservation. All Australians must begin to care about our unique fauna.

Many skilled and learned people, both vets and members of the public devoted to the welfare of animals, have shared their knowledge in the writing of this book, and have patiently read the chapter that pertains to their specialisation. I would like to thank particularly Helen George, Robert Ratcliffe, Jim Gill, Peter Light, Jim Stopford, Derek Spielman and Jenny Readhead. Brian Rich of Wombaroo Products has kindly allowed the use of his tabulated ageing factors in the native animal chapter. Permission was kindly granted by R. Strahan and H. Cogger to use the distribution maps from their informative books on marsupials and reptiles, and written material on the orphaned joey and on birds by veterinarians Richard Speare, Tessa Frazer-Oakley and Ross Perry was invaluable. Thanks also go to Humphrey, Anne and family. Finally, my friend John Readhead deserves special thanks for interpreting some difficult illustrations with patience and skill, and for his enthusiastic creative input.

A life spent living and working with animals is alternatively frustrating and rewarding, funny and sad. It is never, ever dull. Sharing this life with me is another vet who, despite the constant interruptions of a country practice, managed to plough through this manuscript and cheerfully tolerated a wife who became inseparable from her word processor.

Jennie Churchill
Crookwell, 1989

CHAPTER 1

DOGS

The history of the relationship between the dog (*Canis familiaris*) and the human race is still speculative. Wild hunting and scavenging dogs would have obviously benefited from living in close association with man, and *Homo sapiens* would have tolerated an animal that cleaned up the remains of a hunt and warned of impending dangers. Ancient rock paintings indicate that eventually both began to hunt together, and at some stage the dog was accepted as a friend and a useful member of the family group. The process has been called 'mutual domestication', as man and the dog adopted each other. Ever since, dogs have been an integral part of human society.

Dogs make wonderful pets and companions. They are affectionate, trusting, loyal and lots of fun. Many an Australian household would feel empty if it didn't include a dog. However, the dog–human bond that, at its best, provides this special relationship is not easily achieved. Many of these 'average' households contain unhappy dogs with disgruntled owners because the basics of dog ownership are never considered. If you want to own a dog ask yourself the following basic questions.

Can I afford a dog? The larger the dog the more it will consume. The house yard may need to be fenced. Added costs are regular vaccinations and worming, registration, illnesses or accidents, boarding kennels and grooming gear. If you can't afford to desex it, you can't afford a dog.

Do I have the time? All dogs need daily exercise. Long-haired dogs must have daily grooming. You must also have time to spend just giving your dog attention and companionship.

Do I really want a dog? Is this a whim, or will a dog always be welcome in the household? The whole family should make decisions regarding the part the dog will play in the home and, equally importantly, whether they can ensure the dog's happiness.

What type of dog do I want? The decision between large or small should be made on the size of your backyard, the age of the owners (large dogs can be a handful for older people or small children) and the amount of daily exercise the dog will get. You must also decide between a pedigreed dog or a cross-breed. Pedigreed dogs cost more, but apart from this the choice is personal. Also, what sex will be most suitable? In general, female dogs are often cleaner, less likely to roam and are more interested in their home environments than males.

Where do I get my dog? Breed societies can advise on local breeders if you want a pedigreed dog. The RSPCA and similar societies have large numbers of homeless dogs, and may offer a vaccination and desexing scheme as well. Make sure your pup or dog is from clean surroundings with kind caretakers, looks healthy and is outgoing. You can check with your vet to be sure.

What age is best? Beginning with an adult dog may save you the frustrations of house training and puppy antics, but you may get a dog with ingrained bad habits. From four to twelve weeks of age, every puppy goes through a crucial period of socialisation, and this is the time to establish a strong and trusting relationship with your pup. Whether adult dog or pup, always go for an affectionate and friendly manner and avoid timidity or aggression.

BASIC CARE

Socialisation and house training can be immediately successful if you spend the first week at home with your new dog. Puppies especially must feel loved, secure and wanted during this important imprinting stage; they should never be confined or isolated for long periods. Gradually introduce the pup to children, friends, other dogs and cats. Never allow children to play roughly with a puppy—apart from physical injury to dropped or roughly handled puppies, aggressive behaviour could be initiated.

House training means beginning with a set pattern of meals and exercise. After each meal and nap, first thing in the morning and last thing at night (and in between), you must be prepared to stay outside with your puppy for fifteen to thirty minutes. Be generous with your praise each time the pup 'empties' outside. Coin a key phrase (like 'piddle time') that the dog will associate with urinating and defaecating. Confine the pup to a small area of the house until house training is complete; this is less confusing and restricts mistakes. Some mistakes will be made, but punishment is useless unless you catch the pup in the act. Even then punishment usually has negative results—rewarding good behaviour is far more successful.

■ A warm basket with the comforting sound of a ticking clock will often help a lonely puppy feel more secure in its new home.

Remember that your pup will be stressed being in strange surroundings and missing littermates. A hot water bottle or the old favourite, a ticking clock, placed in the pup's basket often provides some comfort at night. Be patient and reassure your lonely puppy. If your dog is to sleep outside, you must provide a warm, dry kennel with a raised floor. The garden must be fenced to prevent the dog wandering and the inevitable car accident. Inside, a particular rug or basket can become the dog's accustomed sleeping place. Your dog will be happier when you go out if it has its own special, secure place in which to stay (or sleep).

The sooner you begin to train your puppy the better. Obedience classes for pups start from three to four months of age, or there are some

excellent books available on the subject of obedience. Routine training has several advantages: as well as producing a well-behaved, disciplined dog that is a pleasure to own, that special bond between owner and dog is strengthened as you work together.

Grooming is an important part of dog care that includes regular flea control, shampoos and brushing sessions. Always use a dog shampoo or pure soap like Sunlight, as shampoos for human use can cause skin problems. Use a dry shampoo between baths if necessary. Pups can be washed from any age, but should be dried

■ A well-trained dog is a pleasure to own, and obedience classes can be rewarding and fun for both dog and owner.

■ All outside dogs should have a warm, solidly built kennel, and a running chain for exercise.

thoroughly and kept warm. Check with your vet before purchasing any insecticides: some flea preparations are unsafe for puppies under three months.

Daily exercise is essential for both physical and mental well-being of your dog, whether it's playing ball games in the back garden or walks in the park. Consider using a running chain if the dog must be tied up regularly.

Your dog must be considered whenever you plan a holiday. Unless you have a particularly reliable relative or neighbour to feed and walk your dog daily, a boarding kennel is the only alternative. Your vet may recommend a good establishment where dogs are well cared for in clean surroundings and receive daily exercise. Good kennels insist on seeing vaccination certificates before accepting a dog.

Sometimes it is possible for dogs to accompany their owners on holiday. Get your puppy used to the car as early as possible, as almost all pups will vomit on their first long trip, but most rapidly become accustomed to travel. Don't feed your puppy just before a car trip, and always take water and stop for fresh air, a little exercise and a drink on the way. If vomiting persists, your vet can dispense tablets.

Finally, your dog must be registered with the local council which will provide you with a numbered disc. A collar should be worn at all times with this disc, and another that shows your address and telephone number and the dog's name. This makes finding a lost dog far easier. Most councils now insist that dogs must be on a lead when taken outside their homes. These laws benefit you and your pet; car accidents involving dogs are all too common.

YOU AND YOUR DOG'S BEHAVIOUR

Dogs are highly social animals; in the wild they live, eat and travel in packs. Domestication has removed the dog from this situation, making the human its substitute companion, and the family, its pack. The wild dog also exercises continually and must hunt to survive. Many dogs today are deprived of an opportunity to vent all these instinctive behavioural patterns. They spend each day in isolation while their owners go to work, they rarely exercise and their natural intelligence is not often exploited. The result is a dog that is bored, unfit, and psychologically stressed.

Excessive barking, destructive chewing, aggressiveness, self-mutilation (lick granulomas) and urinating and defaecating in the house are common behavioural problems of bored dogs. Research studies have shown that most 'problem' dogs are never taken for walks and spend little time with their families. Punishment for these dogs means they are at least getting attention.

Routine is also important to dogs and changes in lifestyle can cause changes in behaviour. A new baby, a new pet, or a death in the family can unsettle the family dog.

Some vets use hormonal therapy to treat unacceptable behaviour, which has variable success. It is best to look closely at the lifestyle of the misbehaving pet and make any necessary changes. Roster family members to walk, play and spend time with the dog each day. Consider starting obedience classes: they are an excellent form of discipline and mental exercise for a bored dog. These activities will probably improve the entire family's quality of life.

NUTRITION

Dogs are classified as carnivores (flesh eaters), which has led to the widespread but incorrect belief that meat alone is all that a dog requires. **Dogs cannot grow and remain healthy on a diet that is composed solely of meat (that is, muscle or flesh).**

The wild ancestors of the domesticated dog ate all parts of their kill: the bones, sinews, intestines and their contents (often vegetable matter), as well as the muscle. This meant that they were getting a varied diet. Meat alone is deficient in most vitamins and calcium, a mineral essential for healthy bone growth. Meat also has an imbalance of calcium to phosphorus and an excess of protein and fat.

The advent of commercial diets— dry biscuits, canned food, or semi-moist food—revolutionised canine nutrition. Dry food has the most kilojoules per unit weight, as canned food contains up to 70% water. Dry biscuits also provide exercise for the teeth. If designated 'complete', both canned and dry food have the correct balance of nutrients.

Puppies

Pups should be weaned on to solid food by six weeks of age. They should have three to four small meals a day until twelve weeks, then two meals a day until six to twelve months of age. If you have a new puppy, find out its previous diet. Any changes needed to the diet should be made gradually to avoid digestive upsets, which is always a good rule to follow for dogs of all ages.

Start your puppy on a 'complete' puppy food, either canned or dry. If dry, moisten it until the pup can handle the dry biscuits. Cereals are traditionally easy, but are very low in calcium and offer little to the pup in terms of good nutrition.

Dogs can go without food for days, but *not* water: it must always be available. Milk is a good food, but should be introduced slowly and initially diluted with water. If diarrhoea results or persists, stop the milk; some dogs are never able to tolerate the lactose in milk.

The feeding of all-meat diets to the puppy can have disastrous effects. Puppies require *twice* the amount of calcium daily as the adult dog (milk does not have enough calcium to compensate), as well as differing levels of protein and other nutrients. Feeding meat means fiddling with vitamin and mineral supplements, usually unsuccessfully (see 'Skeleton' on page 54).

The recommended diet for a puppy to twelve months of age is a mixture of commercial puppy foods such as Puppy Chow, or puppy canned food. Choose well-known brands and vary them. Milk can be given if it can be tolerated. Fresh water must *always* be available.

Adult dogs

After about twelve months of age, one meal per day is sufficient for the average dog (dogs that are perpetually hungry may be more contented on two small meals instead). Bones are greatly enjoyed by dogs of all ages. They help keep teeth healthy and supply calcium, but should be given in moderation to prevent constipation, that is, at most, two to three times per week. The safe bones to feed are large marrow bones, perhaps cut in half by your butcher. *Never* give chicken, fish or sharp chop bones to dogs; they can damage the intestine.

The all-meat diet is just as inadequate for adult dogs as it is for puppies. **A mixture of dried and canned commercial foods is again recommended to form the basis of an adult dog's diet.** Meat may be given as a treat or as a small proportion of the total diet (less than 25%). Milk may be added, and fresh water must always be available.

Further supplementation of adult and puppy diets with vitamins and minerals is unnecessary and can be harmful. The amount of food fed to both growing puppies and dogs depends on their condition; try to avoid obesity. Your task as an owner is to observe the dog's weight, coat sheen and droppings. Any variation from normal should be noted and the animal's diet discussed with your vet.

■ A simple test for obesity: a dog is the correct weight if its ribs are easily felt under a moderate layer of fat.

Old dogs

The need for protein increases with age; old dogs become less efficient at utilising this important nutrient. Unless your dog is on a diet for kidney disease, you can supply good quality protein in the form of eggs, liver, milk and cottage cheese.

Aged dogs often eat slowly and are best fed away from other pets. Unless your dog is fat, several small meals daily are better digested than one large feed.

Obesity

The overweight dog is a common problem, frequently not recognised by owners. To gain an idea of your dog's condition, feel over its rib cage: if you can't feel the ribs the dog is overweight.

Obesity is dangerous. It can shorten a life and puts extra strain on the heart, skeleton, pancreas and other organs. It is rarely 'glandular', or caused by desexing; rather it is almost always due to overfeeding and a lack of exercise.

■ An easy way to determine your dog's weight is to weigh both yourself and the dog and subtract your weight from the total.

With your vet, decide on a desirable weight to work towards. Weigh your pet weekly and keep a record. To weigh a dog, stand on your scales while holding the dog in your arms, then weigh yourself alone and subtract the difference.

A weight loss regimen in the dog involves gradually increasing exercise periods each day together with a change of food. Dogs respond better to a change than to merely reducing the size of their normal portions; they should still feel full, not hungry. Both diets listed below work on the principle of replacing fat (kilojoules) with fibre and poorly digested carbohydrates.

1. Cook together ¹/₂ kg lean meat, 2 to 3 cups of mixed vegetables and 1 litre of water. Remove from heat and add 1 cup commercial dog food and 2 tablespoons of gelatine. Once cooled, this sets rather like a brawn. Feed the same volume of this food daily as the dog's previous diet.

2. Cook together for twenty minutes ¹/₃ cup of rice, ²/₃ cup of bran, 1¹/₂ cups of water, 1 teaspoon of margarine and ¹/₂ teaspoon of iodised salt. Then add ¹/₃ cup of lean meat, 30 g liver and 1 tablespoon of bone meal, and cook for ten minutes.

A vet can supply commercial canned reducing diets if you prefer not to cook the above. Dividing the food into two small meals daily keeps a dog feeling satisfied.

Weight loss

The syndrome of weight loss in healthy dogs is seen mainly in super-active sporting dogs, highly strung pets, or hard working farm dogs. These dogs are so constantly energetic that it is almost physically impossible for them to eat enough to provide the kilojoules to compensate for their activity and excessive use of energy.

A diet based on dry dog food provides the best nutrition for these dogs and should be fed twice daily. Canned food contains about 70% water so supplies fewer kilojoules. The daily addition of one to three tablespoons of margarine or animal fat adds pure kilojoules until the desired weight is gained.

Coprophagy

Coprophagy is the eating of the animal's own, or another animal's, faeces or droppings. It is understandably not well tolerated by dog owners. The reasons behind this habit are still being researched. Many authorities feel it is a digestive problem and a result of enzyme deficiency and/or the feeding of a diet high in carbohydrates. Your vet may prescribe tablets containing enzymes, and a diet with more meat by-products and less carbohydrates could be tried.

Sometimes the problem is behavioural and occurs in dogs that are neglected and in need of attention. Improving the dog's lifestyle might also break the habit.

ROUTINE HEALTH CARE

Vaccinations, worming and desexing are essential components of a health programme for your canine friend. Mark a calendar at the beginning of each year with dates for worming and vaccination (some families make it easy by worming the kids and dogs at the same time!).

PROTECTING YOUR DOG WITH VACCINATION

Despite great advances in medicine there are as yet no effective anti-viral drugs. Antibiotics combat bacteria efficiently, but the important viral diseases of dogs and other animals are very difficult to treat successfully. **The only protection against viral diseases is vaccination.** Many pet owners ask why booster vaccinations are necessary. The answer is that the body's immune response from the first vaccination (the formation of antibodies against that virus) fades with time. Booster vaccinations 'remind' the body to make more protective antibodies.

Canine parvovirus

Compared to other infectious canine diseases, 'parvo' is unique: it appeared suddenly in the United States as recently as 1978, spreading rapidly to all parts of the globe within twelve months.

One reason for this uncontrolled spread was the toughness of the virus

particle. It is extremely resistant to most disinfectants and to extremes of temperature. It is passed out of infected dogs in their droppings, but can also be spread by contaminated feeding bowls, bedding, and shoes and hands of animal workers.

There are two disease syndromes. The virus causes myocarditis, an inflammation of the heart muscle in puppies up to fourteen weeks of age. This is always fatal, and is characterised by the sudden death of an apparently healthy puppy after a short period of breathing difficulties and weakness. There is no treatment. The second, most common effect of the virus is an acute, often fatal inflammation of the gastrointestinal tract. The dog stops eating, becomes very depressed and within the next twelve hours or so begins to vomit and have profuse watery diarrhoea, often containing blood. Severe abdominal pain and extreme dehydration accompanies the infection. Pups can die within twenty-four hours.

Early treatment is essential, and involves the vigorous use of intravenous fluids to combat the severe dehydration. Other drugs are used to treat the pain and vomiting. Puppies under six months of age are most susceptible, but parvo can occur at any age. See 'Vaccination Procedure' over the page.

Distemper

Distemper is another highly contagious, often fatal canine viral disease, to which very young and old dogs are the most susceptible. The virus is excreted from the infected dog in body fluids like saliva and urine. It is then usually inhaled by another dog and begins to move through the body to different organs, causing a variety of symptoms. The dog will have a fever, stop eating, become depressed and develop a discharge from the eyes and nose. Vomiting and diarrhoea begin, as does a cough from developing pneumonia. The virus also affects the brain, causing an encephalitis. Seizures (or fits) and muscle twitches may develop, often after an apparent recovery. These may remain with the dog for life.

There is no specific treatment for distemper. Early veterinary attention can support dogs through the disease and can improve the usual survival rate of around 50%. See 'Vaccination Procedure' opposite.

Infectious hepatitis

Infectious hepatitis is a viral disease that mainly affects the liver and kidney. Affected dogs become depressed and stop eating, with inflammation and swelling of the liver causing severe abdominal pain. Dogs become thirsty, begin to vomit and have diarrhoea.

The virus is shed from infected dogs in the urine and other body fluids. Recovered dogs can excrete the virus for many months. There is no specific treatment for viral hepatitis. See 'Vaccination Procedure' opposite.

Kennel cough

Kennel cough, infectious tracheo-bronchitis, is not as serious as the preceding diseases, but because of its highly contagious nature it can spread rapidly from dog to dog. The disease is hard to control in situations where dogs are in close contact, such as at dog shows and in boarding or breeding kennels (hence its common name).

A mixture of viruses and bacteria are thought to cause kennel cough. The infectious particles are spread in much the same way as the common cold: they are airborne and inhaled after contact with a coughing dog. Affected dogs develop a deep, harsh cough and owners frequently think their dog has 'something caught in its throat'.

There may be a short fever, a period of poor appetite and a chronic cough. Treatment involves medication to relieve the cough, combat the bacterial infection and break up the congestion in the lungs.

Vaccination procedure

The following vaccination regimen applies to parvovirus, distemper, hepatitis and kennel cough. Protection against all these viral diseases is available in a single vaccination.

High-risk situations (cities, breeding kennels, etc.): Puppies should have their first vaccination at six weeks of age, followed by injections every three weeks until eighteen weeks of age.

Low-risk situations: One vaccination should be given at six weeks, followed by one at twelve, then eighteen weeks of age.

Dogs over twelve to sixteen weeks of age: Two vaccinations should be given four weeks apart.

Pregnant bitches: can be safely vaccinated only with certain vaccines. As long as the breeding bitch has regular vaccinations, she will pass on this protection to her puppies. Check with your vet.

All adult dogs: must have boosters every twelve months.

Virus control

Premises where any of the preceding four viral diseases have occurred must be disinfected and kept free of dogs for as long as possible. Parvovirus is the hardest virus to kill. There are good commercial disinfectants available, but a simple homemade mixture is one cup of household bleach to a bucket of water (that is, a ratio of 1:30).

Viruses are incubated insidiously within the body before a disease becomes apparent, which can take many weeks. If your dog has already contracted a virus (for example, a new puppy that has come from doubtful and unhygienic quarters), vaccination will *not* prevent disease.

Full protection after vaccination takes ten to fourteen days. Keep pups away from other dogs if possible during this time. Repeat vaccinations are needed in puppies. Vaccinated bitches pass on antibodies in their colostrum (first milk) that protect their progeny from disease. This important 'maternal immunity' may last from six to sixteen weeks of age, but these protective antibodies can also neutralise the effects of vaccination. Repeat vaccinations cover this risky period of uncertain immunity.

PROTECTING YOUR DOG WITH WORMING

Worming is often a haphazard activity for many dog owners. **Intestinal and heart worms can kill** and should never be ignored.

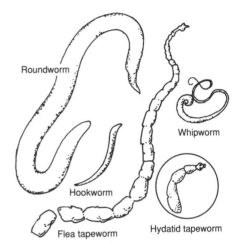

Roundworm

Whipworm

Hookworm

Flea tapeworm

Hydatid tapeworm

■ Important worms of the dog (not drawn to scale).

Roundworms

Toxacara and *Toxascaris* species are the roundworms of Australian dogs. They are long, white and cylindrical, pointed at both ends, can grow to 10 cm and are easily seen in dog droppings. Mature dogs develop an immunity to the roundworm but they cause serious problems in puppies less than twelve weeks of age.

During pregnancy, roundworm larvae inside the bitch travel across the placenta into her unborn puppies. **This means that all pups are born with roundworm larvae, and that they will have adult worms in their intestines within two weeks of birth.**

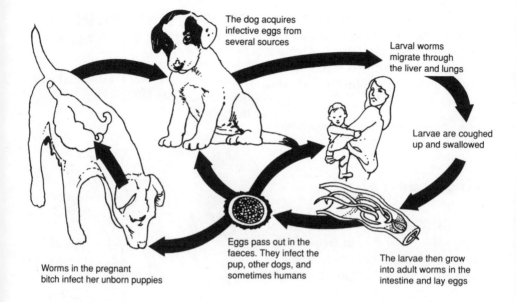

The dog acquires infective eggs from several sources

Larval worms migrate through the liver and lungs

Larvae are coughed up and swallowed

Eggs pass out in the faeces. They infect the pup, other dogs, and sometimes humans

Worms in the pregnant bitch infect her unborn puppies

The larvae then grow into adult worms in the intestine and lay eggs

■ The roundworm life cycle.

A female adult worm lays an incredible 200000 eggs per day which pass out in the faeces (droppings). They have a tough and sticky protective shell and attach to dog hair, feeding bowls, kennel floors etc. In two weeks they hatch into infective larvae that are picked up and swallowed by the puppy. From the intestine they burrow into blood vessels which carry them to the liver, then to the lungs where their migration can cause bronchitis and coughing. From the lungs they are coughed up, swallowed and grow into egg-laying adults in the gut. The cycle takes four to six weeks.

Roundworms are therefore spread in two ways: as larvae from the bitch to her unborn pups, and as eggs passed out in faeces.

The symptoms of roundworm infection in pups include coughing (caused by the larvae migrating in the lungs) and abdominal pain, vomiting and diarrhoea, retarded growth, pot-belly and poor coat from the adult worms in the gut, large numbers of which can fatally block the intestine.

Unless worming is repeated regularly, constant reinfection will occur from the droppings of the bitch and her already infected pups.

A human health hazard: visceral larval migrans: Blindness and brain damage can result from the inadvertent swallowing of roundworm eggs and larvae by humans, usually children. Rather than stay in the gut, these larvae migrate through the body encysting in the brain, eye and other organs. It is most important that all dogs are wormed regularly, and children taught to wash their hands every time they pat their dog or cat.

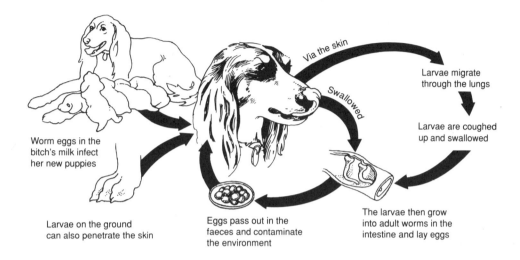

Via the skin

Swallowed

Larvae migrate
through the lungs

Larvae are coughed
up and swallowed

Worm eggs in the
bitch's milk infect
her new puppies

Larvae on the ground
can also penetrate the skin

Eggs pass out in the
faeces and contaminate
the environment

The larvae then grow
into adult worms in the
intestine and lay eggs

■ The hookworm life cycle.

Hookworms

Species of *Ancylostoma* and *Uncinaria stenocephala* are the hookworms occurring in Australia. Despite their small, 1 cm length, these blood-sucking worms are dangerous to dogs of all ages and can cause a fatal anaemia (deficiency of red blood cells). The worms have a hooked tail, and are just visible in the droppings. Bitches again play an important role in passing on hookworms as the larvae pass out in the milk being suckled by their new litters. **Within two weeks, new pups can have adult hookworms in their gut.**

Hookworms are spread in two other ways: eggs passing out in droppings, and larvae penetrating the skin. The eggs in faeces (infective larvae in only six days) are picked up and swallowed, maturing in the gut to egg-laying adult worms. This cycle takes only two to three weeks. Infective larvae that are present in the dog's environment can also penetrate the skin of the abdomen or the pads of the feet. From here they travel to and through the lungs, are coughed up, swallowed and then mature to adults in the intestine.

Hookworms have a well-developed mouth with 'teeth' that attach to a plug of gut tissue, devouring it within thirty minutes. The worm then moves on to a fresh spot leaving behind a bleeding wound. Large numbers of worms can cause serious blood loss, weakness, poor coat, diarrhoea containing blood and a fatal anaemia.

A human health hazard: 'creeping eruption': Hookworm larvae can also penetrate the skin of humans, causing an itchy dermatitis. Always wear gloves when cleaning kennel areas.

Whipworms

Trichuris vulpis is the whipworm of the dog. It is a small worm, growing 4 to 7 cm in length with a distinct shape: one end of the worm is very fine and 'whip-like', easily recognisable in faeces.

The whipworm has a simple life cycle: eggs containing infective larvae are swallowed and travel to the caecum (appendix) of the large intestine, where they attach to the caecal wall and live on the intestinal blood supply. They can cause loss of weight, anaemia, pain, poor coat and dark black diarrhoea that contains blood. Whipworm eggs can survive for years in the external environment. As the life cycle takes twelve to seventeen weeks to complete, the whipworm is normally a problem in dogs older than twelve weeks.

Tapeworms

Tapeworms require an 'intermediate host'. This is another animal, bird, insect or reptile that harbours the worm during a particular phase of its life cycle. Tapeworms are segmented and can grow very long. They can cause loss of weight and mild diarrhoea, but are generally less damaging than other worms. Many types of tapeworm affect Australian dogs; the following are the two that are most important.

Dipylidium caninum is perhaps the most common tapeworm and is spread by fleas. This worm can grow to 50 cm and is detected by the individual segments that pass out in the droppings. These segments look like moving rice grains or cucumber seeds, and are seen in the faeces, or around the dog's anus and tail area. As they are irritating, the dog will drag its bottom along the ground.

The larval flea swallows tapeworm eggs as it feeds on dog faeces. These eggs develop into immature tapeworms in a cyst inside the flea. When a dog scratches and chews himself, he often swallows a flea and the tapeworms hatch out of the cyst and develop into adult worms in the dog's intestine. This cycle takes six to eight weeks.

Hydatid tapeworms: a human health hazard

Echinococcus granulosus is the hydatid tapeworm, important not for its effect on the dog but because it causes fatalities in humans.

Hydatids mainly cause disease in rural areas, but city dogs may on occasion be fed uncooked offal and contract the parasite. The worm is tiny, only 4 to 6 mm in length, and impossible to see in the droppings. The intermediate hosts for this tapeworm include sheep, cattle, goats, kangaroos, pigs and humans.

Grazing animals pick up the hydatid eggs when eating pasture contaminated with dog droppings. Inside the sheep or cow, these eggs grow into large, fluid-filled sacs or hydatid cysts in organs such as the liver and lungs. When dogs eat offal (body organs) containing these cysts they burst, releasing 'eggs' that grow into adult hydatid worms in their guts. They have no effect on the dog.

Humans are also intermediate hosts like sheep and cows. **Humans do not get hydatids from eating offal, but**

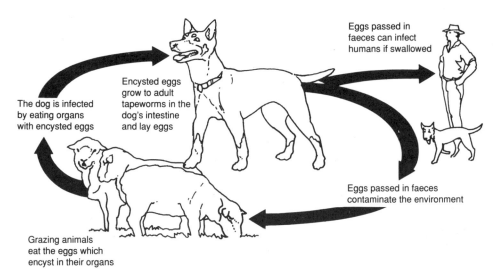

Eggs passed in faeces can infect humans if swallowed

Encysted eggs grow to adult tapeworms in the dog's intestine and lay eggs

The dog is infected by eating organs with encysted eggs

Eggs passed in faeces contaminate the environment

Grazing animals eat the eggs which encyst in their organs

■ The hydatid tapeworm life cycle.

by picking up worm eggs from their dog's coat, feed bowl, or bedding, etc. The hydatid cyst grows inside the infected human's organs, causing serious disease. The only treatment is radical surgery.

Worming procedure

Puppies: Treat puppies at one, two, three and four weeks of age, then at six, eight and ten weeks of age with a preparation like Canex to kill round-worms and hookworms. (This may seem like a lot of worming, but don't forget that pups are being constantly reinfected from eggs in faeces and by suckling.)

Puppies twelve weeks of age: Change to a treatment that will kill whipworms as well as roundworms and hookworms, and begin to treat for tapeworms.

Adult dogs: should be wormed every three months. In high risk situations, such as crowded kennels, monthly worming *at least* will be essential (remember the hookworm cycle can be as short as two weeks). In low risk areas for hydatids (for example, cities), worm adult dogs every three months against tapeworms.

Adult dogs in rural areas: It is crucial that all dogs in the country be wormed every six weeks against tapeworm to prevent human hydatid disease.

Pregnant bitches: should be wormed against roundworm and hookworm starting before mating and continuing *every* three weeks during pregnancy and lactation (suckling).

Heartworms

Dirofilaria immitis, the heartworm, is spread by mosquitoes. It is found wherever mosquitoes are prevalent: in tropical and subtropical climates, and all warm coastal areas and river valleys. The parasite is now widespread over much of populated Australia.

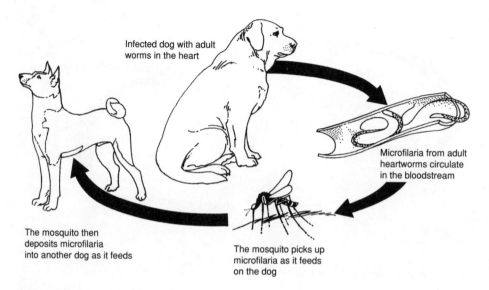

Infected dog with adult worms in the heart

Microfilaria from adult heartworms circulate in the bloodstream

The mosquito then deposits microfilaria into another dog as it feeds

The mosquito picks up microfilaria as it feeds on the dog

■ The heartworm life cycle.

Transmission of heartworm occurs when a mosquito feeds on an infected dog, picking up microfilaria (heartworm larvae) from the bloodstream. After developing inside the mosquito, the larvae are deposited into the skin of another dog, travelling through the skin tissues and bloodstream for several months. They make their way to the heart, growing into adult worms and producing new microfilaria to circulate in the bloodstream. This life cycle is very long and takes six to seven months from the first mosquito bite to adult worms and microfilaria.

You will not actually see this 10 to 30 cm long worm as it lives inside the heart. Large numbers of adult worms can live in the right side of the heart and its major blood vessels. They interfere with blood flow, inflame and thicken vessels and eventually cause congestive heart failure (see 'Heart' on page 48). Early symptoms are coughing, decreased exercise tolerance (dogs getting puffed easily), and laboured breathing.

Heartworm infestation is confirmed by a variety of blood tests and X-rays. Treatment is difficult. Adults and microfilaria must be killed with different drugs, administered three to six weeks apart. During the several months of treatment dogs must be strictly rested, as their bodies can react fatally to the dying heartworms.

Puppies must be started on preventative drugs at eight to ten weeks of age. Adults must have a negative blood test first as these drugs can cause fatal reactions if the dog is already infected.

Preventative drugs are constantly improving. Daily or monthly tablets are available and it is crucial that no treatments are missed. Dogs that live in normally safe areas will need preventative treatment whenever travelling to mosquito-populated areas. See your vet several weeks before leaving: it takes only *one* mosquito bite.

Coccidiosis

Coccidiosis is caused by a microscopic parasite called a protozoan; puppies that are reared in crowded, dirty conditions are most commonly affected. After being swallowed by a puppy, the oocysts (eggs) live in the intestinal walls and can cause bloody diarrhoea, weakness, loss of weight and anaemia.

Microscopic examination of faeces detects the oocysts. Specific drugs like sulphonamides are needed, as ordinary wormers will not treat coccidiosis. Keeping pups in clean surroundings and removing faeces daily is important: the oocysts passed out in droppings are infective within two days in warm, humid conditions.

Internal parasite control

Hygiene is important. Children should be taught from an early age to *always* wash their hands after playing with their dogs. Hygiene for dogs is equally important. Faeces must be picked up daily from yards and kennels to prevent the eggs developing into infective larvae. Kennel runs should be hosed regularly. Always try to observe the following points.

- Worm eggs and larvae survive best in conditions of shade and moisture. Apart from a necessary shelter area, try to have your dog's run exposed to direct sunlight. Concrete is easier cleaned than dirt (larvae and eggs can survive for long periods in dirt).

- Rotate kennels to new fresh areas free of worm eggs.

- Buy worm treatments from a vet, *not* the supermarket to be sure you get an effective one. Weigh your dog properly before worming: weigh yourself holding the dog on the bathroom scales, then subtract your own weight.

- Examination of faeces under a microscope enables your vet to detect specific worm eggs, and so to recommend correct treatment.

- De-flea your dog regularly to combat the flea tapeworm.

- Do not feed raw offal to your dog and don't allow the dog to wander in country areas (well-cooked offal is safer). Farmers must burn or bury all carcases; this prevents the hydatid tapeworm.

DESEXING

Whether to breed or not is a straightforward decision for the responsible dog owner, and their pets, both male and female, are desexed at six months of age. Many people are not so convinced. Below are the pros and cons of the situation.

Contraception

The most effective contraceptives are tablets or injections of progesterone. These can postpone or totally stop a heat cycle.

Their disadvantages are that used continually, these drugs can cause a delayed return to normal heat cycles and a lowered fertility, and can also affect the uterine cells and cause very serious infections.

Mismating and abortion

Mistakes will happen! The vigour with which both male and female dogs climb fences, travel huge distances and escape the confines of home to achieve the act of mating has to be seen to be believed.

Mismatings (that is, unplanned matings between dogs of different sizes and mixed breeds) are common. Injections of the female hormone oestrogen can prevent pregnancy, but must be given within two days of mating.

This drug, however, has the disadvantage of bringing bitches on heat for another three weeks (not helpful for promoting friendly neighbourhood relationships). Side effects of oestrogen injections can be serious and include uterine infections and blood abnormalities. Other drugs that cause abortion in the dog are still at the experimental stage.

If you intended to desex your bitch, it can still be done safely in early pregnancy, preferably the first month after mating. This is the most sensible way of dealing with unwanted pregnancies.

The tubal ligation operation and the vasectomy are rarely performed on dogs as they are in humans, because as well as preventing unwanted pregnancies we need to stop annoying sexual behaviour in our pets. To do this we must remove the main source of their sex hormones: the ovaries and testicles.

Spaying

All non-breeding female dogs should be desexed at six months of age. It is not necessary for them to have a litter before desexing; the operation will not change their personalities; and they will not automatically become overweight after desexing—this fallacy is frequently used as an excuse for overfed and underexercised fat pets. Apart from the prevention of unwanted litters, spaying bitches at six months of age (before their first heat) greatly reduces the incidence of mammary tumours, the most common cancer in female dogs, as well as serious infections of the uterus. Any female dog that has had pelvic injuries from a car accident may have difficulties giving birth and should always be desexed.

Try to plan for the operation when your pet is not on heat. During the heat cycle blood supply to the uterus and ovaries is increased, making surgery more difficult. Surgery on very fat bitches is also more prolonged and complicated.

The desexing operation of female dogs is correctly called an *ovariohysterectomy*, which means the removal of both ovaries and the uterus. It is a major operation and is performed under general anaesthesia in aseptic operating conditions (refer to 'Anaesthetics, Surgery and Medication' opposite). Most dogs are on their feet within eight hours of this surgery and many are able to go home the same day. Your pet may be slightly wobbly from the anaesthetic, so let her sleep it off in a quiet, warm room away from other pets and children. Give her

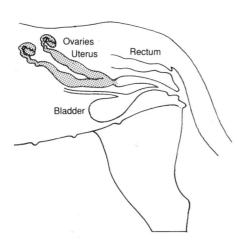

■ Simplified reproductive anatomy of the bitch. The shaded area illustrates the uterus and two ovaries which are removed during the desexing operation.

water, but don't worry about food until the next morning, then offer a small feed. Try to give your pet some extra attention as this is major surgery.

Check the wound daily, and return to your vet for suture removal in seven to ten days. Don't allow your bitch to exercise much until then.

Castration

Desexing male dogs at six months of age is as important as spaying females. The neighbourhood will have fewer unwanted puppies, and you will have a cleaner dog who is generally content to stay at home. Your dog will not become fat as long as he has sufficient exercise and is not overfed. Other problems that castration may help to control include aggressiveness, wandering and hypersexual behaviour (some dogs may masturbate, or mount the nearest available object).

Castration is the removal of both testicles. This involves general anaesthesia, surgery and the removal of stitches as in the spay operation. Check the wound daily, and don't bath your dog or allow him to exercise vigorously until the surgery wound has healed.

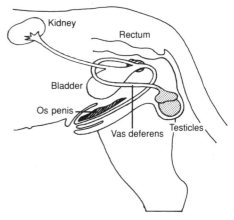

■ Simplified reproductive anatomy of the male dog. The shaded area illustrates the testicles which are removed during the desexing operation.

ANAESTHETICS, SURGERY AND MEDICATION

Anaesthetics are given to animals more frequently than to humans as a means of restraint and to prevent pain and stress during minor as well as major surgery. Short-acting anaesthetics are administered with a single intravenous injection (usually in a front leg and indicated by a small patch of clipped hair). For longer procedures, a tube is then placed down the anaesthetised animal's windpipe, and connected to a machine delivering a mixture of oxygen and anaesthetic gas. Long operations can then be performed with a high degree of safety.

Before an anaesthetic it is *crucial* that your pet have an empty stomach. A light feed the night before surgery is allowed, then all food and water must be removed. An empty stomach is important because when an animal is recovering from an anaesthetic it has no swallow reflex, and if it vomits, food material can fatally block the windpipe.

Surgery is performed using aseptic instruments in much the same way as in human hospitals. Sutures (or stitches) placed internally dissolve over a period of weeks. Skin sutures are non-dissolvable and must be removed, usually seven to ten days after surgery. Always check the surgery wound daily for signs of inflammation. Don't bath your dog until the skin stitches are removed, and keep exercise to a minimum. Vigorous activity can burst the best sutures.

Your pet may be still slightly wobbly from the anaesthetic when discharged from hospital and must be allowed a warm, quiet place to sleep and rest. Place water nearby, but don't worry about food until the dog is bright and alert. Small, frequent feeds are best until normal appetite is regained. Animals undergo the same pain and discomfort as we do after surgery, and they should never be stressed. This means keeping away other pets and playful children, and giving your pet extra attention.

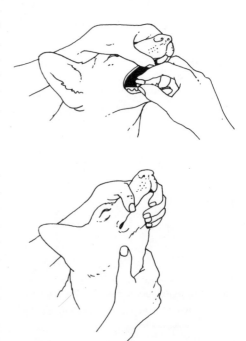

■ A well-trained dog will take tablets obligingly. Grasp the dog's upper jaw, open the lower jaw with the other hand and place the tablet down the back of the tongue. Hold the mouth closed until the dog swallows.

Most animals after surgery will need medication of some sort. Always follow the vet's instructions and finish all courses of tablets even if your dog appears well again.

Training your pup to take tablets without fuss rather than hiding them in food will save a lot of headaches when it is sick and refuses to eat. With the dog sitting, place one hand over its nose and grasp the upper jaw. With the other hand, pull the lower jaw open and quickly place the tablet on the back of the tongue. Hold the mouth closed until the dog swallows. Have someone help you hold small wriggling dogs; the more quickly and cleanly you give the tablet, the less likely you will meet resistance the next time. If you are desperate, try hiding the tablet in a small piece of butter. This is often accepted and slips down easily.

EMERGENCIES

Emergencies are commonplace with small animals, largely due to the proximity of the average dog and cat to busy roads, household poisons and venomous wildlife. In any urgent situation, please remember that vets are there to help you. Always telephone the vet for advice or to say that you are on the way. That one call can save your dog's life.

MOTOR VEHICLE ACCIDENTS

No matter what degree of intelligence you attribute to your dog, it is totally unfair to expect it to learn the rules of the road. The average dog is much more interested in that cheeky black cat across the street than any 'road sense' it is supposed to possess, and it is your responsibility to provide adequate fencing.

Handling injured dogs

Road accidents are traumatic for all concerned. Remember that an injured animal is frightened and in pain, and even the most faithful of pets will bite if hurt while being moved. Approach quietly and calmly. Never pick up a dog off the roadside without first putting on a muzzle. (The exceptions

are those dogs with obvious jaw or facial injuries, and those with distressed respiration). The muzzle can consist of a stocking, a piece of gauze or a bandage. Carefully but firmly tie it on top of the dog's nose, then once underneath the chin, then tie the muzzle behind the ears on top of the head (see below).

Small dogs are easily carried, but large breeds can be transported more comfortably on a strong rug or large

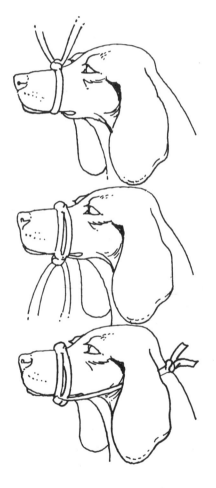

■ The muzzle is first tied above the dog's nose, then again under the jaw. The ends are brought up and tied firmly behind the ears.

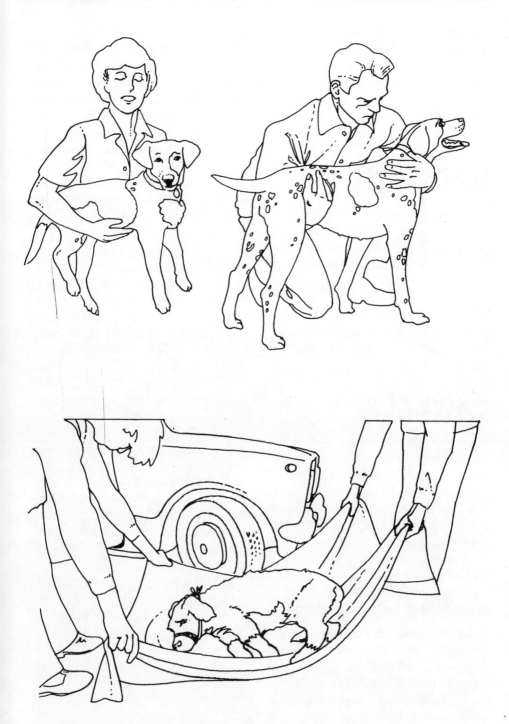

■ These diagrams illustrate ways of safely lifting and carrying injured or healthy dogs.

towel held at each corner. This means that animals with spinal injuries can lie flat. If you are too afraid to move the dog, most vets will do emergency house calls. And, even if your dog is fortunate enough to walk away from a car accident, an examination by a vet is recommended as internal injuries frequently take some time to become obvious.

Legally, the owner of the dog is responsible for any damage done while it is wandering in a public place. Normally of course, it is the dog that sustains the damage, but a Great Dane can remodel the front of a Mini Minor! Don't assume any dog will learn from his traumatic experience to keep away from cars in future; he won't, so mend those fences and keep your dog at home.

POISONS

Dogs, unlike the more fastidious cat, habitually sniff, taste and eat a remarkable variety of substances. They appear to relish many unappetising items, many of which can be toxic. Care needs to be taken to keep poisons out of the reach of pets as well as children.

In addition to the common poisons described below, a huge variety of household products and plants are known to be toxic; many cleaners, solvents and disinfectants, 'health' products such as aspirin, stimulants and sleeping tablets, and poisonous plants such as philodendron, dumb cane (*Dieffenbachia*), foxgloves, oleander, poinsettia, stinging nettles and many bulbs can all be toxic to dogs.

All poisoned dogs need veterinary attention for the best chance of survival. Many owners try home remedies when first confronted by a staggering, slobbering or convulsing dog, forcing salt and water into it to induce vomiting. This is usually ineffective and is dangerous, as convulsing dogs can inhale vomitus onto their lungs. Enforced vomiting can also damage the mouth and oesophagus if a caustic poison has been swallowed. In these cases the dog should be made to drink copious quantities of milk.

Dog owners who live far from a vet should keep syrup of Ipecac on hand. This causes vomiting more effectively than the average home remedy. The dose rate is 1 to 2 mL per kilogram of body weight, roughly one tablespoon for a large dog. This dose can be repeated once only after twenty minutes, as Ipecac itself can be toxic.

When a pet has been poisoned by washing with insecticidal rinses at the wrong concentration, repeated bathing is needed immediately to reduce the amount of toxin absorbed through the skin. The correct antidote should also be administered.

In all cases of poisoning, it is imperative that a vet should be consulted as soon as possible for the correct antidote to be administered. It is very difficult to advise on home treatment, and wasting time with home remedies can lead to the death of a pet. The best advice is to telephone a vet warning him or her of your impending arrival, or to ask advice if you are unable to leave immediately.

Organophosphates

Organophosphates are amongst the most widely used insecticides in agriculture, grazing and on domestic pets. Poisoning occurs from the application of flea, mange and tick rinses at the wrong concentration and from accidental swallowing of the spilled chemical. Poisoning by organophosphates causes constricted pupils, muscle tremors and spasms, profuse salivation and diarrhoea. Prompt treatment by the vet with a suitable antidote such as atropine is usually successful.

Snail baits

Both types of chemical snail killers commonly available are packaged with grain and molasses, making them attractive to pets as well as snails, and both can be fatal if eaten by dogs.

Metaldehyde, the active ingredient in Defender, is green and causes muscle tremors and inco-ordination. It has no antidote but early treatment can still save the majority of dogs. The other type of commonly available snail killer is Baysol, which contains carbamates and is blue. It causes muscle tremors and spasms, excessive drooling, diarrhoea and constricted pupils. Atropine is the specific antidote for carbamates and produces a rapid response if given early.

Anti-freeze

Ethylene glycol, a dangerous chemical present in car radiator anti-freeze and brake fluid preparations, is attractive to pets because of its very sweet taste. Only very small amounts need to be swallowed for fatal kidney failure to result. Symptoms include vomiting, inco-ordination, depression and death within several days. As this poisoning is so difficult to treat, extreme care should always be taken when draining and replacing anti-freeze and brake fluid from motor vehicles.

Strychnine

Strychnine has traditionally been the chemical used in malicious poisonings. It is highly toxic to all pets, and signs of poisoning can occur within ten minutes of ingestion. Strychnine causes severe muscle seizures and convulsions; dogs become totally rigid with the neck and all four limbs stretched out. Affected dogs are also hyperaesthetic (or over-sensitive to external stimuli) and convulsions will be dramatically initiated by any sudden movement, sound or touch.

Treatment involves the prevention of convulsive episodes by muscle relaxation or by general anaesthesia, which may need to be maintained for up to forty-eight hours. Early treatment is essential.

Rat poisons

Most rat poisons are anticoagulants, causing defects in blood clotting by interfering with vitamin K metabolism. Insidious and continual haemorrhage occurs in varying parts of the body; hence, depending on the amount ingested, it can take days before serious symptoms appear. All dogs become weak, pale in the gums, and may bleed from the mouth.

Dogs that are seen eating rat baits should have vomiting induced immediately. Vitamin K is the antidote for these poisons and in early cases is all that is required. Blood transfusions may be needed if the blood loss has been excessive.

1080 sodium fluoroacetate

Cases of 1080 poisoning are seen most frequently in rural areas due to its use as a rabbit exterminator. Violent clinical signs are seen within two hours of ingestion; dogs will wander aimlessly at first, then begin frenzied barking and running fits that end in convulsions and death within twelve hours. This poisoning has a poor prognosis as there is no specific antidote available, but early treatment to control convulsions and metabolic imbalance will sometimes be effective.

Lead

Lead is widely distributed throughout our environment. Some common sources include linoleum, plumber's lead, putty, batteries, golf balls, fishing sinkers and lead paint, still commonly found on older houses. (Lead salts give paint a sweet taste, hence its attractiveness to pets.) Lead poisoning is most often seen in puppies, as they absorb lead more easily than older dogs, and tend to chew strange objects.

Gastrointestinal signs such as a refusal to eat, pain in the abdomen and vomiting will often be followed by nervous signs. Puppies may appear blind, and convulse or exhibit hysteria by biting, barking continually and running wildly.

The red blood cells, which carry most of the lead, can be tested to help make a diagnosis, and treatment involves the use of a chelating chemical that binds the lead into a safe complex that can be excreted via the bile and urine.

VENOMOUS BITES

Australia has a rather large number of dangerous reptiles and insects, and dogs are frequently their victims. As with poisonous chemicals, the sooner treatment is administered the better the chance of your pet's recovery.

Snakebite

There are sixty-five venomous snakes in Australia, with twenty of these being known dangerous species. Their venoms, injected as they bite, contain a wide variety of enzymes and toxins, including a neurotoxin, another toxin that alters blood clotting and one that causes tissue damage. The largest proportion of most snake venoms is taken up by the neurotoxin, which is the poison that immobilises the snake's prey. Injected into a frog or

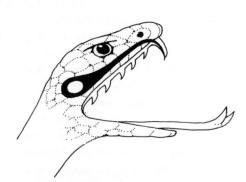

■ The venom gland of most Australian snakes is connected to their large front teeth. The venom is injected through a groove in each tooth into the snake's victim.

mouse, it can render that creature helpless within seconds.

The symptoms of snakebite in dogs vary enormously: each bite injects a variety of toxins, and the age, type and size of the snake is important as is the part of the body it strikes and the amount of venom injected. A snake just out of hibernation will have a full sac of venom for its first bite, whereas one that has recently bitten prey will have far less.

Symptoms include sudden collapse with apparent recovery then relapse, staggering and trembling, dilated pupils, salivation, vomiting, distressed respiration, brown urine and a worsening paralysis. Because all snakes have the same toxins to varying degrees, it is impossible to determine the type of snake involved from the clinical signs.

The anti-venenes used in treatment are specific to certain snakes. Tiger snake anti-venene will successfully treat tiger, black, king brown (mulga) and copperhead snakes, while brown snake anti-venene will combat the bites of brown snakes only. Death adders and taipans have their own anti-venenes. For these reasons, the dog owner's identification of the snake is *crucial*. **Where possible, always bring the entire snake into the vet.** Snakes are correctly identified by the number and shape of scales on different parts of the body, as well as their size and colour. If no snake is seen or found its type must be concluded from the geographical location, or several anti-venenes given.

Puncture marks from Australian snakes are not very obvious and usually difficult to find on a densely coated animal. As the venom is absorbed from the bite wound very quickly, cutting the fang marks has little to no effect and is no longer a suggested part of treatment.

Dogs can die within thirty minutes of a snakebite, so telephone your vet and leave immediately, preferably with the snake. The sooner the anti-venene is administered, the better the chances of the dog's recovery.

Tick paralysis

Tick paralysis, like snakebite, is a seasonal disease and occurs in the warm and humid months of the year. The usual paralysis tick, *Ixodes holocyclus*, occurs mainly on the eastern coastal parts of Australia. Ticks will not survive and breed in cold climates. A tick's normal hosts, which are rarely poisoned, are native animals such as bandicoots, echidnas and brushtail possums. Dogs, cats and humans are accidental hosts and are more vulnerable to a tick's toxin.

Ixodidae ticks are called 'hard' ticks because of the rigid shields on their backs. As each tick grows it needs three host animals for each stage of its development, climbing onto and feeding on each animal before dropping off to mature into its next stage. Depending on the weather at the time, the tick's life cycle takes eight to twenty-four months.

The adult tick, normally a female, injects saliva containing a neurotoxin into a dog as it feeds, but it can take four to seven days before any symptoms appear. Dogs from colder climates often develop symptoms a week after they have returned from a beach holiday. They will often have a strange bark for several days, then paralysis begins with wobbly hind limbs leading on to paralysis of the whole body; the dog will be unable to rise, and will have dilated pupils and difficulty swallowing.

Treatment involves the administration of tick anti-serum as soon as possible. The offending tick must be removed, and a thorough search made for others on the body. Several days of nursing in a quiet environment is usually required before the dog improves markedly.

Immunity after a bout of tick paralysis is not guaranteed and may be short-lived. Don't rely on this as a means of prevention. Keeping your dog free of ticks demands a regular routine in warm, humid climates.

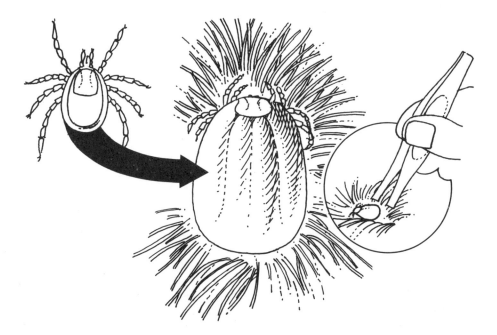

■ The unengorged female *Ixodes* tick has an obvious shield on her back. This appears to shrink markedly once the tick has fed and engorged for several days. Ticks should be removed by grasping firmly at the point where they are attached to the skin with tweezers.

Groom your dog daily, and make a thorough search of its coat. Ticks are removed by grasping them with tweezers near their attachment to the skin and pulling firmly; usually the entire tick is easily removed, but the head will die quickly if it remains embedded. *Do not* douse with methylated spirits or burn with a cigarette as the tick may inject more toxin. Ticks can be notoriously difficult to find and like hiding inside ears, under the tail and between toes. Insecticidal rinses at least once a week will keep both fleas and ticks at bay.

HEAT STRESS

Heat stress is common in dogs that have been confined in cars on hot days, without sufficient air flow and water. Irreversible and fatal heat stress can occur within one to two hours. Puppies, old dogs and brachiocephalic (flat-faced) breeds such as the Pug and Pekingese are the most susceptible.

A heat stressed dog will pant and gasp and have an anxious expression, its gums may be red or purple and vomiting may occur. Panting is the dog's method of cooling down, but excessive panting causes metabolic upsets. Severe dehydration occurs, then cerebral oedema ('fluid on the brain'). The dog becomes unaware of its surroundings, stuporous and eventually comatose. Blood clotting disorders can arise, causing haemorrhage throughout the body.

Rapid treatment is needed to prevent brain damage. If a vet is close by, telephone ahead then leave immediately. Otherwise, the dog should be put into a cold, iced bath while you massage its limbs vigorously. If you have a thermometer, the dog's rectal temperature should be taken every ten minutes until it is down to 39.5°C It is easy to cause over-cooling if the temperature is not monitored.

Once the dog's temperature is coming down, it is imperative that a vet administers treatment as soon as possible to reverse any brain damage and other effects of overheating.

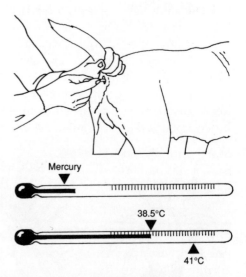

■ Always use a rectal thermometer to take a dog's temperature. Shake the mercury down first, lubricate the tip with oil or moistened soap, and gently insert the thermometer into the dog's rectum for thirty seconds. Normal temperature range is 38 to 39°C. In heat stroke, the temperature will rise as high as 42°C.

Car ventilators are available from pet shops, which fit into car windows allowing adequate air-flow while confining your pet. Always try to park in the shade; check your dog often, and, if you are leaving it in the car for any length of time, take it for a short walk and offer water frequently.

BURNS

Apart from major burns received in house fires or car accidents, minor injuries in dogs result from the use of over-hot hair dryers or clippers, the chewing of electrical cords and from spilling hot liquids.

The correct emergency treatment for all burns is to cool the affected area as soon as possible. Overheated tissue can take a long time to return to a normal temperature. Cooling a burn immediately shortens this period and reduces the pain, swelling and depth of the burn. Cooling will benefit any burn that has occurred within the previous two hours. The animal permitting, ice-water packs should be applied gently to the injured area for at least thirty minutes (use a mixture of ice and water in a sealed plastic bag). Veterinary attention should be sought for the after-care of the burn.

DOG FIGHTS

Dog fights are frightening events for anyone to witness. Resist the temptation to leap in and rescue your dog; you will almost certainly get bitten. A bucket of water or preferably a hose turned on full force are the most effective methods of stopping dog fights.

Once the dogs are separated, take yours to a vet. Puncture wounds from dog teeth inevitably become infected and fight abscesses can be painful and serious. Prompt treatment with antibiotics will prevent infection. Small dogs grabbed by larger breeds can have internal injuries, so a check-up is always essential.

BONES AS FOREIGN BODIES

A dog that is pawing frantically at its open mouth, salivating and constantly moving its tongue and jaws, usually has a bone stuck in its mouth. Often the bone will be across the back teeth on the upper palate.

Strong instruments like pliers will be needed to grasp the bone and pull it quickly off the teeth. If the dog is too distressed, your vet may need to give an anaesthetic before removal.

EYES

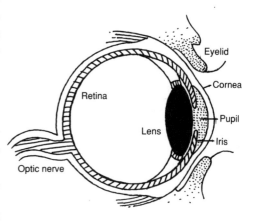

■ The anatomy of the eye.

Dogs are generally regarded as colour blind, or as being able to perceive colours weakly. Shape, brightness and movement are more important factors for visual stimulus. Hunting dogs, for instance, will miss seeing a rabbit close by unless it moves, yet can see a moving object almost a kilometre away.

Like many animals, dogs have a third eyelid, or nictitating membrane, which lies in the inner corner of each eye. This protects and lubricates the eye by 'washing' it with tears.

Eye diseases are characterised by pain, irritation and miserable behaviour in the dog. Eyes are extremely sensitive and react rapidly and seriously to any insult. An injured eye can become blind within hours if the correct treatment is not initiated.

Conjunctivitis

Conjunctivitis results in 'red eyes' and is perhaps the simplest and most common eye problem. Caused by dust, windy weather, injury, or some other irritant, it occurs in both eyes and responds well to treatment as long as the initiating cause is removed. All red eyes, however, are not conjunctivitis, and if pain or blindness accompany these symptoms more serious disease such as glaucoma or retinal problems may exist. Play it safe for your pet and contact your vet.

Corneal ulcers

The cornea is the fine sheet of transparent cells that covers the pupil, lens and other interior parts of the eye. It is the first line of defence for the eye and is frequently injured, usually from a cat scratch, or from foreign bodies such as grass seeds. Any break in the corneal epithelium is termed an ulcer, and ulcers allow bacteria to enter the eye. If infection occurs the eye may be lost entirely or, at best, a bluish-white scar will result that can impair vision.

Ulcers are extremely painful, so your dog will resent bright light, will blink frequently and its lids will swell. Don't expect to locate the foreign body yourself; most seeds find their way deep behind the third eyelid and require local or general anaesthetic for removal.

Ulcers are diagnosed using a special green dye that is taken up only by the injured cornea. As well as medication to prevent infection, treatment of the ulcer often involves suturing the dog's eyelids together. This provides a moist healing environment for the ulcer (it is rather like wearing an eye patch).

Cataracts

The lens is that part of the eye that transmits and focuses light on the retina. It consists of water and protein inside a thick capsule. The lens reacts to disease or injury by becoming less transparent and this opacity is called a cataract. The 'blue eye' that is seen commonly in older dogs is called nuclear sclerosis, and results from normal changes to the lens protein in ageing dogs. The dog's vision is often not greatly impaired.

Cataracts can be genetic, due to injury or secondary to disease, such as diabetes. Hereditary cataracts are well-documented in many breeds of dog and the severity of vision loss they cause varies. There is as yet no medical cure for cataracts, and surgical removal is the only choice. Old-age cataracts are not candidates for surgery, nor are those that are secondary to some other disease. Surgery to remove the cataract can be successful, as dogs, unlike humans, can see quite well without a lens. Nevertheless, it is difficult and must be performed by a veterinary ophthalmologist.

Eyelid disease

Eyelid diseases are quite common in certain breeds, and have a hereditary basis. 'Ectropion' and 'entropion' are the terms for the turning outwards and inwards of the eyelids respectively. Entropion causes irritation, weeping and eventual corneal ulceration as the inturned eyelashes rub against the corneal surface of the eye. Ectropion allows dirt and tears to collect inside the loose lower lid, and the conjunctiva often becomes red and inflamed.

Surgical correction is simple, but the dog owner should remember that the breeding of animals with eyelid disease is not recommended.

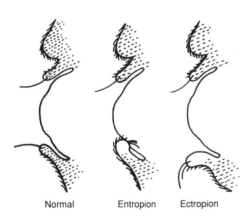

Normal   Entropion   Ectropion

■ Entropion describes the inward curving of the lashes and eyelid; continual rubbing of the lashes on the cornea causes irritation and ulceration. In ectropion, the lid is floppy and hangs outwards, disturbing the normal flow of tears and allowing debris to collect inside the lid.

Watery eyes

In most dogs' eyes, tears pool in the corner of the eye before draining down the tear duct to the nose. An eye that is weeping excessively can mean simple conjunctivitis, a serious ulcer, or abnormalities of the tear duct; certainly it indicates that a problem exists that needs attention.

Although not a medical problem, the large eyes of short-faced dogs such as Pekingese sit in a shallow socket, causing the tears to spill over and drain down the face. In white-coated dogs with similar large eyes weeping becomes especially noticeable as proteins in tears stain the face red-brown. A particular antibiotic can bind these proteins and prevent staining, but its long-term use is not recommended. Pet shops have lotions that can be helpful in removing the stains.

'Popped' eyes

'Popped eyes' describes the total dislocation of the eye from its socket. It occurs during dog fights, car accidents, or is commonly seen in flat-faced breeds (for example, Pekingese and Pug) that have large, protruding eyes sitting in shallow sockets. In these dogs only slight pressure may be needed to dislodge the eye.

The condition is an emergency and immediate treatment is essential. **Telephone a vet, then keep the eye continuously wet as you make your way there** by using artificial tears, saline, or clean water flowing over the eye constantly. This is *crucial.*

Usually a general anaesthetic will be required to replace the eye, then the eyelids will be stitched over to help hold it in place. Rigorous treatment to reduce the swelling and inflammation in and around the eye will then be needed to try to preserve sight.

Blindness

Blindness, whether from injury, cataracts, inherited factors or just old age is not uncommon in dogs, but most pets with failing sight cope remarkably well. Dogs rely heavily on their sense of smell even when they have full sight, and if the blindness has developed gradually, they can adapt very well. Taking care not to change the dog's environment is important; for example, don't alter the placement of furniture in the house. In familiar surroundings, providing it is healthy in all other respects the blind dog can still take an active part in family life.

Treating eyes

When treating eyes, eye drops are the easiest to apply, but eye ointments remain in the eye longer. You may need a helper to hold a wriggly dog's head still while you hold the lids open. Steady your hand on the dog's head while you put one to two drops or a small amount of ointment into the eye. The medication should be placed into the conjunctival sac: you should *never* touch the eyeball.

Never be tempted to use left-over, out of date or human eye preparations in a dog's eyes. Use only drops prescribed for each particular problem; an eye ulcer can worsen rapidly and become irreversibly infected if the wrong chemicals are used.

EARS

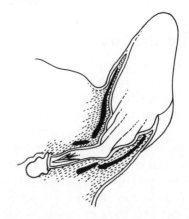

■ The dog's ear canal is quite long, and foreign bodies such as the grass seed illustrated must be removed by your vet.

Dogs have longer ear canals than humans with an approximate right-angle in the middle, making them difficult to examine properly without the correct instrument (an otoscope). They also provide a deep, hidden environment for foreign bodies and for infection. Any ear problem will cause affected dogs to shake their heads and hang them towards the side of the diseased ear. Never neglect these symptoms as the ear can quickly become seriously inflamed.

Otitis

'Otitis' is the term describing inflammation of the ear. Otitis externa, which is inflammation of the outer ear canal, is very common in dogs, especially those with floppy ears such as spaniels, hounds and bassets. A sudden bout of head shaking or hanging the head to one side should indicate to you that something foreign is inside your dog's ear. Don't expect to see it, as grass seeds and other foreign bodies travel down the ear canal rapidly and sit close to the eardrum, where they can cause great pain, inflammation and infection. If these ears are neglected, chronic and painful infection results.

The bacteria that cause ear infections are some of the hardest to treat. Affected ears first need flushing to remove the pus and discharge, then the infection can be treated with ear drops and tablets. Sometimes a swab will be made to determine exactly which organisms are causing the problem. The most severe cases can be helped with a surgical procedure that removes the upper part of the ear canal while creating a new opening. The remodelled ear canal is shorter and easier to treat and keep healthy.

Otitis interna, or middle ear infection, is not as common. It can result from a blood-borne infection or from a ruptured eardrum. The structures of the inner ear are necessary for normal equilibrium, so infection will cause inco-ordination, general loss of balance and result in a dog that walks in circles.

Any suspected ear problems should receive prompt attention. This may save your dog a great deal of pain and misery.

Aural haematoma

An aural haematoma is a rather large 'blood blister' of the ear flap, or pinna. The pinna contains many blood vessels which, if traumatised, can burst and bleed, slowly filling the space between the skin and the cartilage

that keeps the ear erect. Haematomas are usually caused by a bite or scratch from another animal, or a problem inside the ear that causes the dog to scratch furiously. Over a number of days, a fat, drooping ear flap develops. A general anaesthetic is required in order to open and drain the blood clot, and to then stitch the skin to the cartilage to prevent further haemorrhage.

The unfortunate aftermath of an aural haematoma is that your dog's ear may never return to a nice, erect shape because of damage to the cartilage.

■ The aural haematoma is caused by injury to the ear flap. The affected ear (here, the dog's left ear) appears swollen and hangs at an odd angle.

Ear mites

Otodectes cynotis is a tiny mite just visible to the naked eye that can inhabit the ear canal causing intense itchiness and irritation. The mite is very contagious and often every pet in the family will become infected.

Using an otoscope, your vet will see small, white mites moving around on the typical dark brown discharge that builds up inside the ear. The mites feed on this debris and undergo their entire life cycle on the dog, most of it in the ear canal. An ear full of wandering mites is very irritating to the dog who will shake its head constantly and scratch at its ear. Chronic infestations lead to bacterial infection and otitis.

Insecticidal ear drops are very successful at eliminating the mites. An insecticidal rinse should also be used over the whole dog, as often these very mobile mites will be travelling over the body when they're not residing inside the ear.

Fly worry

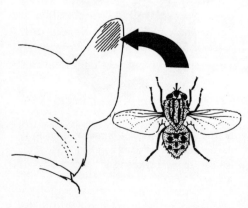

■ The large, pointed ear tips of dogs such as German shepherds often become inflamed from the bites of the stable fly during hot weather.

Dogs with upright ears are candidates for attack by the stable fly, *Stomoxys calcitrans*. These insects will bite and feed on the vascular and sensitive ear tips, and the edges of the pinnae (ear flaps) will become crusted with oozing blood and serum. Affected dogs (usually breeds such as collies and German shepherds) can become quite irritated by the constant fly worry.

Fly repellent creams applied twice a day will help if the dog is unable to be kept in fly-proof premises.

Deafness

Deafness can be a normal part of ageing and senility; many old dogs lose their hearing along with their sight. It can also be inherited, and certain breeds, such as the blue cattle dog, have a higher incidence than others. This type of hearing loss is untreatable. The occasional dog will have impaired hearing from excessive dirt in the ear canal, but it will usually show other symptoms such as head shaking.

Treating ears

Ear medication dispensers have long nozzles that should be placed gently down the ear canal and squeezed lightly. Try not to flood the ear. Massage the dog's ears to distribute the lotion throughout the canal and wipe away any excess with cotton wool. Avoid using cotton buds for cleaning; they can damage the sensitive lining of the ear canal.

As with eye medications, you should never be tempted to use leftover, out of date or human preparations in a dog's ears. Overuse of ear drops that are not prescribed can lead to resistant bacterial infections in the ear.

SKIN

The skin is the largest organ of a dog's body. Due to its complexity, it is a very sensitive organ and any insults rapidly cause irritation, inflammation, pain and/or itchiness. Dermatoses are probably the most common group of diseases presented to the veterinarian.

The itchy dog

Itchiness is a non-specific symptom of skin disease. It is also extremely annoying to a dog and its owner, and can be frustrating to treat. External parasites such as fleas and mange mites, irritating substances in the dog's environment, even the boredom of a lonely pet can start that common itch-scratch-itch cycle.

'Atopic' is the description given to that itchiest of pets, the allergic dog. In humans, atopy is characterised by asthma, hay fever and some skin disease. In dogs, allergy is almost exclusively manifested by itching: eyes and face are rubbed, paws are chewed and most parts of the body are scratched almost constantly. Allergic animals react to antigens from the environment such as pollens, house dust, flea saliva, plants, even feathers and wool. Atopic dogs are sensitive to a wide range of substances.

Atopy has a strong hereditary basis, and certain breeds are more likely to develop multiple hyper-sensitivies, in particular, the Dalmatian and all types of terriers. The problem begins at one to two years of age and remains for life. Initially the dog may only itch during certain seasons, but as more and more allergies develop the scratching becomes continuous.

A correct diagnosis is essential, as although every atopic dog is itchy, not every itchy dog is atopic; flea control may be all that is required. Diagnosis involves testing the dog with a number of common antigens injected into the skin. Reaction to a large number of these will indicate possible atopy.

Treatment in the past has relied strongly on the use of corticosteroids, which are very useful for providing short-term relief from itchiness but have well-known debilitating side effects. A more effective treatment, which can provide more permanent relief, is to desensitise the dog with a series of injections of the antigens to which it is allergic. The disadvantages of this treatment are that it may require referral to a specialist clinic, and the success rate can be variable.

Atopy can never be cured, only controlled, and it requires much patience on the part of dog and owner.

Flea allergy dermatitis

Flea allergy dermatitis is by far the major cause of itchiness in Australian dogs. The warmer and more humid the climate the happier the flea. Dogs in cold and very dry areas will have some respite during winter and a dry summer when the flea temporarily disappears from the scene. Unfortunately, most of populated Australia has a climate suitable for fleas. Difficulties can also arise if a pet owner refuses to acknowledge that his or her precious mutt may be carrying fleas. Flea infestation is not a social disease, it is a fact of life.

Another major obstacle to effective treatment of flea allergy dermatitis arises because fleas do *not* live on the dog—they only hop on the dog to feed. Fleas live and lay their eggs in dirt, in cracks and crevices of buildings and kennels and, frequently, in your best carpet. **This means that both the dog and its environment must be treated.**

Ctenocephalides felis is the most common flea variety of dogs and cats. This wingless, bloodsucking insect is a shiny, dark brown, and moves very quickly through the coat. After egg laying, in warm and humid weather, adult fleas will emerge from a pupa in a little over two and a half weeks. The adult flea can survive for prolonged periods—up to a year—without a blood meal.

Flea faeces, or 'flea dirt' is detected more easily than the flea itself. It is deposited on the skin over the rump and back and looks like tiny black specks of dirt. When wet, flea droppings turn red as they contain the blood ingested by the flea as it feeds.

The average dog can live happily with fleas, giving an occasional scratch that notifies his owner that a shampoo and flea rinse is in order. Allergic dogs, however, the real sufferers of this disease, become acutely sensitised to fleas and can develop severe skin problems. During feeding, fleas inject saliva into a dog's skin. The saliva contains irritant substances that cause all dogs to react, and also a hapten, or type of allergic protein, and antibodies form in allergic dogs that react to this substance each time a flea bites.

Dogs allergic to fleas scratch and chew constantly, developing wheals and papules (tiny pimples) and raw and eventually bald skin in specific areas: over the rump and lower back, the base of the tail and inside the hind

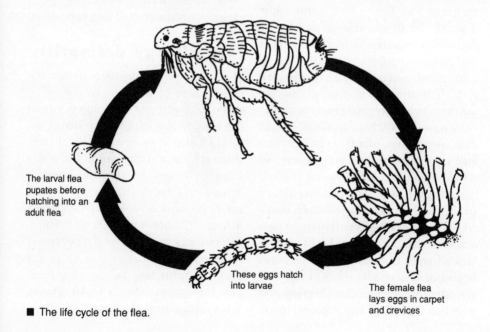

The larval flea pupates before hatching into an adult flea

These eggs hatch into larvae

The female flea lays eggs in carpet and crevices

■ The life cycle of the flea.

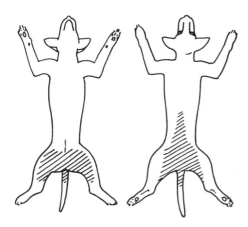

■ Dogs that are allergic to the flea will develop dermatitis over the areas shaded: the lower back, rump and tail, and under the flanks and groin.

limbs. This self-mutilation in untreated dogs leads to the skin becoming grey, hairless and thickened. Puppies as young as three months can become allergic to the flea, and the problem will stay with them for life. The reasons why some dogs and not others become allergic are not yet fully understood.

To keep fleas at bay, a combined attack must be made on the environment and the dog. For dogs, there are numerous products available: flea collars, powders, 'spot' treatments and insecticidal rinses (remember, *all* insecticides are potentially dangerous). Applied once a week, or twice a week in severe infestations, rinses are the most efficient method of keeping fleas off your dog. Ask a vet for advice as flea resistance to certain insecticides has already been detected. A dog that has developed a dermatitis will also need medication to heal the trau-matised skin. Any treatment must be combined with flea control.

The environment is much more difficult to 'treat'. In overwhelming flea plagues a commercial pest controller may be necessary. Regularly washing your pet's rugs and spraying kennel areas will help. 'Foggers' to treat the inside of the house are now available through vets; they are easy to use and safe for both animals and humans.

In Australia, as in many parts of the world, we must accept that flea control is an important part of pet care. Both dogs and the home environment must be subjected to regular flea control efforts, and allergic dogs in particular must have a routine programme of grooming and treatment that will enable them to be as itch-free as possible.

Mange mites

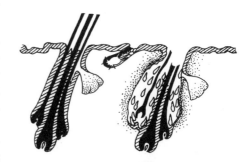

■ (Left) A normal hair follicle. The round fat mite burrowing into the skin is a sarcoptic mange mite, laying her eggs in the tunnel as she progresses. The demodectic mange mite (right), invades the hair follicles in large numbers, causing inflammation and destruction of the follicle and hair fibre.

There are two microscopic mites that cause skin conditions in dogs: *Sarcoptes scabiei* var *canis*, which causes scabies, and *Demodex canis*, which causes demodectic mange.

This particular scabies mite is better adapted to the dog as its host, but pet owners can catch a short-lived dose of the dog variety and scratch furiously for a week or two. The female mite burrows into the upper skin layers and makes tunnels. Here she stays for three to four weeks, feeding on skin cells and fluids and laying eggs until she dies. These eggs hatch into immature mites, which burrow into their own tunnels and develop into adult mites within three weeks.

The scabies mite is highly contagious and dogs of any age, breed and sex are at risk. The mite can only live away from its host for very short periods, so contact is necessary for spread. The disease causes intense itchiness, and constant scratching by the dog results in reddened skin with tiny lumps, ulcers and scabs. The lesions begin on the ears, elbows, hocks and lower limbs and the abdomen and chest. Eventually, the entire body surface can become affected and the dog appears quite moth-eaten.

Demodectic mange has a different pattern, as the mites are found in small numbers in the hair follicles of healthy skin in most dogs. Mites are transmitted from healthy bitches to their pups in the first few days of life.

The disease primarily affects dogs under eighteen months of age, but why the mites suddenly cause disease is not well understood. Dogs with a lowered immune response are sus-

ceptible, as are pedigreed dogs, especially certain short-haired breeds. It has been suggested that dogs with obvious demodectic mange should not be used for breeding.

There are two types of demodectic mange. The localised form occurs generally on the face and head and consists of small, hairless patches. These are red and scaly, but may not be itchy. Generalised demodicosis begins with a few isolated hairless and itchy areas on the face, feet or neck. Untreated, this mange can be fatal as the skin lesions spread to cover most of the body, and frequently secondary bacterial infection develops often involving the bacterium golden staph *Staphylococcus aureus*.

Mange mite infestations are confirmed by taking scrapings of the affected skin. This scraped material is examined under a microscope for the presence of mites.

Although mange has traditionally been a difficult disease to treat, effective miticidal washes and an oral treatment are now available. The washes may need to be given once a week for at least six weeks.

Ringworm

Ringworm is not a worm, but a fungal infection of the skin. In dogs, three types of fungus are commonly involved. Some inhabit the soil, while others are transmitted to and from animals and man. (Many parents have had the experience of having to treat both puppy and child simultaneously for ringworm.) The fungi invade the superficial layers of the skin and the hair follicles of young animals and humans. The classical lesion, the growing, circular, hairless patch that lends itself to the term 'ringworm', develops anywhere on the body. Dogs that love to dig in the garden will often develop a soil fungal infection on the top of their noses.

Ringworm is highly contagious and can spread to cover large areas of the body. Affected animals should be isolated from other pets in the family and from children. Rugs, leashes and grooming gear should be sterilised.

Some fungal infections will fluoresce a bright green under ultraviolet light; others may need to be grown in a laboratory for correct diagnosis. Medication involves a course of griseofulvin tablets combined with anti-fungal shampoos and creams.

Contact dermatitis

As the name suggests, dogs with contact dermatitis have come into contact with something in the environment that irritates their skin. Redness and inflammation and sometimes pain or itchiness will occur on the specific parts of the body that are contacting the reactive substance.

Often a new woollen rug or an old rug washed in a new washing powder, will cause irritation on the dog's abdomen. Many dogs will react if they are washed in their owner's shampoo for a change. A new garden fertiliser may be sniffed and licked, causing inflammation around the muzzle. A multitude of possibilities exists, and the vet and owner must play detective to track down the cause.

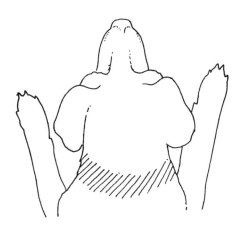

■ Contact dermatitis can result from any irritant substance, here caused by the chemicals in a flea collar.

Endocrine skin disease

An excess or deficiency of reproductive, adrenal or thyroid hormones can change the skin's texture, thickness, hair coat and degree of pigmentation. In general, hormonal skin problems are not itchy, and often occur in a symmetrical pattern over both sides of the body. Skin disorders are only a small part of the symptoms of these diseases, and diagnosis is definitely a task for your vet.

Pyoderma

Pyodermas are acute skin infections, better described by their common name of hot spots. They are usually initiated by a minor skin inflammation, ear infection, impacted anal gland or similar annoyance which causes the dog to lick and scratch vigorously. Such is the degree of self-mutilation that a raw, moist and exceedingly painful infection results, often within twenty-four hours.

Other pyodermas may result in dogs that have natural but exaggerated skin folds on the face and vulva, such as spaniels and Pekingese. These wrinkles are constantly moist and are a prime site for infection. If surgical correction is not possible, the owner must try to keep these areas washed and dried daily.

Acute hot spots must be carefully clipped and cleaned, and dogs treated for infection and irritation (as well as the original cause). Often an Elizabethan collar—a collar that makes it impossible for the animal to reach its body—is required to prevent dogs traumatising a wound until it is no longer painful and itchy (see illustration opposite).

Oil or paint on the coat

Often dogs will lie under a vehicle that is dripping oil, or will brush against a newly painted surface. Don't use turps or other irritant removers; instead, trim any thick lumps of matted hair with scissors, then soften the remainder with mineral or vegetable oil for as long as possible. Shampoo repeatedly until the coat is clean.

Lick granuloma

Lick granulomas are lesions that also result from self-inflicted injury, but develop over a long period of time and are often intitiated by boredom. Lick granulomas usually occur on the upper surface of the lower front or hind limbs, an area that is easy for a

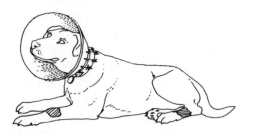

■ Lick granulomas occur in places the dog can reach easily with its mouth, such as the upper surfaces of the front and back legs. Often an Elizabethan collar is required to break the 'lick cycle' to allow healing.

dog to lick. They develop into circular, raised lesions up to several centimetres in diameter, and can be very difficult to treat.

Small lesions can be removed surgically. Otherwise, dogs must be prevented from continuing to lick a granuloma by using Elizabethan collars or buckets on their heads, as well as drugs to stop the chronic cycle of licking and irritation.

A critical examination of an affected dog's environment is essential. Many pets with lick granulomas are spending prolonged periods without the company of their owners or another animal, and are receiving little exercise or outdoor activity. Most animals, like humans, are gregarious and have a strong need for companionship. They also need to be entertained, exercised and involved in interesting pursuits if boredom and bad habits are not to result.

Skin tumours

Over one third of all tumours in dogs involve the skin. Numerous types exist that vary in their location on the body, their growth rate and appearance and their malignancy. Most occur on older dogs, but certain tumours develop at specific ages and in specific breeds.

As with all types of cancer, prompt attention provides the best chance of a successful outcome. It is relatively easy to remove and treat a small tumour; any abnormal lumps should be examined by a vet.

Nail care

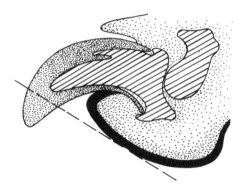

■ Dogs that miss frequent exercise will need to have their nails clipped regularly to keep them short and healthy. The nail should be clipped below the blood vessel that runs down the centre of each nail. This is easily seen as a pink area on white nails.

The nails of the dog have a tender, vascular 'quick' like those of humans. The main blood supply extends down through the centre of the nail, which is seen most easily in non-pigmented or white nails. Dogs that have regular exercise on hard surfaces rarely deve-

lop nail problems. However, inactive dogs that spend their lives on carpet develop long nails, with the blood vessel inside growing down with the nail, and once this happens it is very difficult to trim the nails properly. The aim should be to trim to just below the pink blood vessel line (this involves a little guesswork in black nails so ask your vet to help).

Don't panic if you cause bleeding when cutting your dog's nails. Just keep firm pressure on the nail with cotton wool and the bleeding will stop in a few minutes.

Check your dog's nails regularly, especially the dewclaw nail (the inner claw that doesn't touch the ground), which can go unnoticed in long-haired dogs and become painfully ingrown.

GASTROINTESTINAL TRACT

The gastrointestinal tract comprises the organs that ingest and digest food and pass the finished product. The tract begins with the mouth and teeth and finishes with the anus. In between are the oesophagus, stomach, intestines, liver, pancreas and salivary glands, all of which produce different substances that aid digestion by breaking down different food particles. The dog has a relatively large stomach, with a capacity of up to 3 litres (the horse's stomach only holds 8 to 15 litres). The small intestine is about 4 m long, the large intestine shorter.

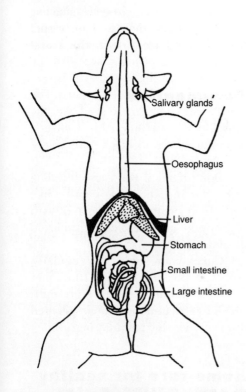

■ Simplified anatomy of the dog's gastrointestinal system.

Labels on diagram:
Salivary glands
Oesophagus
Liver
Stomach
Small intestine
Large intestine

Teeth

As dogs are carnivores, their teeth are adapted to eating meat. The four long canine teeth at the front of the mouth were used for catching prey and for tearing flesh. The molars at the back of the mouth bite meat into smaller pieces for swallowing.

All permanent teeth are present by six to seven months of age. After about twelve months of age it is difficult to age dogs, as teeth vary with diet and eating habits (some dogs love playing with stones, behaviour that wears down even the healthiest teeth).

Inherited defects of the mouth and teeth

The most common examples of inherited problems involving teeth are **over** and **under-shot jaws**. Dogs will have either a lower jaw that is much shorter or much longer than the upper jaw. These dogs must be fed a diet they can easily manage.

Cleft palates result from a malformation of the upper palate. There is usually a piece missing in the middle of the palate, and this allows fluid to pass out of the mouth and into the nasal cavity. Milk will dribble out of a pup's nostrils as it sucks or drinks, causing it to splutter and cough. Surgery can help this condition.

Dogs with such obvious defects as over/under-shot jaws and cleft palates should *never* be used for breeding.

Retention of deciduous teeth

■ Retained temporary canine teeth must be removed by your vet to prevent incorrect positioning of the permanent teeth.

Many dogs, especially smaller toy breeds, retain some of their deciduous teeth after the permanent ones have erupted. The teeth involved are usually the canines, the four long teeth at the front of the mouth. Two teeth, instead of the normal one, will be seen in the same tooth socket. The retained teeth push the permanent teeth out of line and must be removed as soon as possible. If they are not removed they may cause malocclusion, a condition where teeth become crooked and don't meet correctly when the mouth is closed. Unless the teeth to be removed are very loose, a short anaesthetic will be required.

Dental plaque and calculus

Wild dogs always had good strong teeth because their diet included bones and other tough foodstuffs. Domesticated dogs often have a relatively soft diet and develop the same dental problems as humans do.

Plaque is the layer of food, saliva and bacteria that remains on teeth after eating. Plaque eventually mineralises and forms a hard, yellow material called calculus, or tartar. Calculus invades gum margins, allowing bacteria to flourish in food particles. (See 'Home Care for Healthy Teeth' opposite.)

Halitosis

Halitosis, or bad breath, may result from any disturbance or inflammation of the oral cavity, including infections from trauma, foreign bodies (grass seeds in the mouth), tartar, perio-dontitis or tumours. Dogs with failing kidneys will also develop bad breath. (See 'Home Care for Healthy Teeth' below.)

Periodontitis

The periodontal membrane is the tissue that lines the tooth socket; an excess of bacteria in the mouth may cause infection of these tissues. This may be secondary to disease, or helped along by plaque and calculus. The gums become red and inflamed, infection occurs in the tooth socket and eventually the tooth loosens. The dog will have bad breath, drool excessively and may have a poor appetite. As the dog eats, food may be dropped in pain. (See 'Home Care for Healthy Teeth' below.)

Home care for healthy teeth

The problems already described above —dental calculus, infection of the tooth socket and halitosis—can largely be prevented or corrected if teeth care becomes a routine for your dog. Most essential is a good diet. Healthy teeth need chewing exercise to keep them clean, which can be achieved by feeding your dog dry dog biscuits, rawhide chew strips and non-splintering marrow bones.

Many small breeds of dog are unable to cope with large bones or hard biscuits and their owners must be prepared to clean their dog's teeth. Use a soft infant toothbrush or soft rag wrapped around your finger moistened with hydrogen peroxide or baking soda, or, better still, use a dog toothpaste, available through a vet (don't use human toothpastes as they contain too much detergent).

Teeth should be cleaned once a day or once a week, depending on the extent of the dog's problem. The aim is to remove as much food debris as possible to prevent plaque formation.

If obvious problems exist, a vet will need to clean your dog's teeth professionally. This is a very common procedure in dog and cat practice, and usually involves a short general anaesthetic, scaling and cleaning all tooth surfaces and removing any loose and infected teeth. This may need to be done annually.

Gastric torsion

A gastric torsion occurs when the stomach twists and blocks off, preventing the normal passage of food and fluid. It usually occurs in large, deep-chested dogs such as bassets, Dobermans and German shepherds, frequently after the dog has had vigorous exercise following a large meal, or in greedy dogs that eat quickly. The dog will suddenly appear to be in great pain, salivating and retching frequently. The upper part of the abdomen distends rapidly, the dog becomes shocked and then collapses. Major blood vessels are obstructed by the distending stomach.

This is an emergency and a dog will die unless surgery is performed quickly. The surgical procedure involves emptying the stomach and returning it to its usual position and size. It is then stitched to the abdominal wall in an effort to prevent recurrence of the torsion.

Vomiting

Any disease or inflammation of any part of the gastrointestinal tract can cause vomiting and/or diarrhoea. It is important to realise that both vomiting and diarrhoea are symptoms of an underlying disease.

Dogs can vomit easily, which is helpful if garbage or poison has been ingested. The occasional vomit is considered normal in an average dog, but if it becomes persistent a vet must be called.

Puppies have particular problems. They are rubbish eaters and frequently swallow stones or small household items that can irritate or obstruct the stomach and intestines. They will often vomit if carrying a heavy worm burden. Newly weaned puppies that vomit after each meal may have one of several birth defects that interfere with the normal passage of food down the oesophagus (food pipe). Although it is hungry, the pup still vomits after each meal.

Ulcers of the stomach occur in dogs, sometimes from stress (just as humans get ulcers from stress), from disease such as kidney failure, or from the incorrect use of certain drugs such as aspirin. Ulcers cause dogs to be nauseous, off their food and sometimes vomit blood.

Dogs that are vomiting become dehydrated and thirsty. Allowing the dog to continue drinking usually leads to persistent vomiting and worsening dehydration (an excessive loss of body fluids). If your dog has only vomited several times and is still bright and alert, remove all food and water for at least twelve hours to allow its stomach

■ Water, electrolytes and the withholding of food may be all that is required for dogs with simple diarrhoea. Continual diarrhoea or vomiting will rapidly cause dehydration and intravenous fluids via a 'drip' may be needed.

to rest and heal, and observe it closely. If vomiting persists during the next few hours you must call a vet immediately. **Continual vomiting may indicate serious disease.**

Diarrhoea

Diarrhoea is caused by an imbalance in the movement of intestinal salt and water. Usually, very little body water passes out in the faeces; diarrhoea disrupts this normal pattern and most of this fluid is lost, causing dehydration. Many of the diseases causing vomiting also cause diarrhoea. Heavy worm infestations, the eating of garbage, diseases such as parvovirus, and tumours can all have diarrhoea as a symptom.

Dark black faeces indicate bleeding near the stomach and upper small intestine, while red droppings may mean haemorrhage in the large intestine. Pale, fatty faeces may indicate one of the malabsorption syndromes (inadequate digestion and absorption of nutrients as the food moves through the intestine). Dogs with malabsorption problems are usually thin and ravenous despite being well fed, as their body misses out on its normal nutrition.

Simple diarrhoea can be treated at home *if* the dog is still bright and not vomiting. As the cells lining the intestine are constantly being renewed, the removal of all food for one to two days will often allow an inflamed gut to heal. The crucial thing is to prevent dehydration, a major problem following diarrhoea. Test for dehydration by pulling up the skin on the dog's neck with your fingers. In normal dogs, the skin springs back into place. If the dog is dehydrated, it remains elevated.

Dehydrated animals must be given small, frequent drinks of water, preferably with electrolytes such as Vytrate and Lectade from your vet. These contain sodium and potassium salts, which are lost in large quantities in diarrhoea. Milk products and other foods high in lactose should be avoided in dogs with diarrhoea. Once back on to solid food, the diet should consist of small meals of bland, low-fat, low-lactose food such as boiled rice or potatoes, cooked mutton, chicken, boiled eggs or cottage cheese. Gradually change back to the dog's normal diet.

Severe diarrhoea, like vomiting, must never be ignored. A dog that is obviously weak and dehydrated should be seen by a vet. A vet can immediately combat serious dehydration with intravenous fluids while investigating and treating the underlying disease.

Constipation

Constipation, or the inability to pass faeces, is very common in dogs. Usually droppings are very hard and result from a big feed of bones or garbage several days before. Obesity can make passing faeces difficult, and inflammation of the prostate gland in male dogs causes pain and reluctance to defaecate (see 'Reproductive Tract' on page 65). Injuries to the bony pelvis and diseases of the rectum and anus, such as hernias and diverticula (a large pocket of stretched bowel that allows faeces to build up in the rectum) can also be the causes of constipation.

Unless your dog is used to bones, allow it only one marrow bone to chew once or twice a week. Avoid large, infrequent meals of bones as constipation can almost be guaranteed. Sharp pieces of bone travelling through the intestinal tract can also cause damage.

The obvious sign of a constipated dog is continual, ineffective straining. This may be accompanied by yelps of pain. If faeces are not passed, the dog becomes depressed, vomits and dehydrates. Faecal softeners such as Coloxyl may work if used as soon as the dog begins to strain. The longer the dog is constipated, the harder will be the faeces and the more inflamed the bowel. Your vet will need to administer enemas to the dog, often under anaesthesia, to gently break up and flush out the blockage.

Flatulence

Flatulence is the passing of excess gas from the gastrointestinal tract. Gas is produced normally by bacteria in the bowel, most of which is absorbed. Any person who lives with a flatulent dog well knows the unpleasant odour that accompanies excess gas production.

Diet is the first consideration; many dogs react to a particular commercial diet that may suit other pets. Some dogs love vegetables, but beans, peas and cauliflower, for example, can cause gas production. Diets with a very high protein content may have the same effect. Large amounts of milk can cause a very mild enteritis with a growth in the number of gas-producing bacteria. You may have to experiment with different brands and types of food to keep flatulence under control. Dividing the total food volume into several small feeds daily can help by allowing more efficient digestion after each feed.

Pancreatitis

The pancreas is a small organ lying near the stomach that has two functions: to produce the hormone insulin, and to release enzymes that are used in the digestion of food. Pancreatitis is inflammation of the pancreas. The acute form of the disease is frequently fatal, and is seen in middle-aged, overweight, female dogs that scavenge, or that have had a large fatty meal within the past twenty-four hours.

The disease is characterised by sudden severe abdominal pain, vomiting and diarrhoea, shock and collapse. The inflamed pancreas cells begin a cycle of self-destruction as they release enzymes that attack other pancreatic cells. Peritonitis can result. **Intensive, early treatment is needed to save a dog suffering from acute pancreatitis.** The dog is maintained on intravenous feeding and antibiotics to rest the pancreas, combat shock and dehydration and control infection.

Chronic pancreatitis is the occurrence of repeated, less severe bouts of the disease. Diabetes mellitus will sometimes result from such continual pancreatic damage.

After-care for dogs that survive must include a constant, healthy, low-fat diet and the curtailing of any scavenging habits.

Anal glands

The anal sacs are two small organs that lie just under the skin on either side of the anus of both male and female dogs. The lining of the sacs contains glandular cells that produce an oily, rather foul-smelling fluid. This is passed with the droppings. The actual function of these glands is obscure, but it is thought that dogs in the wild used the scent to mark their territory. Useful or not, the anal sacs often become impacted, and annoy and irritate the dog. Licking and biting the affected area, the dog often drags its bottom along the ground.

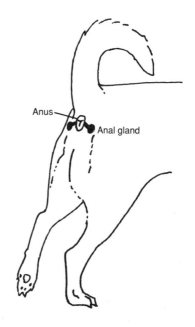

Anus
Anal gland

■ The anal glands, which lie on either side of the anus, can become impacted, causing the dog to drag its bottom along the ground.

Impaction is easily relieved by expressing the glands. If the problem occurs often, your vet will show you how to do this at home. Using well-lubricated, thin plastic gloves, the forefinger is placed just inside the anus. The thumb puts gentle pressure on the outside of the gland, and the impacted material is expressed. Always do this in the garden and never wear your best clothes!

Anal gland abscesses are also common. Infection inside the sac will rupture to the outside and the dog will have a draining wound. Antibiotics need to be administered to hasten healing. Anal glands that are continual problems can be removed surgically.

HEART

The heart is a tireless, muscular organ that is responsible for supplying the body with oxygen, carried by red blood cells. It has four sections, separated by valves. Veins bring the used blood from all over the body into the right side, from where it is pumped to the lungs. Here, carbon dioxide is exchanged for oxygen and the oxygenated blood returns to the left side of the heart. Arteries then carry this blood to every body tissue.

The heart can be affected by various things including infection, parasites (see 'Heartworms' on page 15), cancer and birth defects. Congenital heart problems are quite common and are often diagnosed at a pup's first vaccination when the vet listens to the heart as part of a routine examination. Such puppies may be weak and inactive compared to the rest of the litter. Some of these defects respond well to surgery.

Congestive heart failure

This is by far the most common heart syndrome seen in dogs, and is usually the end result of chronic disease in the heart muscle and heart valves. One study of dogs diagnosed valvular disease in 58% of dogs over nine years of age. Often the cause is unknown.

Congestive heart failure occurs as the heart gradually becomes less able to efficiently move blood around the body. The body tissues become starved of oxygen and try to compensate by making the heart beat faster. The heart enlarges in order to hold more blood, and the kidneys respond by retaining water and sodium to try to increase the amount of blood circulating.

Congestive heart failure can be right or left-sided, or both. Right-sided heart failure means the blood in the veins is not returned to the heart promptly. Blood 'backs-up' in the veins, causing them to be overloaded or congested. Organs like the liver also become enlarged and congested, and some of the excess fluid leaks out of the veins into the abdomen, causing it to swell.

Left-sided heart failure causes inefficiency in the return of blood from the lungs and its pumping around the body. The end result is lung congestion. The dog often has difficulty breathing, gets puffed easily after exercising and develops a moist cough. This is most noticeable at night

■ Congestive heart failure causes the heart to enlarge, the liver and lungs to become congested, and the accumulation of fluid in the abdomen.

when the dog is lying down.

There is no cure for the ailing heart, but good control can be gained from medication, rest and correct diet. A low-salt diet is essential; in heart disease, excess sodium causes the body to retain fluid. Table scraps are *not* allowed, nor are salty foods such as devon, ham, milk or animal hearts. Foodstuffs low in salt include rice, pasta, egg yolks and low-salt milk; canned food is saltier than dry biscuits. Canned heart diets are available through your vet.

Exercise must be restricted and the dog rested according to the stage of the disease. If the dog can tolerate daily walks, these should be continued. Also, as obesity causes the failing heart to work even harder, weight loss is an important part of treating heart disease. When diet and exercise control can no longer maintain heart function, daily medication is necessary. Various drugs are used to help the heart muscle beat more efficiently, to dilate blood vessels and to help the kidneys pass excess body fluid.

Regular check-ups, the correct diet and a caring home environment free from stress will comfortably prolong the life of an old pet afflicted with heart disease.

LUNGS

The primary function of the lungs is gas exchange. As a dog breathes, carbon dioxide from the body and oxygen from the atmosphere are exchanged in the blood cells which are circulating through the lungs.

The lungs, like all organs, are susceptible to parasites, tumours, and infections that may cause bronchitis or pneumonia. Traumatic injuries from car accidents, for example, are a common cause of respiratory tract problems.

Pneumothorax

Pneumothorax literally means 'air in the chest'. The lungs normally expand and contract within a vacuum inside the chest cavity. If air leaks into this cavity, either via a penetrating wound or from damaged lung tissue, the lungs have difficulty expanding, and may collapse. Car accidents are the major cause of pneumothorax. Dog fight wounds may also open the chest. An injured dog will have difficulty breathing and will refuse to lie down, sitting up or standing in an effort to take in enough oxygen.

Animals showing these symptoms should be taken to a vet immediately. Transport the dog as quietly and calmly as possible, as stress will only cause further breathing problems. The vet will remove excess air from the chest. This may need to be done repeatedly until the torn lung seals over, and the dog must be hospitalised and kept under constant observation.

Diaphragmatic hernia

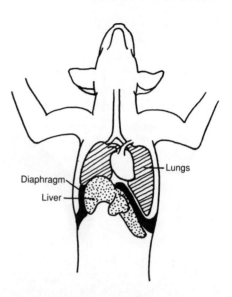

■ Trauma such as car accidents can result in diaphragmatic hernias. The tear in the diaphragm allows the liver to slip into the chest cavity, preventing the lungs from expanding efficiently.

The diaphragm is the sheet of thin muscle tissue that separates the abdomen and chest cavity, thereby maintaining the vacuum around the lungs. Trauma (usually the result of a car accident) can tear the diaphragm. As the dog moves, abdominal organs such as intestine and stomach can slide in and out of the chest cavity, putting pressure on the lungs and preventing their expansion. The symptoms are the same as pneumothorax: the dog sits or stands and has obvious breathing difficulties.

Treatment involves surgery to remove the abdominal organs, stitch the tear in the diaphragm and ensure the lungs are correctly expanded.

URINARY TRACT

The urinary tract consists of the organs that produce, store and transport urine, the main fluid excreted by the body. The kidneys are bean-shaped organs cushioned by fat that lie against the spinal column. A thin tube, the ureter, leads from each kidney to the bladder, from where the urine is carried out of the body by another narrow tube called the urethra.

The kidneys act as filters for the bloodstream. They maintain a crucial balance between body fluid and salts, and help to excrete certain waste products of metabolism. They are also involved in the manufacture of red blood cells. Kidneys are frequently exposed to infection, poisons and other chemicals, and drugs such as aspirin will concentrate in the kidneys, causing damage.

Chronic progressive renal disease

Chronic progressive kidney disease is a syndrome of kidney failure that is common in many old dogs and cats. Any disease processes that have inflamed the kidneys can ultimately cause this condition.

Unlike the liver, which is able to regenerate after illness, damaged kidney cells are not always replaced or healed, often becoming scarred and useless. Kidney disease can be insidious and symptoms may not show until about 70% of the renal tissue is altered.

As the kidneys become less able to function, the delicate balance of body water, electrolytes and waste products becomes disrupted; excess water passes out in the urine, while toxic substances like urea build up in the bloodstream. The large amounts of water lost as urine causes dehydration and make dogs thirsty. Hence, the first signs of kidney disease are often increased drinking and subsequent passing of large volumes of urine. Despite constant drinking, the dog may still become dehydrated.

Excess protein is also lost in the urine, causing the body to become malnourished and high urine protein levels to occur. The build-up of urea and other metabolic waste products in the bloodstream causes the dog to become depressed, lose appetite, develop bad breath and mouth ulcers and begin to vomit. Anaemia may result from interference with red blood cell production.

Although degenerative kidney disease is impossible to cure, careful medical management, avoidance of stress and good home nursing can give affected dogs a longer and more comfortable life.

The aims of treatment are to maintain a good urine output, reduce the work load of the kidneys and replace those substances that are being lost in the urine. Once the initial veterinary treatment has stabilised the dog, dietary management at home is very important. A kidney-saving diet must be high in carbohydrates and fat and low in protein.

Protein molecules are large and make the failing kidneys work too hard. Protein is, nevertheless, essential, so high-quality protein should be fed in low quantities. Red meat is a poor-quality protein and should be avoided; substitutes include cooked eggs, cottage cheese and chicken. Kilojoules that provide energy and maintain body weight must be supplied by the carbohydrate and fat portion of the diet. Suitable foods include spaghetti and other pasta, rice, bread, butter, cream and ice-cream.

The water-soluble vitamins B and C should be supplemented; ask your vet for advice on other supplements as calcium and salt are sometimes needed in certain kidney disease.

Large amounts of fresh water must *always* be available, as dogs with kidney disease easily become dehydrated.

Dividing this low-protein/high-carbohydrate diet into three to four small meals a day reduces the work-load of the kidneys. To make things easier, there are now commercial canned kidney diets available from vets which supply these nutrients in the correct proportions.

Once a dog is stabilised and on the correct diet, it is essential that treatment of chronic renal disease is extended to the home in the form of affectionate and caring nursing and a strict avoidance of stress.

Cystitis

Cystitis is inflammation of the bladder. It can result from infection that enters via the urethra, bladder stones and injury or nerve damage that causes the bladder to retain urine. Affected dogs, male or female, will be miserable, depressed and strain frequently. Only small amounts of urine, often

containing blood, will be passed.

Antibiotics usually clear simple infections, but sometimes the urine must be cultured in a laboratory. This tells the vet which bacteria are causing the infection and therefore what medication he or she should use.

Urinary calculi

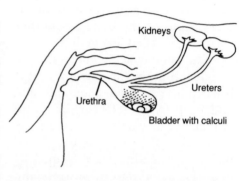

Kidneys

Ureters

Urethra

Bladder with calculi

■ Simplified anatomy of the female dog's urinary system, showing 'stones' or urinary calculi in the bladder.

'Stones' in the bladder, also known as calculi or uroliths, are caused when crystals of mineral salts or other metabolic products clump together in the bladder. Continual depositing of crystals onto this original core can result in calculi several centimetres in diameter.

Bladder infections are the primary cause of calculi formation. Certain bacteria make the urine very alkaline, and compounds that normally dissolve in the urine crystallise instead. These compounds are commonly phosphates with calcium, magnesium and ammonium ions. Symptoms of bladder calculi are the same as those of cystitis: frequent straining with the painful passage of small amounts of urine.

Stones are generally removed surgically, analysed and the diet adjusted accordingly to try to prevent recurrence, while alkaline urine is treated with urinary acidifiers. Medication is now becoming available to vets that can dissolve certain types of stones.

Calculi can also occur inside the kidney and in the urethra and ureters. Dalmatians have a unique uric acid metabolism and urate calculi form in this breed, often lodging in the kidneys.

Male dogs have a rare anatomical feature—a bone inside the penis called the os penis. Urethral calculi can pass from the bladder and lodge near this bone, blocking the passage of urine and causing a sudden onset of severe pain and continual straining. **This type of blockage is an acute emergency and a vet should be called immediately.**

Urinary incontinence

Incontinence is the inability to voluntarily control urination. It can be caused by infections of the bladder, spinal and pelvic injuries that affect the nerves to the bladder, and by a lack of hormonal control.

Hormonal factors are usually involved in the incontinence of old dogs of both sexes. The dribbling of urine occurs mainly during rest and sleep, and is especially noticeable in dogs that have previously always been well house trained. These dogs have often been desexed many years before. Treatment is simple and effective: your vet will prescribe medication with low doses of male and female sex hormones.

HORMONAL DISEASE

Hormones are the chemical messengers of the body. They are produced by glands and travel in the bloodstream, helping to maintain normal body functions and metabolic balance.

Diabetes mellitus

Diabetes mellitus, the common diabetes of humans, occurs quite frequently in dogs and cats. It results from a deficiency of the hormone insulin, which is secreted by the pancreas. Factors such as obesity, genetics, pancreatic disease and the overuse of drugs such as corticosteroids are thought to be involved in diabetes.

Without insulin, tissues are unable to absorb and utilise glucose, the body's sugar. Cells begin to starve while high levels of glucose build up in the bloodstream, and protein and fat are instead broken down to provide energy. The result is a dog that is eating well but starving.

High levels of blood glucose cause excessive urine production, and a cycle of increased drinking and urination begins. Coupled with increased appetite in a dog that is still losing weight, these are the first symptoms of diabetes. Eventually, cataracts develop in the eyes and kidneys and liver become diseased. Untreated dogs become very sick.

Diabetes mellitus is diagnosed by detecting high levels of glucose in the blood and urine. There is no cure, and like their human counterparts affected dogs must have injections of insulin once or twice a day and have their urine tested several times a day. After stabilisation in a vet hospital, the dog must be maintained on a consistent routine of controlled exercise and diet. Sudden changes will affect the amount of insulin needed and de-stabilise the dog's condition. Diabetic diets must be nutritious, consistent in quantity and quality and, above all, low in sugar and other carbohydrates.

Long-term treatment of a diabetic dog involves a major commitment from the owner and an acceptance by the dog of the new routine. It is very difficult to stabilise a diabetic dog, but determined and enthusiastic owners can cope successfully.

Diabetes insipidus

Diabetes insipidus is another type of diabetes that involves the antidiuretic hormone ADH, that is, the hormone that normally controls urine output and concentration. Lack of ADH results in large volumes of dilute urine, a thirsty dog and subsequent increased drinking. Hormone replacement therapy is successful in treating diabetes insipidus and this type of diabetes is easier to control than diabetes mellitus.

SKELETON

Bones and joints form the solid framework of a dog's body. Strong and healthy bones, perhaps more than any other tissue, are dependent on a well-balanced diet.

Dogs can suffer from a large number of skeletal diseases that can be related directly to poor nutrition, especially during crucial times of bone growth. Many owners tend to overfeed their pets and over-supplement with minerals and vitamins, and large breeds of dogs in particular can grow too heavy too quickly. Other problems relate to imbalances of minerals such as calcium and phosphorus (see 'Nutrition' on page 5).

Nutritional secondary hyperparathyroidism

Secretion of the parathyroid hormone is inversely related to blood levels of calcium: low levels cause excessive production of the hormone. Diets low in calcium, high in phosphorus and low in vitamin D_3 will cause low calcium blood levels. The hormone, in trying to balance blood calcium, takes it from the bones and replaces it with fibrous tissue. The bones become weak, often bowed, or may break after the slightest injury. Affected puppies will have a variety of symptoms, from mild lameness to a total inability to walk, and bones that will be painful to handle and may fracture easily. In adult dogs, the jaw bones become weak and teeth become loose in their sockets. This is often called the 'rubber jaw syndrome'.

The most common diet causing this problem is the 'all-meat' diet, which has imbalances of calcium and phosphorus (see 'Nutrition' on page 5). Commercial puppy foods contain the proper balance of required minerals.

Puppies must be treated with calcium and rested until their bones strengthen, however, it is important not to over-supplement with calcium as this can be just as harmful. Check with your vet who will prescribe the correct dosage.

Fractures

Dogs are so frequently the victims of trauma, especially on the roads, that fractured bones are commonplace (a fractured bone is the same as a broken bone). Most fractures are 'simple', that is, the bone is broken through and the ends separated but there is no opening in the overlying skin. 'Compound' fractures, however, are very serious because the broken bone has penetrated the skin and is immediately vulnerable to infection. 'Green stick' fractures occur mainly in puppies and are more like fine cracks; the bone remains in the same shape. These heal well if the pup is on a good diet; they are usually treated with a cast or other fixation.

Fractured bones are usually obvious. The dog will be in pain and is unable to walk on the affected limb, which may be very swollen and hang at an odd angle. Don't try to splint the leg yourself; this is usually unnecessary and causes more pain, and you may get bitten. Dogs are usually able to hold the leg comfortably themselves.

The fracture will need to be X-rayed to enable the correct treatment to be undertaken. Plaster casts are rarely used as lighter, more pliable casting materials are now available. However, internal fixation is generally preferred to casting. This involves the use of non-reactive metal pins, plates, screws and wires to hold the bone ends firmly in place until they are healed. Internal fixation is performed under sterile surgical conditions with the dog under general anaesthesia. These surgical methods make it easier to stabilise broken bones for the average six weeks required for healing. Some of this 'hardware' is removed after healing, while other pieces are left in for life.

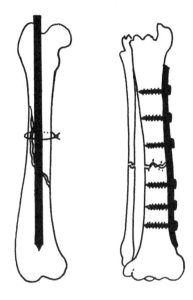

■ Broken bones are often repaired most efficiently by 'internal fixation'. (Left) A metal pin has been inserted inside the bone and special wire encircles the fracture to provide extra stability. (Right) The bone has been repaired using a metal plate and screws.

Dislocations

A dislocation is a disruption in the manner in which bones articulate, or move, within a joint. Normally, ligaments and other tissues hold bones firmly in definite anatomical relationships. Injury to these tissues can allow the bones to slip out of place, and the joint to no longer bend or straighten correctly.

Dislocated hips are common in dogs. In this ball and socket joint, a dislocation causes the ball to slip out of the socket. A general anaesthetic is required to replace most dislocations in the dog, and the limb may be strapped in place for several weeks to allow the joint to recover.

The patella, (or kneecap), which sits over the stifle joint on the back leg, can also dislocate. In small dog breeds such as poodles, inherited defects of the joint allow the patella to slide out of place, causing lameness and eventual arthritis. Fortunately surgery can reposition the patella permanently.

Any suspected dislocation must be treated as soon as possible by a vet. The longer a bone is out of place, the more difficult it becomes to return it to its correct position. Without treatment, the dog will have a malfunctioning joint and be constantly lame.

Amputations

The amputation of a limb is only performed when there is no hope of saving that limb for normal function. The limb may be damaged beyond repair, often from a car accident. Permanent paralysis of nerves such as the radial nerve in the front leg may mean the leg is continually dragged rather than lifted. For whatever reason, amputation is a valid way of saving a dog's life. Dogs cope on three legs remarkably well, and don't appear to suffer the painful aftermath of surgery as do human amputees.

Hip dysplasia

The hip joint in the dog is a ball and socket joint. When this is more mobile than normal, subluxation (a very slight dislocation) occurs and the head of the femur (the 'ball') and the acetabulum (the 'socket') become malformed and misshapen. The cartilage covering the bones wears and erodes, leading to osteoarthritis.

The hip dysplasia seen commonly in large, heavy dogs such as labradors, German shepherds and Rottweilers is an inherited disease. The severity and symptoms of this condition, which can occur in both sexes, vary enormously. Dogs may show hind-limb stiffness and lameness as early as six months of age, while other dogs are healthy until middle age.

The only reliable method of diagnosing hip dysplasia is by radiography. X-rays are taken of the hips at specific angles and positions with the dog under general anaesthesia to provide maximum relaxation. Rest combined with weight loss in fat dogs can alleviate pain in many cases, as drugs can only provide temporary pain relief. Several surgical techniques can be used to give affected dogs a better quality of life.

The major problem with this disease is its heritability. Adult dogs that have normal hips on X-ray can still produce puppies with hip dysplasia. Dogs with any suggestion of the disease should not be used for breeding. It is important that anyone contemplating owning, and especially breeding from, a large breed of dog obtain that dog from kennels that regularly have their breeding stock X-rayed.

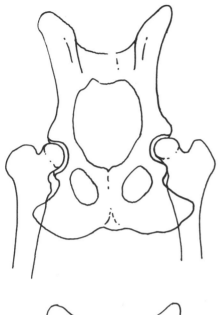

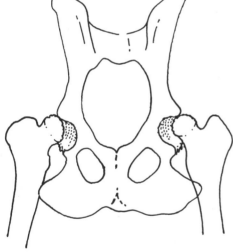

■ (Above) healthy hip joints. (Below) hip dysplasia, showing the subluxation and roughened bone surfaces of the 'ball and socket' joint.

Arthritis

Arthritis, the inflammation of a joint, can result from inherited problems such as hip dysplasia, from injury and from infection.

Osteoarthritis is a chronically degenerative disease that is the most common arthritis of older dogs, occurring in one or more joints. The dog gradually becomes stiff and less flexible and is often in pain. Degenerative arthitis has no cure. Fat dogs benefit greatly from a loss of weight, and in mild cases this may be enough to alleviate signs. Rest combined with anti-inflammatory medication often provides effective pain relief. Dogs that need to be maintained on these drugs for prolonged periods should be on as low a dose as possible.

Home nursing is important. Old dogs with arthritis should *never* be allowed to get cold: always provide warm and well-padded sleeping quarters.

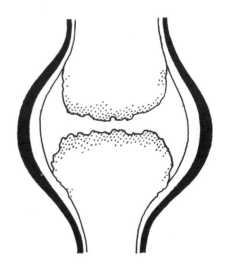

■ In osteoarthritis, the cartilaginous and bony surfaces of a joint become roughened and painful.

NERVOUS SYSTEM

The nervous system consists of the brain, spinal cord and a vast network of connecting nerves. Electrical impulses carry messages along nerves to and from the brain. These messages help to co-ordinate all parts of the body.

Traumatic injuries

Brain and spinal damage is very common after car accidents. Characteristic symptoms include inability to move (paralysis), varying states of consciousness, pupils of different sizes, or pupils unresponsive to light. Paralysed dogs must be transported carefully—a thick blanket held by two people, or a solid sheet of plyboard will keep the injured animal as still and flat as possible.

Brain or spinal injuries should be treated as emergencies and rapid professional treatment is required to decrease swelling of the brain and spinal cord. It is often difficult to assess whether an animal may recover full function after such injuries. Usually nerves are unable to regenerate if totally severed—they will heal rapidly if only mildly injured—or they can take weeks or even months to fully regain their usefulness. Many owners have been rewarded by their dog's return to normal after weeks of patient nursing.

Epilepsy

A convulsion, fit or seizure is caused by a sudden excess of electrical energy in the brain. This causes the nerve path-ways to be activated rapidly and repeatedly, and then the 'typical' seizure occurs: the animal falls to its side with limbs stretched stiffly and head drawn back, the whole body undergoing severe muscle spasms and twitches.

Idiopathic epilepsy (which means cause unknown) is a convulsive disorder that occurs repeatedly with the same pattern. The disease is quite common in dogs and mimics human epilepsy. Certain breeds such as poodles appear to have a high incidence of epilepsy, but all breeds and sexes can be affected, the first fit usually occurring after twelve months of age.

Epilepsy has three phases and it is important for the owner of an epileptic dog to recognise this pattern. The 'aura' phase precedes the actual fit; it can last from a minute to several days and is noticeable by changes in the dog's behaviour. Pets may become more affectionate, more restless, or appear frightened. The 'ictus' is the actual fit, which usually lasts less than five minutes. The 'postictus' is the time of recovery after the epileptic fit

■ Following a car accident or similar trauma, different sized pupils can indicate brain oedema or swelling. Consult your vet immediately.

when the dog may appear confused and disoriented. This phase may last from a few minutes to many hours, but usually the dog returns to normal quite quickly.

Epileptic seizures usually become more frequent with time. If the fits occur rarely and are only very short, treatment may not be necessary. More regular attacks require continual medication with anticonvulsant drugs. The owner of an epileptic dog should note the length and severity of the fits and the dates on which they occur, enabling their vets to prescribe suitable treatment.

Dogs that are convulsing can be dangerous. Apart from removing any nearby objects that could injure the dog, handling should be avoided. True epileptic fits are almost always of short duration, so any dog that convulses for longer than five minutes should get immediate veterinary attention.

Intervertebral disc disease

The spinal cord lies within the spinal canal, which is a 'tunnel' enclosed by the bony vertebrae. These are separated by flexible cartilaginous intervertebral discs that act as shock absorbers, distributing the pressures of movement up and down the spine.

Degeneration of these discs is a normal process of ageing, but occurs faster and earlier in certain breeds such as the dachshund, corgi and Pekingese. As the discs degenerate they lose their elasticity and flexibility, eventually becoming calcified and rigid. The centre of the disc begins to protrude and pushes up into the

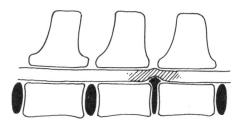

■ Intervertebral disc disease results from pressure on the spinal cord as a prolapsed disc protrudes into the spinal canal.

spinal canal, putting pressure on the nerve roots and spinal cord.

The symptoms of disc disease vary with the nerves that are affected. They include pain, stiffness and a reluctance to walk up steps or jump into the car. This may progress in a few days to wobbliness of the hind limbs and problems with urination. If the disc is putting enormous pressure on the cord, the dog may develop total hind-limb paralysis, drag both hind limbs and be unable to pass urine.

As with all nervous diseases, prompt veterinary attention can relieve inflammation and swelling. The longer the nerves are being damaged, the longer will be their return to normal function. Drugs are used to decrease the swelling and pain, but most importantly, strict rest is essential and it is usually advisable for the dog to remain hospitalised until signs of improvement are obvious. Patience and devotion are required of owners as nursing at home is important. The dog must have total rest, especially when on drugs to alleviate pain, and the urinary bladder may need to be expressed by the owner until nerve function returns.

■ Some dogs with permanent hind-limb paralysis from intervertebral disc disease lead happy and surprisingly active lives on custom made 'gigs'. These support their hind limbs and allow them great mobility.

Surgery is advised when the paralysis is severe or the dog has repeated attacks of disc disease to remove the protruded discs and parts of the vertebrae. This will relieve pressure on the spinal cord.

REPRODUCTION

The bitch, or female dog comes into heat between six months and two years of age, then on average every six to seven months. The oestrus cycle lasts three weeks. For the first eight days, the bitch will have a blood-tinged discharge and swollen vulva. Male dogs will be attracted to her but mating will not take place. For the next one to two weeks the discharge becomes clearer, and during this time mating will occur.

When dogs mate they usually 'tie', that is, they turn back to back and remain like this for up to forty minutes. The end of the male's penis swells and he is unable to pull away. Don't try to separate tying dogs; be patient, this is normal behaviour.

PREGNANCY

The bitch, or female dog, has a Y-shaped uterus or womb that can accommodate over a dozen pups. Most litters are smaller, averaging four to eight pups, or less for a dog having her first pregnancy. The length of pregnancy in the dog averages sixty-three days, or nine weeks (it can vary from fifty-seven to over sixty-eight days).

A vet can help confirm a pregnancy by palpating the dog's abdomen between twenty-one and twenty-eight days after mating, when the developing embryos feel like a series of golf balls. After forty-two days, the bones of the growing foetuses will be calcifying and will show clearly on an X-ray.

Pregnant bitches will need moderate exercise; unfit dogs will often have trouble whelping (giving birth), and they should not be allowed to become fat, as obese dogs also tire easily and have poor muscle tone. A balanced diet is essential, and the volume of food given should be gradually increased during the last third of pregnancy to help the bitch feed herself as well as the rapidly growing pups in her uterus. Young dogs mated on their first heat may need extra nutrition throughout to enable their own bodies to finish developing properly; some bitches can come on heat as early as six to seven months of age.

Bitches should be wormed every three weeks during pregnancy (see page 15). Tell the vet your dog is pregnant as administering the wrong drugs can be dangerous for unborn puppies.

Several weeks before she is due, the bitch should be introduced to a whelping box or area (place her normal bedding here to encourage her to use the area). This could be a wooden or cardboard box, large enough for her to stretch out comfortably. Cut one side down for easy access, and you may want to include a 5 cm wide narrow ledge that also reaches 5 cm from the floor, to prevent a bitch from squashing the puppies against the sides of the box.

A corner of a room is an adequate spot for a whelping box as long as the area is warm, draught-free, quiet and easily cleaned. Some breeders use heat lamps or pads, which are excellent but must be used with care as it is easy to overheat the bitch and pups. Hygiene is important, so use thick layers of newspaper which are warm and easily replaced.

Despite all your organisation, your pet may still choose to have her pups under the bed! After the event, she may allow you to carefully move her litter into the planned location.

BIRTH

In the six to twelve hours before birth a bitch becomes restless, may refuse to eat, and 'nests' by scratching up the newspaper and bedding in her box. Her temperature will drop to about 37.5°C in the twelve to twenty-four hours before birth commences (you can check this using a well-lubricated thermometer placed gently in the rectum for thirty seconds). The mammary glands should by now contain milk.

As birth begins the first pup moves into the vagina (birth canal), accompanied by obvious labour contractions and the rupture of placental membranes. The released fluid will be relatively clear, then a black-green discharge accompanies the pups as they are born.

Pups are expelled still inside membranes called amniotic sacs. The bitch tears these open, bites off the umbilical cord and eats the attached placenta. (The instinct that drives bitches to eat the membranes is protective. In the wild it was a method of hiding all signs of a recent birth, thereby hopefully protecting the new litter from predators.) She will lick the new pups vigorously to clean them and stimulate breathing.

It is wise to observe the birth process, but you must let your pet be your guide. Stress of any sort, particularly the presence of other animals, can cause a bitch to delay whelping. Some like their owners to be close by, others prefer solitude for whelping. In any case, don't interfere unless it is absolutely necessary.

A maiden bitch (one that is whelping for the first time) may be slow at first to break the amniotic sac. Using clean hands you can do this for her, then clean the pup's nose and mouth. If she is still uncertain and not licking the pup, rub the pup gently but firmly with a clean towel while holding it upside down to stimulate breathing and drain excess fluids from the nose and mouth. You may need to tie off the umbilical cord with clean cotton about 2 cm from the abdomen, then cut below this with clean scissors. Most dogs learn rapidly to follow their instincts, so give your bitch the benefit of the doubt and don't jump in to help too soon.

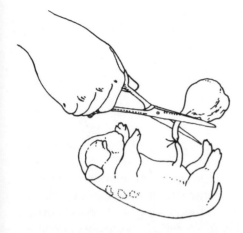

■ When an inexperienced bitch neglects to sever her pup's umbilical cord, it can be tied with clean cotton about 2 cm below the umbilicus. Cut below this with clean scissors.

LACTATING BITCHES

The lactation period is the time to feed your pet well as the bitch needs enough food to maintain her own body weight and at the same time to produce sufficient milk for her puppies. Bitches nursing a litter of pups may require up to three times their normal food intake. The diet should be well balanced, preferably including dry biscuits, and small meals should be offered two to four times a day. Water must always be available.

The three-weekly worming routine begun during pregnancy should be continued while a bitch is feeding puppies.

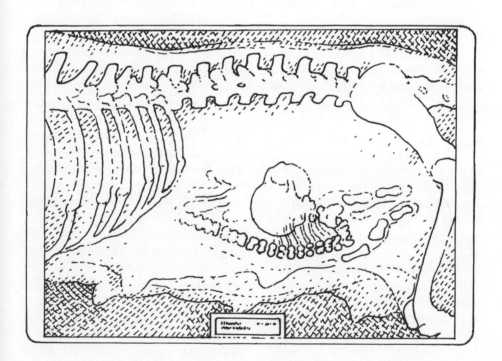

■ X-rays can be helpful when diagnosing whelping difficulties. Illustrated here are the bones of a very large pup with head turned back, indicating the need for a caesarian section.

BIRTH PROBLEMS

Whelping times vary enormously from three to over twelve hours. The bitch may rest for over one hour between pups, or may have them in rapid succession. Problem births may result when the mothers are inexperienced, when puppies are too large, and from uterine inertia. Inertia means that the uterus muscles can no longer contract and push out the pups. This can be from tiredness, or from low calcium and hormone levels. Your vet can treat inertia with simple injections.

Caesarian sections are performed on bitches when it is obvious that whelping will not occur naturally. This operation is performed under sterile conditions with a light general anaesthetic, allowing the bitch to wake up rapidly and begin feeding her new puppies.

It is important to know when to call your vet. A bitch that strains and contracts continually for one hour without producing a pup needs professional help. She may be tired and distressed, a pup may be visible at the vulva, or birth may not follow membrane rupture. Never ignore these signs.

Retained membranes

As a birth proceeds, make sure each pup is followed by a placental membrane. Occasionally these will be retained inside the uterus, causing serious infection. A foul-smelling discharge from the vulva will indicate uterine infection, but don't wait until your pet is sick: if necessary, a vet can give a simple injection to help the membranes pass soon after whelping.

Eclampsia

Eclampsia, or milk fever, is caused by low blood levels of calcium, a mineral essential for normal muscle tone and function. Bitches producing a lot of milk can lose considerable calcium each time their litter suckles.

Milk fever usually occurs in the first three weeks after birth, rarely during pregnancy. An affected bitch is initally nervous, anxious, panting and resents her pups feeding. A stiff hind limb action and muscle twitches develop, and she will soon be unable to stand.

Milk fever is an emergency and the bitch will die unless treated professionally with intravenous calcium to reverse the symptoms. You will have to feed the pups for the next twenty-four hours until the bitch is stabilised. If the puppies are three weeks or older, it is advisable to wean them. Otherwise, supplement the bitch's diet with calcium lactate or calcium gluconate from a vet.

Mastitis

Mastitis is inflammation of the mammary gland tissue. One or more of the bitch's teats will become hot, painful and swollen, and the milk produced will usually be thick, lumpy and discoloured. The bitch herself will become ill and the infection may also affect the puppies. A daily check of the bitch's teats will pick up any abnormalities. Mastitis is treated with antibiotics from your vet.

PUPPIES

Puppies must have constant warmth, frequent feeds and a clean environment. Contented puppies suckle, sleep and make appreciative squeaks; hungry, cold or ill pups will cry continually.

Colostrum, the high protein milk made by all mammals in the first twenty-four hours after birth, contains antibodies that give the newborn protection from disease. It is essential that all pups have their first drink within a few hours of birth, preferably from their mother, so they may absorb colostrum. After twelve to twenty-four hours, a pup's intestine can no longer absorb this important milk.

Cold and hungry pups may need to be fed with an eye-dropper, or warmed near a hot water bottle before being placed back with the bitch. Continued signs of weakness indicate professional attention should be sought, as pups easily become dehydrated or develop diarrhoea, and a sick puppy can die within hours.

Dewclaws and tails

Dewclaws are small, non-functional claws attached by skin, muscle and/or bone to the inside of the lower limbs. They can become floppy and a nuisance in adult dogs. They are snipped off at the base by a vet, leaving a small wound that doesn't require stitches.

Tail docking is done only to conform to breed standards. It is of no benefit to the dog, and there is absolutely no reason why crossbred dogs should be deprived of their tails. For pedigreed dogs it is preferable that owners know the correct length for tail docking in their particular breed. Tails are cleaned, swabbed and cut off with sharp scissors, then the skin is stitched.

The removal of tails and dewclaws must be done in the first week of life. As pups get older, this procedure becomes much more complicated and a general anaesthesia may be required.

Weaning

Pups' eyes open between eight to twelve days of age. From this time on they become more active and interested in their surroundings and should be given lots of affection and attention over the next month or so to ensure they enjoy the company of humans. They will then be ready to leave the security of their mother and littermates.

Worming should begin at one to two weeks of age (see page 15: pups are born with roundworms and are soon infected with hookworms). Vaccination against important viral diseases should start at six to eight weeks of age (see page 10).

When the pups are three to four weeks old, start offering them solid food. Canned puppy diets are soft and easy to begin with, enabling an owner to avoid cereals and meat (see 'Nutrition' on page 5). During weaning, gradually reduce the bitch's food and drink intake to normal to help her reduce her milk production. All pups should be weaned by six to eight weeks of age.

Orphan puppies

Rearing an orphan pup is hard but rewarding work. Commercial milk formulas such as the Wombaroo product make the task easier, and contain all essential nutrients. Cow's milk is inadequate, being too low in protein, fat and calcium and too high in lactose for puppies. Nurser bottles with small, pup-sized teats are available also.

If at all possible, try to feed colostrum from the pup's mother, or another newly whelped bitch, in the first twenty-four hours. Start on the milk formula at half strength, working up to full concentration over several days to enable the pup's digestive system to adjust.

The chosen formula should be divided into four to six feeds a day for the first few weeks; feed small amounts at frequent intervals, giving as much formula as the pup can comfortably drink without overfeeding. Weigh the pup every day to make sure growth is steady. This is ·the most important guide to the pup's health. Introduce solid food as soon as possible to encourage early weaning.

All bottles and teats must be sterilised after use, and milk fed at body temperature. Until puppies have learnt to urinate and defaecate, you must stimulate these processes. After each feed, gently massage the lower abdomen area with a lubricated finger; this mimics the bitch's licking and cleaning.

Orphan pups must be reared in a stress-free, clean, constantly warm environment. Ambient temperature should be 30 to 32°C for the first week, reduced to 24°C over the next four weeks. Heating pads are excellent, but make sure the puppies have room to move away from the heat source if necessary. Refer to the sections on worming (page 11) and vaccination (page 9).

REPRODUCTIVE TRACT

The following problems can occur during reproduction, or in the reproductive tracts of both male and female dogs. Complications of whelping and lactation are discussed under 'Birth Problems' on page 63.

False pregnancy

False pregnancies are common in the bitch, and are thought to be the result of excess production of certain hormones such as progesterone during the heat, or oestrus, cycle. Bitches experiencing false pregnancies think and behave as if they were pregnant. The condition occurs in all breeds and types of dogs, usually between two and six years of age. It is thought to be partly heritable.

Enlargement of the mammary glands six to twelve weeks after a heat cycle is usually the first sign. Fluid, which may be milky or clear, can be expressed. Bitches will often have temperament changes, for example, docile dogs may become nervous, excitable and lose their appetites. Occasionally bitches will 'nest' as if preparing for birth. Treatment is usually not necessary, as symptoms will generally disappear within six weeks. Hormone treatment will sometimes help, but desexing is the only permanent cure.

Pyometra

Pyometra, literally a 'pus-filled uterus', is an extremely serious infection of older, non-desexed bitches. In most cases, it is thought to occur after excessive progesterone causes the cells of the uterine lining to proliferate or become cystic. The uterus is then vulnerable to bacterial infection. Continual use of oral contraceptives can have the same effect on a uterus. Signs are seen within twelve weeks of a heat cycle.

If the cervix (the outside opening to the uterus) remains open, the pus is able to drain away. A bitch will have a thick, yellow discharge from the vulva and may be depressed and have little

Ovary
Infected uterus
Closed cervix
Vulva

■ Pyometra is a life threatening infection of the uterus. It can be avoided by routine desexing of the young female dog.

appetite. This infection can become chronic.

A pyometra with closed cervix becomes life-threatening, as the infectious material cannot escape and continually builds up inside the uterus. An affected bitch becomes extremely sick, drinks and urinates excessively, loses her appetite, and may vomit. The kidneys are damaged with by-products from the overworked immune system.

Surgery for both types of pyometra must be performed to remove the infected uterus, as well as the ovaries. Intensive treatment with intravenous fluids and antibiotics may be required to save the bitch.

Desexing bitches early in life prevents pyometra. Breeders should also consider desexing older, non-breeding bitches.

Prostatic disease

The prostate gland is present in many male animals, but is developed and functional mainly in dogs and human males. It secretes a fluid that passes out with the sperm during copulation.

In a large proportion of dogs over six years of age, excessive male hormones change the nature of the prostatic cells and the gland enlarges. Sometimes infection causes the prostate to swell and become painful and on rare occasions it becomes cancerous.

The gland lies over the neck of the bladder, just beneath the rectum. When the diseased prostate gland enlarges, often partially obstructing the flow of urine, it puts pressure on the overlying rectum causing pain so

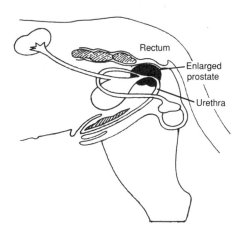

cation, although a general anaesthetic may be required to open the prepuce. If paraphimosis is not treated early, part of the penis may die from loss of blood supply.

As this condition seems to recur in oversexed pets, castration is advisable. In valuable breeding animals, the prepuce can be enlarged surgically.

■ Disease of the prostate gland is common, particularly in older male dogs. The enlarged prostate gland places pressure on the urethra and rectum, disrupting the normal passage of urine and faeces.

that the dog refuses to pass faeces. Constipation and dribbling of small volumes of urine result.

Changes to the prostate from male hormone imbalance can be helped by injections of female hormones. Repeated attacks are best treated by castration, which provides more permanent relief.

Paraphimosis

'Paraphimosis' describes an erect penis that cannot be retracted into the prepuce, or sheath. The act of copulation or sexual excitement enlarges the end of the penis, which is engorged with blood vessels. The prepuce becomes a tight muscular ring that prevents the penis from retracting while at the same time cutting off its blood supply.

Paraphimosis is an emergency. Early cases can be replaced back inside the prepuce with adequate lubri-

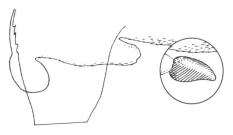

■ Normally, a dog's penis sits inside the prepuce. The inset illustrates paraphimosis, when the penis, unable to be withdrawn into the prepuce, becomes swollen and deprived of blood supply.

Cryptorchidism

When one or both testicles fail to descend into the scrotal sacs, the animal is called a cryptorchid. In a normal male both testicles are present at birth, but in a small percentage of cases they may take several months to descend. Many drugs have been claimed to 'bring down' the retained testicles, none of which has been proven scientifically. As this condition is highly heritable, cryptorchids should never be used for breeding.

The retained testicle sits anywhere in the abdomen from the kidney to just above the scrotum. It frequently becomes cancerous in old dogs, so castration is usually recommended.

CANCER

Cancer is not uncommon in dogs and cats, occurring more frequently in older pets, and although the word is frightening, not all cancers are untreatable and hopeless. Methods of cancer therapy improve continually and early treatment is often successful.

Benign cancers or tumours are those that rarely invade surrounding tissues. They often have a slow growth rate, don't spread through the body and rarely recur after treatment. Sometimes benign tumours become malignant with time. Malignant tu-

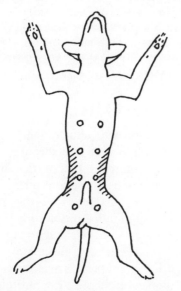

■ Sertoli cell tumours may occur in retained testicles. They produce hormones that cause symmetrical hair loss on the flanks, enlarged nipples, and the shrinking of the remaining testicle.

mours have a fast growth rate and spread aggressively throughout the body and surrounding tissues. They will often recur.

Treatment varies with the type of cancer and includes surgery, radiation therapy, cryosurgery (freezing) and chemotherapy. Always have your vet check any abnormal lumps—these are the obvious cancers and are usually easiest to treat. Others involving the blood cells, bones and internal organs are more insidious, but not necessarily fatal. Every cell type in the body has its own cancer; several are more common in dogs and are described below.

Mammary tumours

Twenty-five per cent of all tumours in the female dog occur in the mammary glands, usually in older animals. They grow into a series of knobbly lumps in and around the teat and milk-producing tissues.

Spaying bitches before their second heat cycle greatly reduces the incidence of mammary tumours. Surgical removal is very successful, but must be done as soon as possible as these tumours can become malignant. Chest X-rays are usually taken first to ensure that the tumour has not spread to the lungs.

Lipomas

Lipomas are benign tumours of fat cells and are very common in older, overweight animals. They start as small, firm, round lumps in the fatty tissue just beneath the skin, and occur usually on the body rather than the limbs. Many lipomas remain small for life, while others continue to grow to a huge size. Surgical removal of small lipomas is usually successful.

Sertoli cell tumours

Sertoli cell tumours occur in the testicles of older male dogs, often in those that are retained (refer to 'Cryptorchidism' on page 67). Sertoli cell tumours can produce female sex hormones that cause a feminising syndrome in affected dogs: the nipples enlarge, the normal testicle shrinks and there may be symmetrical loss of hair over the flanks. These tumours can become malignant, so early removal is advisable. After successful surgery, feminising signs disappear in several months.

OLD AGE

More and more pet dogs are surviving to old age. Ageing brings with it changes in the body: the cells become less able to function efficiently, and the number of functional cells within an organ decreases. Older animals have less 'reserve', taking longer to heal and recover from illness and injury and coping poorly with stress and change.

The ageing of individual dogs varies; the average life expectancy is twelve years, but less for large, heavy breeds and often considerably more for small dogs. Regular vaccination and worming should be continued, bearing in mind that older dogs become more susceptible to disease.

Teeth should be cleaned of tartar regularly and nails clipped as required (nails tend to grow longer as exercise decreases).

Common disease problems that affect older pets include congestive heart failure, chronic kidney disease, blindness, deafness and arthritis (refer to these specific diseases). Most of these are incurable and slowly progress.

Obesity is a common disease of aged dogs and is certainly reversible. Diet must be tailored to suit the decline in exercise of old dogs, and owners who manage to successfully slim their dogs will be rewarded by a happier, fitter and more active pet. Older dogs eat slowly and should be fed several small feeds daily, away from other pets. Vitamins and minerals are recommended if your pet's appetite is diminishing.

Warmth is most important. A coat is useful, and a bean bag or trampoline bed will keep an old dog comfortable and raised off a cold, hard floor.

Vets and owners must work together to combine medical treatment and home care in an effort to ensure relief from pain and discomfort. Many diseases of old age can be kept under control for long periods with diligent care. There is no substitute for tender loving care: old animals especially respond to plenty of affection and attention and a stress-free environment.

There may come a time when dog owners know their old pet's quality of life is diminishing despite constant care. Euthanasia may then be considered. If required, euthanasia is a fast, painless and kind way to end a life; it involves a single, intravenous injection of concentrated barbiturate, or anaesthetic. The animal literally 'goes to sleep' and dies quietly and quickly. Euthanasia can save a pet from prolonged periods of pain and discomfort. Always feel free to discuss the subject with your vet, who is trained to guide you through this difficult decision.

CHAPTER 2

CATS

The feline is a fascinating creature. Since domestication about three thousand years ago, the cat has compelled humans to sit up and take notice. The ancient Egyptians used cats to guard their granaries. They held them in high regard, and worshipped a cat-headed goddess of hunting, love and pleasure. Statues and talismans were made in the cat's likeness, and to kill a cat incurred the death penalty. In the Middle Ages cats became the witch's companion and black cats and eyes that glowed in the dark were feared and distrusted.

Since then, the cat (*Felis domestica*) has continued to appear as a favourite subject of artists, writers, cartoonists and poets. The Cheshire Cat from Alice in Wonderland, Tom and Jerry, Felix and all the cats from the pen of T. S. Eliot have been intelligent and humorous, reflecting the cat's prominence amongst domestic creatures.

Few people today can resist the cat, and most households play host to this inscrutable, independent but very expressive pet. There is an indefinable rapport between humans and cats that makes the question 'Why do you want a cat?' seem rather superfluous. Nevertheless, before you do introduce a cat to your family, ask yourself the following questions.

Can I afford a cat? Cats need to be fed, vaccinated, wormed and desexed and there will always be inevitable illnesses, boarding catteries and baskets to afford.

Do I have the time? Cats may be independent, but they need affection and resent boredom and inactivity. You will need to spend time talking and playing with your cat, and long-haired cats will need daily grooming.

What kind of cat do I want? Do you want a pedigree, or a moggy from down the street? The main difference is price, unless a particular feline appeals. Cats have individual personalities regardless of their origins. Both desexed male and female cats are clean once house trained. Long-haired cats need *daily* grooming, while short-haired cats excel at their own coat care. White cats may be deaf, and cats with white noses, eyes and ears are susceptible to sun cancer.

Where do I get my cat? Breed societies can advise on pedigreed cats, otherwise the RSPCA and other animal shelters have many unwanted cats and kittens available, and will often have a vaccination and desexing scheme. Choose the kitten in the group that is the most outgoing, friendly, sturdy and healthy. Avoid the runt or the timid

■ Familiarise your new kitten with the rest of the family's pets quietly and carefully. Given the right sort of introduction, dogs and cats often become inseparable.

cat: they may never respond to humans.

What age is best? Kittens respond best to new surroundings and house training. Adult cats may come with difficult habits, but if the personality appeals this could be the cat for you.

BASIC CARE

Regardless of the age of the cat you are bringing home, you *must* keep your new pet inside the house for several days—frightened and insecure cats will often disappear quickly. Try to spend most of the first week with the cat, making it feel secure and loved. Kittens in particular benefit from kind, caring attention, and between the ages of six and twelve weeks they are very responsive to their surroundings. Good or bad habits, fear or security are all learnt, often irreversibly, during this crucial time.

Teach children to be gentle from the start: show them how to hold, pat and carry their new friend. Introduce the cat carefully and slowly to any other pets in the household. Observe any interactions until they establish the inevitable pecking order. Have a new litter tray, basket and food bowls waiting, and confine the cat to a small, well-defined number of rooms. Develop a feeding pattern that your new cat can rely on.

After a few days, the cat will be relaxed and confident of its territory inside the house. Then you can begin taking it outside for short periods just before meals, until it has obviously decided 'this is home'. Your cat must also establish itself in a hierarchy with the neighbouring cats; this may entail spats and hisses, or even fighting.

House training is usually simple in cats: they are naturally clean creatures, and their mothers began their training at an early age. Confine the cat to certain areas of the house at the start with the litter tray conveniently nearby. Place kittens in the tray frequently, especially after meals. The litter tray must always be clean, as cats resent dirty trays and may resort to another more appealing location, thus breaking house training.

Find out what your new cat has been used to eating, then change its diet slowly if necessary. Refer to 'Nutrition' on page 76 for the correct diet for cats.

Cats are naturally very playful. Catnip toys can give hours of amusement to a kitten at home alone. A cat scratch post should also be provided

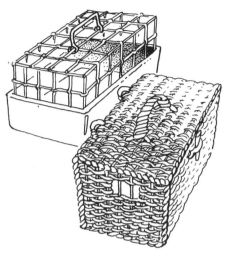

■ Cats are notorious escapees and should always travel in sturdy and safe baskets.

■ Cats keep their nails short and sharp with regular scratching sessions. A simple cat scratch post of carpet attached to a wooden frame can save many favourite armchairs.

from the start to prevent your best chairs being used as claw sharpeners. Use a cat repellent spray if furniture has been clawed; both posts and spray are available from pet shops.

It is preferable to have your cat *always* sleeping inside, especially if you live near a busy road. Darkness means exploration time for cats, and is the time most cat fights and car accidents seem to occur. A new kitten may appreciate a basket with a well-wrapped hot water bottle for the first few nights.

Cats must be considered when you plan a holiday. A reputable boarding cattery is the safest place to leave your cat for any length of time. Make sure the cat's vaccinations are up to date. Sturdy cat-carrying baskets are essential for any car trips. Most cats hate travelling and a frightened cat roaming the car can be quite off-putting to the driver. Tranquillisers may be necessary, but try the cat without them first; if the basket is strong and allows the cat a good view, most will settle down quietly, albeit unhappily.

If you are moving house, be aware that your cat is a creature extremely sensitive to its environment—many cats have been lost during a house move. Board the cat if necessary until the family has settled, then apply the same rules as those for introducing a new cat: keep it inside for up to a week, establish normal routines so the new house becomes familiar, and accompany the cat outside until you are satisfied it feels secure.

Your cat should wear a collar with a light, engraved name plate that also bears your telephone number. Light but noisy bells such as those found on budgerigar toys will spoil a cat's hunting success. Note that all cat collars *must* be elasticised to allow the cat to escape easily if it is caught in vegetation.

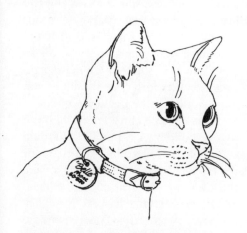

■ Collars with bells attached can save the birds in your garden, and a name and address tag provides quick identification if your pet is injured or lost. An elastic insert allows a cat to escape if tangled in tree branches.

Grooming a cat can be pleasant for both owner and cat. Short-haired breeds rarely need combing (but might appreciate the attention). However, long-haired cats must be groomed daily, and should be trained from the beginning to tolerate grooming. There are excellent metal cat combs available that have rotating teeth designed specifically for long-haired cats. Severely knotted long-haired cats may require general anaesthesia and close clipping to remove the tangled mess.

Occasionally you may have to wash a cat that has a skin problem, or that has grease or dirt on its coat. Before you begin, be prepared with towels, plastic jug, shampoo, warm water and a hair dryer. Unless your cat is very amenable, you will have to hold it firmly throughout the entire procedure keeping a firm grip of its scruff, which is how a mother cat controls her kittens. Having somebody to wet, shampoo and rinse the cat while you keep a firm grip can be very helpful. Most cats quickly learn to enjoy a warm hair dryer (*not* hot) played over their coat: this is the fastest and easiest way to dry a cat. Alternatively, place the cat in an open wire basket in the sun or near a heater and take care not to overheat.

Feral cats

A feral cat is any domestic cat that obtains food by hunting and scavenging. Since early European settlement, feral cats—abandoned pets and their offspring, and cats deliberately released in an effort to keep rabbits under control—have existed. They are distributed widely over Australia from sub-Antarctic Macquarie Island, where they are in densities of over nine cats per square kilometre and are estimated to eat over 50 000 native birds each year, to the Gibson Desert and Cape York Peninsula.

Born survivors, feral cats destroy native mammals, birds and reptiles and compete with them for food. All Australians must take responsibility for their cats by spaying them at six months of age, or by taking all unwanted kittens to a vet or the RSPCA.

YOU AND YOUR CAT'S BEHAVIOUR

Although cats have always been described as independent and aloof, when we take a cat into our homes we are removing this independence and encouraging reliance on a human family. We expect the cat to adapt to our way of life, forgetting how it once lived in the wild.

The cat's wild forbears hunted for survival, which required intelligence, agility, fitness and speed, as well as constant awareness of their surroundings and acute development of all five senses. Cats throughout time have always spent a large part of their day sleeping, but the remainder was filled with activity and purposeful living.

Often today cats are expected to spend long periods confined and isolated until their owners return from work. They have little chance for exercise and rapidly become bored with their immediate surroundings. Their natural playfulness is restricted, and they are unable to use their high energy levels. This constitutes stress.

For a cat that is very involved with the household, other stresses can include moving house, a new baby, divorce or a death in the family and, particularly, the introduction of another pet to the home.

Stress-induced behaviour includes destructiveness—you may come home to find the curtains torn, or the lounge scratched. The cat may lick and groom excessively, pulling out lumps of hair, or creating lick granulomas (see page 103). Some cats lose their appetites; others develop a habit of sucking either their tails or perhaps a woollen blanket. The most common manifestation of stress is the perfectly house-trained cat that suddenly starts to urinate in the house. Stressed, spayed females may even begin to 'spray' urine like a tomcat.

If you suspect your cat is suffering from stress, have your vet give the cat a thorough examination. If it is healthy, you must assume that it can no longer cope with its environment and you must assess its surroundings critically. Often all members of a family work; in that case consider getting two cats initially instead of one. Introducing a second cat later for companionship can cause, rather than alleviate, stress. Spend as much time as possible playing with the cat and, when you go out, leave it with catnip toys, the radio playing and a scratching post.

Seriously stressed cats may need hormone therapy from a vet, which can be very useful but it is not treating the cause of the problem. It has been said that it is impossible to separate the behaviour of a cat from that of the humans in its home. Use this as a key to your cat's stress problems.

NUTRITION

■ Small rodents were the basis of the cat's natural diet. A combination of good quality canned and dry food provides the same correct balance of essential nutrients.

The cat has been described as an 'obligate carnivore'. Whereas the dog has quite a flexible digestive tract and nutrient requirements, cats *must* have a certain amount of animal tissue to survive. Cats are unique in that they cannot manufacture specific nutrients that most other animals can; these nutrients must be constantly supplied in their diet and include vitamin A, taurine and certain fatty acids.

Vitamin A is essential for many body functions and is found in such foods as liver, kidney and fish oils. Taurine is an amino acid required for retinal function (in the eye), and deficiencies of it cause blindness. Arachidonic acid is a fatty acid manufactured by dogs, but not cats and a deficiency of this nutrient will result in dry and scaly skin. All of these nutrients occur in animal tissues.

Cats also require an incredibly high 30 to 40% protein level in their diet, up to four times the average mammalian requirement. The need rises even further in pregnant and lactating queens. High fat levels are also necessary and well tolerated, reflecting a cat's high energy (kilojoule) requirements. Fat and protein add palatability and must come from animal tissues (cats have no known need for carbohydrates and usually dislike vegetables).

It is therefore obvious that cats cannot survive on a diet of dog food. Dog food is too low in protein and animal fat and lacks essential nutrients.

Knowing, then, the strict carnivorous eating habits of cats, the distinction must be made between meat (muscle or flesh) and meat by-products (bones, liver, etc.). **Cats cannot survive on an all-meat diet.** This is especially crucial for kittens. In the wild, cats ate *all* their prey: bones, feathers, tendons and internal organs, and not just the muscle. This provided the correct balance of protein, fat, vitamins and minerals. An all-meat diet (muscle or flesh only) has imbalances of calcium, phosphorus and vitamins.

Despite persistent stories to the contrary, many cats *can* tolerate milk well. Always introduce it diluted with water first and gradually increase the milk to full strength. If diarrhoea persists, you know your cat can be given only water. Fresh water should always be available, both inside the house and outside.

The feeding of bones to cats is a contentious issue. The major advantage is better dental hygiene as bones are excellent for cats' teeth. In general, cats can cope with chicken bones, for example. They are careful eaters and rarely gulp their food, slicing it well with their molars before swallowing.

There are several 'rules' to feeding cats. Always serve cat food at room temperature, not straight from the fridge. Warmed food 'smells' better and a strong odour makes food more palatable to the cat. Also, avoid excesses of raw fish or liver. Certain raw fish contain an enzyme that destroys vitamin B_1 or thiamine, resulting in seizures, and liver contains high levels of vitamin A, which can cause skeletal deformities (refer to 'Skeleton' on page 116 and 'Nervous System' on page 119).

An understanding of cat behaviour helps you to establish a feeding pattern. As the modern cat's ancestors were solitary hunters, most cats like to eat alone, leisurely and quietly, in a safe, secure place without competition. Place feed bowls apart in a multi-cat household, and always feed dogs and cats separately.

Kittens

Kittens should be totally weaned by six to eight weeks of age. If you have a litter, start encouraging them with canned food at about three to four weeks of age. Kittens should be fed four times a day until three months of age, then gradually reduce the feeds to twice a day after six to twelve months. A newly introduced kitten should have any necessary changes to its previous diet made slowly. Switching diets suddenly in cats of any age will lead to digestive upsets.

Cats can become inordinately fussy eaters! They can decide at an early age that one particular brand of fish food, or a food such as liver, is all they require. Serious bone deformities can be the result, or, if a fussy cat is ill, it becomes extremely difficult to tempt it with food. Changing the fixed eating habits of an adult cat is almost impossible. Bearing this in mind, feed a varied diet from the start. Don't bow to pressure; remove uneaten food and replace it with fresh food at the next meal until your kitten accepts the food placed before it.

As already mentioned, a diet composed solely of meat should *never* be fed to a growing kitten. Calcium, which is found in low quantities in meat, is required for a healthy skeleton and kittens on a meat diet develop weak and painful bones; even jumping off a low chair can cause a fracture (see 'Nutritional Hyperparathyroidism' on page 116).

'Complete' commercial cat foods are totally balanced and do *not* need supplementing; vitamins and minerals in excess are harmful. Bear in mind that expensive usually means best when comparing commercial diets. Canned food is the most palatable for a cat but contains a large percentage of water, while dry foods provide more protein and kilojoules weight for weight. Dry biscuits also help keep teeth healthy and are excellent for the cat that likes to nibble throughout the day (although they do increase the cat's need for water).

The correct diet for a growing kitten consists of a mixture of commercial canned and dry foods. Buy well-known brands and vary them constantly. Milk can be given if the kitten can tolerate it. Fresh water must *always* be available.

Adult cats

Mature cats require feeding morning and night and sometimes in between (unless they are overweight). Cats have a relatively small stomach and can't eat huge portions, so feed them small amounts often.

As with kittens, **a varied mixture of canned and dry food is the best diet.** Adult cats may be given meat as a treat, or as a small percentage (less than 25%) of the total diet only. Milk can be fed if tolerated and fresh water must always be available.

Obesity

Obesity is not a common problem in cats. If your cat is the correct weight, you should still be able to feel its ribs. If a cat is overweight, feed it mainly canned food (it contains a lot of water), don't allow constant nibbling or self-feeding on dry food and encourage the cat to exercise by taking walks around the garden, or try a catnip mouse toy for games and play.

Sick cats

A cat's sense of smell is an important component of eating: food must have a tempting odour as well as taste. Sick cats, especially those suffering from respiratory disease, often have a diminished sense of smell. Be prepared to experiment and try strong smelling foods such as tinned fish, liver and pâté, and always serve foods that are warmed to room temperature.

ROUTINE HEALTH CARE

Vaccinations, worming and desexing are essential for healthy pet cats, and are important responsibilities for each cat's owners. Mark a calendar at the beginning of each year with dates for worming and vaccinating your cat.

PROTECTING YOUR CAT WITH VACCINATION

Cats are vulnerable to certain contagious diseases, only some of which are preventable by vaccination (the

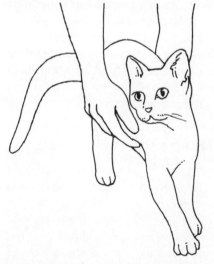

■ Obesity can be tested simply by feeling your cat's ribs. A healthy, slim cat should have only a moderate layer of fat over easily palpable ribs.

remainder are discussed under 'Infectious Disease' on page 93).

Vaccination is the *only* way to protect against viral disease. It is a way of stimulating the cat's immune system into producing antibodies, or defence cells, against each virus to prevent it from causing disease.

Feline infectious enteritis

The enteritis (inflammation of the intestinal tract) caused by the feline infectious enteritis virus can be extremely sudden, severe and fatal. The disease is highly contagious and especially affects very young and very old cats. It is a very tough virus, resistant to most chemicals, and it can remain infectious for over a year (at room temperature). It can be spread by human hands, by objects such as food bowls and bedding, and by sick cats in their vomitus, diarrhoea and saliva.

The virus acts in several ways: in young kittens, or susceptible adults, it causes an acute onset of profound depression, abdominal pain, vomiting, diarrhoea and dehydration. Kittens may die within hours. Pregnant queens that become infected can pass the virus across the placenta to their unborn kittens, causing abortion or the birth of dead or inco-ordinated kittens.

There is no specific treatment and affected cats must be given intensive care to have any chance of survival. Unfortunately, even with prompt veterinary attention, over 50% of cats will die. Refer to 'Vaccination Procedure' overleaf.

Feline respiratory disease

Feline respiratory disease, commonly known as 'cat flu', is very contagious and can be fatal in old or young cats. It is usually a debilitating and uncomfortable disease that can persist for three weeks or more.

The first sign of infection is often an occasional sneeze. Many cats just sneeze and go off their food for several days. More severe cases develop a fever, ulcers on the tongue and thick discharges that block the eyes and nose. Without a sense of smell and with a sore throat, cats lose all interest in eating and drinking, rapidly becoming dehydrated and losing weight. Occasionally pneumonia or a chronic sinusitis will develop, giving the cat permanent 'snuffles'.

There are two viruses involved in cat flu, which are spread by cats in their saliva and nose and eye discharges. A single sneeze can pass on the disease. Recovered cats can become 'carriers', shedding the virus into the environment for long periods.

There is no specific cure for feline respiratory disease; the most successful treatment is good nursing. Imagine yourself with a good dose of flu and you will understand how miserable your cat feels. Your vet may prescribe antibiotics for secondary infection, anti-viral eye drops and vaporiser treatment. Most cats can be treated at home unless they become dehydrated and weak. The sick cat at home should be kept constantly warm, allowed to sleep and have its eyes and nose cleaned of discharge twice a day with warm water. A continual array of strong smelling food must be offered to stimulate the animal's appetite.

Vaccination procedure

Protection against feline infectious enteritis and the respiratory disease complex is packaged conveniently into a single vaccine. The following regimen applies to both of these diseases:

High-risk situations (cities, catteries, etc.): Kittens should have their first vaccination at eight weeks of age, followed by repeat vaccinations at twelve and sixteen weeks of age.

Low risk situations: Vaccinate at eight weeks, then again at twelve weeks.

Cats over twelve weeks of age: Two vaccinations should be given four weeks apart (the second vaccination need only be for feline respiratory disease).

Breeding queens: should be vaccinated before mating, as only certain vaccines are safe for unborn kittens. Ask your vet.

All adult cats: require booster vaccinations every twelve months.

Virus control

A useful disinfectant for premises known to have harboured any of the cat viruses is made by adding one cup of household bleach to a bucket of water (this is a ratio of 1:30).

Full protection after vaccination takes ten to fourteen days. Booster vaccinations are then needed, because immunity wanes and a cat's body must be restimulated to make fresh protective antibodies.

Kittens under three months of age need repeat vaccinations. The queen, or mother cat, passes antibodies to her kittens via colostrum (first milk), providing important but temporary disease protection. These antibodies may interfere with vaccination until about twelve weeks of age.

Certain vaccinations, including that for cat flu, require an initial course of two injections to stimulate good immunity.

PROTECTING YOUR CAT WITH WORMING

A recent survey in Brisbane showed that over 80% of all cats were infected with hookworms (only one of many worms that can affect cats). Apart from intestinal worms, cats can also be infected by the lung worm (refer to 'Lungs' on page 111). The canine heartworm is very rare in cats but has been recorded, notably in Queensland. This worm's life cycle and the symptoms of illness in cats are similar to those found in dogs.

Roundworms

The main roundworms infecting cats, *Toxocara cati*, are easily seen in the droppings (or vomitus of severely affected kittens) as long, white worms up to 10 cm in length. There are three main routes of infection in the cat: kittens are infected immediately after birth by the larvae that pass through their mother's milk; eggs in the environment can be swallowed; and hunting cats can pick up roundworms by eating mice, birds and beetles that have previously swallowed worm eggs.

Kittens can have adult round-worms before they reach four weeks

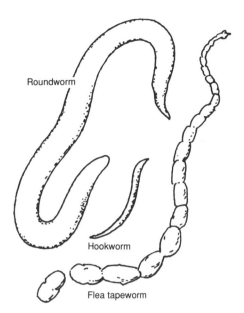

■ Important worms in the cat (not drawn to scale).

Roundworm

Hookworm

Flea tapeworm

Roundworms can lay an amazing 200 000 eggs per day, which all pass out in the faeces thus contaminating the environment. They are tough eggs, with a sticky, thick surface that attaches to dirt, feed bowls, bedding and litter trays. Symptoms of roundworm infection are most severe in kittens and include a potbellied appearance, rough coat and stunted growth rate, diarrhoea and vomiting, often of adult worms. The migration of the larvae within the lungs can cause coughing.

Reinfection of kittens is continual, both from their mother's milk and from worm eggs picked up from the environment. Repeat treatments are essential (see 'Worming Procedure' on page 83).

Hookworms

Species of *Ancylostoma* and *Uncinaria* are the hookworms affecting cats in Australia. They are tiny, white worms visible in faeces and are about 1 cm long with a distinct hook on the tail. They enter the cat via three routes: to kittens in the queen's milk; as eggs

of age. The larvae swallowed from their mother's milk migrate through body tissues to the liver and lungs. Eventually they are coughed up the windpipe and reswallowed, growing into adult egg-laying worms in the intestine. This cycle takes four to ten weeks.

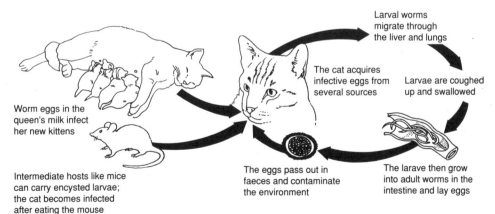

Larval worms migrate through the liver and lungs

The cat acquires infective eggs from several sources

Larvae are coughed up and swallowed

Worm eggs in the queen's milk infect her new kittens

Intermediate hosts like mice can carry encysted larvae; the cat becomes infected after eating the mouse

The eggs pass out in faeces and contaminate the environment

The larave then grow into adult worms in the intestine and lay eggs

■ The roundworm life cycle.

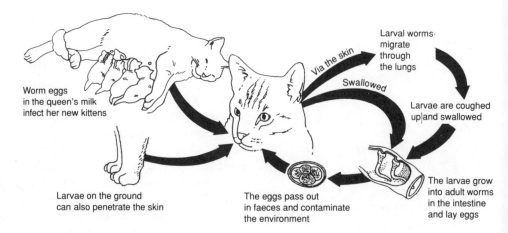

Larval worms migrate through the lungs

Via the skin

Swallowed

Worm eggs in the queen's milk infect her new kittens

Larvae are coughed up|and swallowed

Larvae on the ground can also penetrate the skin

The eggs pass out in faeces and contaminate the environment

The larvae grow into adult worms in the intestine and lay eggs

■ The hookworm life cycle.

swallowed from the environment; and by penetrating a cat's skin.

Eggs passed in faeces can become infective larvae in just a few days. These larvae penetrate the skin between the cat's toes, migrate to the lungs and are then coughed up and reswallowed to grow into egg-laying adult worms in the intestine. Eggs picked up and swallowed go straight to the intestine, and can mature into adults in less than three weeks. Kittens can have a hookworm burden by the time they are four weeks of age.

Hookworms are blood suckers. They attach to the intestinal wall, feeding on these tissues before moving on, leaving bleeding wounds. Heavy infections can cause anaemia from blood loss, dark red diarrhoea and weakness in cats of all ages.

Tapeworms

Cats can be infected with a number of tapeworms (but not the hydatid tapeworm), the most common of which are described below. Heavy infections can cause loss of weight, a rough coat and diarrhoea.

Tapeworms are segmented, usually very long and commonly seen as separate segments in the faeces. They develop in an intermediate host, such as an animal, bird, insect or reptile. This is then eaten by the final host, the cat, and the worm matures to an adult.

Dipylidium caninum is spread by fleas. The tapeworm egg is swallowed as a flea feeds on cat faeces, then the flea plus developing worm are swallowed by a grooming cat. The worm then grows into an adult in the cat's intestines. The cycle takes six to eight weeks. This tapeworm can grow to 50 cm, but usually only single segments are seen, passing out in faeces or moving around the tail and anal area where they look like mobile rice grains. Irritated, infected cats groom and lick their anal areas vigorously.

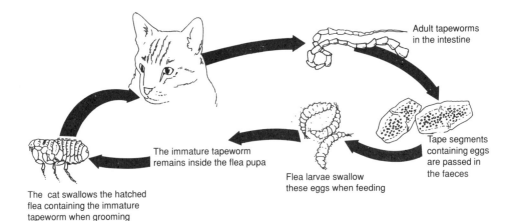

Adult tapeworms
in the intestine

Tape segments
containing eggs
are passed in
the faeces

Flea larvae swallow
these eggs when feeding

The immature tapeworm
remains inside the flea pupa

The cat swallows the hatched
flea containing the immature
tapeworm when grooming

■ The flea tapeworm life cycle.

Spirometra erinacei is the 'zipper' tapeworm. It is wider and longer than *Dipylidium*, growing to 100 cm with a flat body with a ridge down the centre, giving the distinct appearance of a zipper. This worm requires two intermediate hosts for development. The first hosts are freshwater crustaceans, which are eaten by frogs and birds. These second hosts are then eaten by cats; hunting cats are therefore the most commonly infected. As *Spirometra* requires different treatment from most tapeworms, you should contact a vet for advice.

Worming procedure

Always ask your vet for a worming preparation that is safe for cats.

Kittens under twelve weeks of age: Treat at four, six, eight, and twelve weeks of age with a product such as Felex Paste against roundworms and hookworms (this helps to control the constant reinfection from milk and faeces).

Kittens at twelve weeks of age: can now also be treated for tapeworms.

All cats over twelve weeks of age: Treat for roundworms, hookworms and tapeworms every three months. In high-risk areas, such as catteries or multiple cat households, treatment for hookworms in particular may need to be much more frequent so ask your vet for advice.

Pregnant queens: should be treated every three weeks throughout their pregnancy and lactation (suckling). Make sure the vet knows that your cat is pregnant before treatment is dispensed.

Internal parasite control

Purchase worm treatments from a vet, not the supermarket to ensure they are efficient. Make sure they are for cats, as many dog wormers are unsafe.

Teach your children to *always* wash their hands after playing with the cat.

The larvae of the roundworm in particular can cause problems in humans. Observe strict hygienic measures for your cat too. Clean litter trays at least once a day. This removes the eggs before they can become infective larvae. Routine flea control will also help to control some tapeworms.

If you suspect a worm problem, ask your vet to examine the cat's faeces under a microscope for worm eggs.

DESEXING

The discussion on the feral cat should convince responsible cat owners that *all* pet cats must be desexed. Here is a comparison of all the alternatives to give you the complete picture.

Contraception

Tablets or injections containing the female hormone progesterone are the most effective contraceptives for cats. Treatment regimens can postpone or completely stop a cycle, however, used continually these drugs cause problems. In breeding animals they can cause delayed heat cycles. More importantly, serious infections of the queen's uterus may result. Diabetes mellitus can be another side effect.

Mismating and abortion

Your vet can prevent an unwanted pregnancy with an injection of another female hormone, oestrogen. This must be done within two days of mating. Unfortunately, this will lead to the cat coming on heat again, often for several weeks. The drug can also be dangerous and side effects include uterine infections, bone marrow depression and blood abnormalities.

The easiest way to avoid unwanted pregnancies in a pet cat is to have her desexed in early pregnancy. As long as this is done in the first month after mating it is perfectly safe.

Spaying

The spaying operation should be performed routinely on all non-breeding female cats at six months of age. It is unnecessary for cats to have a litter first—this has no effect on their personalities. Neither will spaying make them fat. The reasons for obesity are almost always underexercising and overfeeding.

Spaying to prevent the birth of unwanted kittens is a responsibility of all pet owners, but there are other good reasons for this operation. Any

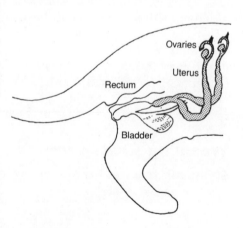

■ Simplified reproductive anatomy of the queen. The shaded area indicates the ovaries and uterus which are removed during the desexing operation.

cats with pelvic deformities from injury or from poor nutrition will have breeding difficulties and should always be desexed. Cats that are spayed before their first heat have a much lower incidence of mammary cancer than entire, or non-desexed females; they will also never develop the uterine infections common in older queens.

The actual spaying operation is called an *ovariohysterectomy*, which means the removal of both ovaries and the uterus. Thus the cat cannot become pregnant and there are no annoying heat cycles.

The spay is a major operation, performed under general anaesthesia and in sterile operating conditions similar to in a human hospital. (Refer to 'Anaesthetics, Surgery and Medication' overleaf).

Most cats can go home the night of their operation. Your cat will be slightly 'groggy' from the anaesthetic and will need a quiet, warm and cosy spot to sleep and recuperate. Offer her water and only a very small feed if she is hungry. Check the stitches daily, and contact your vet if they are red or moist. Keep the cat inside and allow her only minimal exercise until the stitches are removed in seven to ten days.

Castration

The tomcat, or male, reaches puberty when he weighs about 3.5 kg beween six to eight months of age. Like females, all pet tomcats should be castrated at six months of age. A desexed male is a pleasant pet unlike his entire counterpart. He doesn't smell, urinate over your couch, or

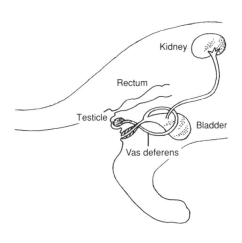

■ Simplified reproductive anatomy of the tomcat. The shaded area indicates the testicles which are removed during desexing.

have numerous fight abscesses from battles of supremacy with other male cats. He will defend his territory, but will not roam, preferring to be at home.

The castration operation is simple compared to the spay, but it still requires a general anaesthetic to prevent pain and stress. Both testicles are removed and there are no stitches involved. When your cat arrives home, he will need a warm spot to sleep off the anaesthetic.

Vets are often asked why vasectomies or 'tying the tube' operations are not performed on cats. The testicles and ovaries produce most of the hormones that cause heat cycles and male urine smells. As well as preventing unwanted pregnancies, the spay and castration stop these annoying sexual traits.

ANAESTHETICS, SURGERY AND MEDICATION

Short anaesthetics make many tasks easier, painless and less stressful for both cats and vet! To prepare your cat for an anaesthetic a small evening meal may be given, then all food and water removed overnight. If your cat is a hunter, confine it to ensure it can't catch and eat a mouse. It is crucial that cats have totally empty stomachs before an anaesthetic, as they temporarily lose their swallow reflex during recovery and any food vomited can fatally block their tiny windpipes.

Before an anaesthetic, a small patch of fur will be clipped off the cat's front leg and liquid anaesthetic injected into the vein. For longer procedures, the cat's larynx is then sprayed with local anaesthetic and a small tube is placed down the windpipe, which is connected to a mixture of oxygen and anaesthetic gas.

Surgery is performed in veterinary hospitals using sterile instruments and technique. Internal sutures (stitches) are self-dissolving, while skin sutures must be removed seven to ten days after an operation. After surgery, check your cat's wound daily and report on any redness or inflammation. Keep the wound dry (don't bath your cat) and restrict exercise. Cats that leap over the back fence two days after surgery stand a good chance of breaking their stitches.

Surgery causes pain and discomfort. After an operation, put your cat in a quiet, warm room and let it sleep off the anaesthetic. Give it water, and start food the next morning, offering only small feeds at first. Until the stitches are removed, keep the cat away from other pets or playful children, and give it lots of extra attention.

Training your kitten to take tablets at an early age will avoid many battles. Sit the cat on a table and stretch one hand across the top of the cat's head. Bend the head backwards and the mouth will partially open. With the tablet between the thumb and

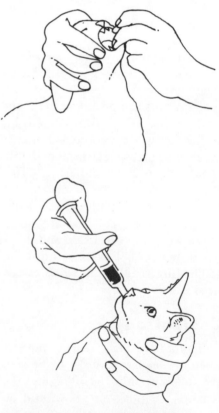

■ The well-trained cat will take medication amicably. When giving tablets, the head must be held firmly while the other hand quickly places the tablet at the back of the cat's tongue.

forefinger of the other hand, open the lower jaw by pressing on the incisor teeth with your third fingertip and drop the tablet onto the back of the tongue. Follow through with your forefinger to poke the tablet quickly down the back of the throat.

For fractious cats, have a helper lean over the sitting cat from behind and hold the front legs firmly, or wrap the cat gently and firmly in a blanket leaving only the head exposed. Use blunt tweezers instead of your fingers to drop and push the tablet down behind the tongue. Hold the cat firmly by the scruff just behind the ears as you bend the head back (this is how a mother cat carries and disciplines her kittens), or use liquid medication where possible (hold the cat's head in the same way, but administer the liquid through the side of the mouth instead).

When desperate, try placing the whole tablet deep inside a piece of meat, pâté or butter. Crushing tablets in food will deceive very few cats.

■ Some cats may need their front legs held to prevent scratching while being dosed. Really intractable cats can be wrapped securely in a blanket and controlled with a firm grasp of the scruff.

EMERGENCIES

Once domesticated, cats are confronted by a wide range of unnatural dangers and predators: poisonous substances, hot stoves, the motor car and the freeway. Hunting cats still fall foul of snakes, and tick paralysis is not uncommon. Your cat will be very fortunate if it survives to old age with nine intact lives.

Ensure that you have your vet's telephone number in a handy spot. In any emergency, always ring first: vets are there to help you and your pets in any crisis.

MOTOR VEHICLE ACCIDENTS

Keeping your cats inside every night is the best possible prevention against car accidents. Most cats are hit by cars after dark when they are off exploring the neighbourhood. Cats trained to use litter trays cause few problems, and nightly restriction also prevents nasty fights with the local delinquent strays.

■ Various ways of safely and securely carrying injured or healthy cats.

Remember that dogs can be fenced in, but not so the agile feline. It is quite irresponsible to throw your cat outside each night if you live on or near a busy road.

Handling injured cats

Always approach an injured cat quietly and calmly: even *your* cat may scratch when distressed and in pain. Frightened cats will also better accept one person than a team of well-meaning neighbours. Have a thick blanket and a sturdy box or carrying basket handy. Speak gently and stroke the cat's head first before attempting to lift it. If the cat is unable to walk, slide it onto the blanket with one hand under the hips and one under the shoulders, then place the animal in a box large enough for it to lie out flat.

If the cat resents handling, take a firm grip of the scruff behind the neck with one hand and place the other hand under the hips and tail before gently lifting. The only way to handle really fractious cats is to drop a thick

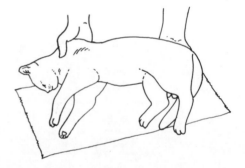

■ Cats injured in car accidents that are unable to walk should be supported evenly when transported.

blanket over the entire cat, wrapping it around to keep the head and feet inside (to protect yourself from teeth and claws). Then place the whole bundle inside an escape-proof box. You will need to do this quickly: Houdini had nothing on the average cat, and a frightened, hurt cat can inflict a lot of damage.

POISONS

Cats' slow and fastidious eating habits prevent many poisonings. They care-

■ The cat's fastidious nature and meticulous grooming habits make it very susceptible to any poisonous substances on its coat.

fully inspect prospective food, unlike dogs who eat first and ask questions later. However, cats' fussy attention to cleanliness can cause problems if toxic substances are licked from their coats during grooming. And cats are also much more susceptible to many medicinal drugs and household chemicals than most other animal species.

Symptoms of poisoning may include trembling, drooling, staggering, or falling to the ground convulsing. Such symptoms should *never* be ignored. The treatment of poisoned animals involves specific antidotes, and requires immediate veterinary attention. Because of these specific antidotes and because inducing vomiting in a poisoned cat can be dangerous, recommending home treatment for poisonings is difficult. If a cat is convulsing or semi-conscious, it may inhale vomitus onto its lungs and survival will be complicated by pneumonia. If the poison is corrosive, vomiting may damage the mouth and oesophagus.

Telephone a vet for advice if you are unable to go there immediately. It is far safer to describe the symptons to your vet and follow his or her instructions than to attempt home remedies. Syrup of Ipecac is the safest drug if you do need to induce vomiting at home. The dose rate for animals is 1 to 2 mL per kg of body weight, about two teaspoons for the average cat. (Don't overdo this, as Ipecac itself can have toxic side effects.)

Household drugs and chemicals

Cats are far more sensitive to many potential toxins than dogs or humans. Biochemical differences between the species mean that cats lack certain body chemicals that dogs use to help break down and excrete toxins from their bodies.

Paracetamol, or the common human pain-killer, acetaminophen, is extremely toxic to cats and just one 500 mg tablet can be fatal. The most obvious symptoms of this kind of poisoning are puffy swelling of the face, dark brown urine, bluish gums and distressed breathing.

Aspirin, or the pain-killer salicylic acid, is also toxic. One to three tablets can cause ulceration of the intestinal tract with vomiting of blood, anaemia and nervous symptoms such as staggering, flickering pupils and hyperexcitability.

Other household chemicals such as disinfectants (especially those containing phenol), food preservatives such as benzoic acid, insecticides used by professional exterminators (board the cat out for several days at least after the house has been sprayed) are a few of many substances that can be toxic to cats.

Sometimes cats are poisoned by incorrectly mixed insecticidal washes. They must be rinsed in warm water repeatedly to prevent the insecticide being absorbed through the skin. Take your cat quickly to a vet for administration of the antidote.

Organophosphates

Poisoning by these insecticides is common, and can be caused by the misuse of flea rinses and sprays, or by accidental ingestion. Organophosphates cause muscle tremors, excess salivation, constricted pupils, inco-ordination and diarrhoea. Early treatment with a suitable antidote such as atropine is usually successful.

Cats incorrectly rinsed in organophosphates should be washed repeatedly and taken to a vet for administration of the antidote.

Snail baits

Both chemical snail killers Baysol and metaldehyde (the active ingredient in Defender) are manufactured with grains and cereals that make them attractive to cats as well as garden pests. They can both fatally poison cats.

Metaldehyde, which is coloured green, causes muscle tremors and spasms, a staggering walk and eventual collapse. Baysol, which is coloured blue, causes similar muscle tremors and inco-ordination with excessive drooling, diarrhoea and pin-point pupils. Poisoning with either chemical *must* be treated promptly by a

vet—most cats will respond well if treated early enough.

Anti-freeze

This dangerous chemical appeals to the cat because of its very sweet taste. Ethylene glycol, which causes kidney failure, is the active chemical in motor vehicle anti-freeze and brake fluids.

Even very small amounts can cause cats to vomit and become inco-ordinate and depressed, and most cats die within twenty-four hours. Always take care when draining and replacing brake fluid.

Rat poisons

Unlike the poisons mentioned above, common rat baits are insidious, often taking several days before symptoms of poisoning are obvious. These poisons cause death by interfering with vitamin K metabolism and hence with blood clotting. The disruption to blood clotting causes cats to haemorrhage and they become very weak, pale in the gums, and may bleed from the mouth.

Cats must eat the equivalent of one poisoned rat per day for a week to absorb enough toxin. This is possible for a hunting cat perhaps, but is less likely than eating the powder, which is packed with grains and cereals. Any cat seen eating rat bait must be taken to a vet immediately for induction of vomiting and treatment with vitamin K injections. Very sick cats may also need blood transfusions.

VENOMOUS BITES

Even old, lazy, domesticated cats will transform into a powerhouse of muscle when confronted by a snake. Cats' ingrained hunting instincts often cause problems in Australia, a land of dangerous reptiles and insects.

Snakebite

Snakebite in cats is a very common occurrence, especially in country areas. Fortunately, cats are one of the most resistant species to snakebite and survival rates are generally high.

Snake envenomation involves many variables. Each snake has its own composition of venom: some toxins attack the nervous system, some cause tissue inflammation, some cause bleeding. Other important factors include the amount of time since the snake's last kill (a snake that has been hibernating will have very full venom sacs) and which part of the body the snake strikes. Despite all these variables cats respond to snakebite with very specific symptoms: the pupils become dilated and a flaccid paralysis develops. Affected cats become progressively weaker, floppy and unable to stand, eventually lying out flat. In severe cases, they are too paralysed to even flick an ear.

Each type of snake has its own specific anti-venene, with little cross-protection between them. Tiger snake

■ Cats affected by snakebite have dilated pupils and become progressively floppy and paralysed, unable to even lift their heads.

anti-venene will successfully treat bites from the tiger, black, king brown (mulga) and copperhead snakes, while brown snake anti-venene combats bites by brown snakes only. Death adders and taipans have their own anti-venenes. Therefore, identification of the snake is *crucial*. If possible, take the entire snake into your vet to identify it (colour is confusing: snakes are correctly identified using numbers and patterns of scales).

It is advisable for cats bitten by snakes to be hospitalised. While paralysed, cats cannot control their body temperature, so heating pads are used to maintain warmth, and dehydration and infection must be prevented. Close observation is required to monitor the cat's condition.

Tick paralysis

The paralysis tick, usually *Ixodes holocyclus*, is found mainly on eastern coastal areas due to its needs for warmth and high humidity. The ticks normally live on native animals such as long-nosed bandicoots, brushtail possums and echidnas. These animals are rarely poisoned and are an essential part of a tick's life cycle. Cats and other animals are accidental hosts.

Ixodidae ticks, which have a hard 'shield' on their backs, must find three host animals for development. Once the eggs hatch, larval ticks climb onto an animal host, feed and drop off. This pattern is repeated by nymphal ticks and again by adults. The whole cycle can take eight to twenty-four months.

Adult females are usually responsible for tick paralysis. As they feed, they inject a neurotoxin contained in their saliva. After four to seven days, cats will develop signs of toxicity. Although cats are generally more resistant to a tick's poison than dogs, symptoms are similar and affected cats progressively become more paralysed. Initially, the larynx is affected and the cat may have a strange miaow. The back legs then begin to wobble, and the paralysis works its way up the body until the cat is unable to stand. The pupils will be dilated and the cat will have difficulty swallowing and laboured breathing.

Tick anti-serum *must* be administered by a vet as soon as possible, and the cat searched and any ticks removed. Although there is a danger of reaction to this injection, without it the paralysed cat will die.

Cats living in tick areas should be groomed every day and sprayed or rinsed every week with a safe insecticide. Ticks will attach anywhere on the body and are easily removed by grasping firmly with tweezers at the point where they are embedded in the skin. Try to remove the entire tick, but remnants will quickly die and cause no problems. *Do not* use methylated spirits or cigarette butts as this may cause the tick to inject more toxin.

HEAT STRESS

Heat stress is rare in the cat; it appears that cats can tolerate higher temperatures than dogs. Nevertheless, it can occur after an animal has been left in a car on a hot day without provision for fresh air and water, and rapid action is required as irreversible damage can occur and even death within one to two hours. Refer to 'Dogs' page 28 for more information on heat stress.

Cats should always be transported in sturdy, escape-proof cages so car windows can be safely lowered to provide adequate fresh air on hot days. Always park your car in the shade if you are carrying any animals.

BURNS

There are several potential dangers for thermal injury, or burns, to your cat in the domestic situation. Cats can be burnt by accidentally walking over a hot stove, having hot liquid spilt on their skin, or by hair dryers that malfunction during a drying session. The extent of tissue damage after a burn depends on the time the tissue remains overheated. Fast cooling shortens the duration of overheating and reduces pain, swelling and the depth of the burn.

All burns should be cooled as soon as possible. Place a mixture of ice and water in a plastic bag and hold over the injured area for at least thirty minutes. Your vet will need to prescribe medication for follow-up treatment of the burn.

CAT FIGHTS

Most cat fights occur at night, so it is unusual for them to be witnessed by worried owners. In any case, they are extremely difficult to stop and, as for dog fights, a bucket of water or a blast from a hose are the best ways of separating the warring cats.

Abscesses caused by scratches and bites inevitably result from cat fights, and these are discussed under 'Skin' on page 99. It is important that cats be treated with antibiotics after a fight to prevent these infections occurring.

INFECTIOUS DISEASE

Cats are susceptible to a number of infectious diseases that appear to be unique to this species. Feline infectious enteritis and viral respiratory disease are discussed under 'Protecting Your Cat with Vaccination' on page 78, and the feline leukaemia virus is discussed under 'Cancer' on page 128.

Feline infectious peritonitis

Feline infectious peritonitis (FIP) is a very serious, usually fatal, viral disease exclusive to cats. As the virus involved is fragile and easily destroyed, close contact between cats is usually necessary for its spread. The greater the cat population the more common this disease. Fortunately however, the vast majority of cats that come into contact with the virus quickly develop antibodies and hence immunity: most will not develop the disease, others may have only a mild infection and then recover.

There are two recognised forms of FIP. In the 'wet' form, the chest and abdomen may fill with fluid, causing breathing difficulties and/or a swollen abdomen. The cat will usually have a high, persistent fever, a slow weight loss and will be depressed. The so-called 'dry' form of FIP has very

variable symptoms as the virus attacks most tissues of the body including the liver, kidneys, eye (the eye becomes cloudy) and the brain (the cat may have seizures).

Up to 50% of cats that have FIP are often also infected with the leukaemia virus. Unfortunately, the prognosis for both these diseases is very poor. At this stage, there are no available vaccines, although current research may change this situation in the near future.

Feline infectious anaemia

Feline infectious anaemia (FIA) is caused by a microscopic organism, a rickettsia called *Haemobartonella felis*, which attaches to the surface of a cat's red blood cells, damaging them so they are removed by the body from circulation. Affected cats can become very anaemic. The organism is thought to be spread by bites from other cats or from biting insects.

Normally there are few signs of disease, and many apparently healthy cats carry *Haemobartonella* passing it on to other cats. Stress, which might occur after a cat fight or another disease, appears to cause the organism to proliferate in a cat's circulation. For example, FIA often occurs in conjunction with infectious peritonitis.

In an acute attack of FIA cats become weak and tire easily, have a fever, stop eating, and have pale conjunctiva and gums. In other cats the organism causes repeated bouts of anaemia with apparent remissions in between.

The disease is diagnosed by detecting the parasites on blood cells, which can be difficult. Treatment may be prolonged, consisting of weeks of antibiotics and other drugs to treat the anaemia. Some cats may still not respond well to therapy.

Feline immuno-deficiency virus

The feline immunodeficiency virus was isolated only as recently as 1987, but blood samples since tested in Australia indicate the disease has been here since the early 1970s at least. The virus is thought to be transmitted by cat bites so the disease is seen commonly in older, non-desexed tomcats. It is not transmissable to humans.

Very little is known about this disease apart from it being a chronic illness that causes a cat's condition to fluctuate. Symptoms of the disease are very variable, however, it is thought to cause poor appetite, loss of weight, chronic inflammation of the gums and upper respiratory tract, diarrhoea, fever, nervous signs and swelling of the lymph glands.

Toxoplasmosis: health hazard to humans

Toxoplasma gondii is a worldwide microscopic protozoan parasite that infects a wide range of animals and birds, including humans. The organism has little effect on the cat, but it can cause serious disease in adult humans and unborn babies.

Stray cats are without doubt the primary contaminators of the environment with the *Toxoplasma* organism. Only in the cat does the organism have a true life cycle, reproducing in the intestine so that oocysts, or eggs, are passed out in a cat's faeces. In all other animal and bird species, *Toxoplasma* encysts in body tissues. Serious disease is infrequent, although it may cause sheep and goats to abort, and dogs to develop pneumonia. Marsupials appear to be the most vulnerable species of all to this parasite.

Oocysts on the ground are picked up by birds, dogs, rodents, all grazing animals (including kangaroos) and humans, where they encyst in body tissues. A cat eats these animal tissues when hunting birds and mice or when being fed raw meat, and the parasites mature in the cat's bowel, where they begin to reproduce.

On the rare occasions it causes disease in adult humans, the organism produces a fever, tiredness and swollen lymph glands. Infection in pregnant women can cause abortion or retardation of the child.

To prevent the disease occurring in humans, you must observe the following:

■ Have no contact with cat faeces or the ground where it is buried.

■ Cook all animal or bird tissues before eating.

■ Avoid feeding the family or any cats raw meat (freezing meat makes it safer).

■ Wear gloves when gardening or cleaning litter trays *especially* when pregnant.

■ Clean litter trays daily as the oocysts can become infective after two to four days.

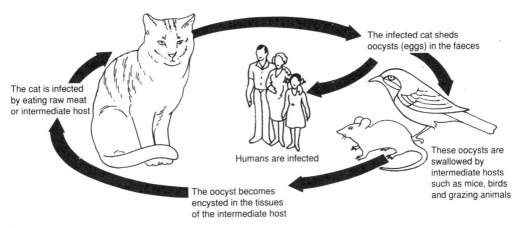

The cat is infected by eating raw meat or intermediate host

The infected cat sheds oocysts (eggs) in the faeces

These oocysts are swallowed by intermediate hosts such as mice, birds and grazing animals

Humans are infected

The oocyst becomes encysted in the tissues of the intermediate host

■ The toxoplasma life cycle.

■ Cover children's sand boxes to prevent cats using them as toilets.

■ Wash your hands after handling cats.

■ If possible stop cats hunting and eating birds and rodents.

■ If you're pregnant do not acquire a new cat.

Although widespread, the *Toxoplasma* parasite rarely causes disease. It is nevertheless an important health hazard of which to be aware.

EYES

Cat's eyes are adapted for hunting and are sensitive to movement—they can miss a stationary mouse! (Like dogs, cats have apparently very little colour vision, relying more on movement and varying light.) Their large size gives the cat a wide field of vision and allows maximum absorption of light: if you notice a cat's pupils their shape and size vary enormously, enlarging to let in the small amounts of light available after dusk and becoming slits in harsh sunlight, allowing them to focus better.

Most nocturnal animals are best adapted for night vision, but cats can see well both during the day and at

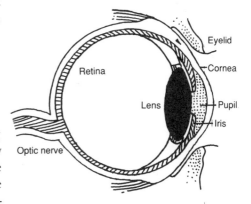

Eyelid

Cornea

Retina

Lens

Pupil

Iris

Optic nerve

■ Anatomy of the eye.

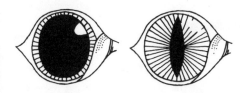

■ Cats' pupils are very mobile, changing rapidly from mere slits in bright sunshine to full circles in the dark. This enables them to see efficiently both day and night.

night. The shiny 'cats' eyes' you see in the dark are the tapetums, structures in the back of the eye which humans lack that reflect light at night.

Eyes are extremely sensitive organs and react so rapidly to injury and disease that sight may be lost within hours. Always regard eye problems seriously and get professional attention as promptly as you can.

Inherited problems

Compared to the dog, the cat is relatively free of inherited eye disease. Exceptions are Siamese cats which are notorious for producing cross-eyed kittens (called strabismus), and Persian cats which are continually bred with very flat faces causing tear duct problems and a resulting overspill of tears onto the face. Entropion, or the inward rolling of the lower eyelid, also occurs in Persians, whereby the cornea becomes irritated by eyelashes and hair. It is inadvisable to breed with cats with these problems.

Conjunctivitis

The conjunctiva are the tissues attaching the eyelids to the eye; when diseased they become red, swollen and covered in discharge.

Conjunctivitis in the cat is usually caused by infectious agents. The herpes and other viruses of cat 'flu' can be so severe in kittens that their eyelids adhere together with thick discharge, sometimes causing the cornea to become ulcerated and damaging the tear ducts. Infected eyes should be washed gently and the lids kept open using warm water. Anti-viral eye ointments, available from your vet, are also helpful.

Another contagious conjunctivitis is caused by organisms called *Chlamydia* or *Mycoplasma* which are similar to bacteria, and which can often be a problem in catteries and breeding colonies. Queens can infect whole litters of kittens which develop swollen eyelids and thick discharges. Isolate infected cats and clean their eyes twice a day. Your vet can prescribe the specific antibiotic ointment required for treatment.

Prolapsed third eyelids

The third eyelids, or nictitating membranes, are located in the inner corner of each eye of the cat. They protect the eyes and help keep them clean and moist. These third eyelids may 'prolapse' across the eyes, giving cats a distinctly peculiar appearance. This is not a disease, but rather tells us that the cat is not well, for whatever reason. Often the cat may have diarrhoea, or is carrying large numbers of worms, or the eyes themselves may be inflamed. Always have your vet examine the cat thoroughly to discover the underlying cause.

Prolapsed eyelids will not harm cats, but they frequently take weeks or even months to go back to a normal position.

■ Third eyelid prolapse can be caused by any illness, from worm infestation to simple diarrhoea. It is a non-specific indication of a health problem needing investigation.

Corneal ulcers

A scratch from another cat or a foreign body like a grass seed will often cause an ulcer (or break) in the cornea, the fine membrane that covers and protects the eye. Corneal injuries leave eyes vulnerable to infection and can cause a loss of sight. Often a blue-white scar will remain on the surface of affected eyes.

A dye called fluorescein is often used to stain a suspected ulcer bright green, as they can be hard to see with the naked eye. Often the vet will stitch the eyelids together for one to two weeks, which doesn't worry the cat and allows the ulcer to heal in a moist, protected environment.

An eye ulcer causes extreme pain and swelling, constant blinking and avoidance of bright light. Don't ignore these symptoms.

Cataracts

A cataract is a disease of the lens, that part of the eye that transmits and focuses light on the retina. The lens always reacts to disease by becoming more opaque, which causes the blue-white cataract seen in the back of an eye.

Inherited cataracts are unknown in the cat. Most result from disease such as diabetes, or, in kittens, from contracting certain diseases before birth. Cataracts in old cats are due to normal changes that occur in the lens with ageing.

Surgery is possible on certain types of cataracts, for which the cat is usually referred to a specialist veterinary ophthalmologist.

Watery eyes

Flat-faced cats such as Persians frequently have watery eyes. These cats have large eyes but shallow bony sockets, so the normal pooling of tears in the corner of their eyes can't be accommodated. Often there are malformed tear ducts as well, which can also result from severe viral conjunctivitis. The tears overflow onto the face and proteins in the tears stain the face red-brown. Long-term antibiotic therapy can bind these proteins but is not advisable. Tear-stain removers are sold by pet shops.

If inflammation and pain are evident with a weepy eye, the problem is usually serious—take the cat to your vet.

Tumours

The feline leukaemia virus can cause failing vision due to deposits of certain white blood cells within the eye.

On the external surfaces the common squamous cell carcinoma (see 'Skin' on opposite page) occurs frequently on the eyelids of non-pigmented (white) cats, usually due to excess sunlight.

Blindness

Blindness can be a result of injury, cataracts, incorrect diet or disease, but given the right environment blind cats can survive remarkably well, learning instead to rely on their already well-developed senses of smell and hearing. Sometimes a second pet in the family will take on a 'guide dog' role. Keep the cat's environment stable and it will adapt well. Don't move furniture, change patterns of feeding and sleeping, or introduce a new pet.

Treating eyes

Eye drops and ointments are placed in the eye by holding the cat's head to one side and opening the eyelids with one hand. The other hand should rest lightly on the cat's head, enabling the medication to be placed accurately and gently into the eye. Only one to two drops or a small amount of ointment are required, which will be spread over the eye as the cat blinks. Avoid touching the eyeball.

Your vet will prescribe different eye preparations depending on the problem. Never use human or out of date eye medication as eyes can rapidly worsen if incorrect drugs are applied.

EARS

Cats' ear canals are long and have a bend in the middle, so it is necessary for your vet to use an otoscope to examine all parts of the ear canal properly. Despite this deep, narrow ear canal, cats have far fewer ear problems than dogs. Serious chronic infections of the canal, called otitis externa, are uncommon in cats.

The symptoms indicating an ear problem in the cat include: shaking the head constantly, hanging the head to one side and scratching that ear, and a discharge visible at the top of the ear canal. In rare middle ear infections, the cat will be unbalanced and may walk in circles. Depression often accompanies these signs as ear diseases are very painful, so get prompt professional attention if you notice any of these symptoms.

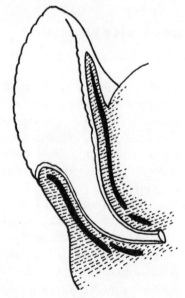

■ The cat has a long ear canal and foreign bodies must be removed by your vet.

Ear mites

Ear mites, *Otodectes cynotis*, are tiny insects that live on the debris and dead skin tissue inside the ear canal. As a vet examines the ear, the light from the otoscope warms the canal and the white, pinhead size mites can be seen moving around on the dark brown discharge that is typical of this problem.

The mites spend their entire life cycle on the cat, mostly inside the ear. They cause intense irritation and affected cats will shake their heads constantly.

Treatment is essential to prevent a chronic infection and to prevent their spread to other pets in the family: these mites are very contagious. Insecticidal ear drops are effective against the mites, but cats should also be rinsed with an insecticide as the mites often wander elsewhere over the body and can reinfect the ear (your vet will advise on safe insecticides to use on your cat).

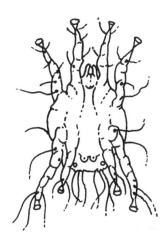

■ The ear mite, *otodectes*, is a tiny insect that can invade the cat's ear canal causing intense irritation and inflammation.

Deafness

Deafness can be inherited, especially in blue-eyed white cats, otherwise it is usually a part of the ageing process. Always be alert to your deaf cat; many cats like to sleep under the family car, but if they're deaf they won't hear the engine start.

Treating ears

Ear-drop preparations have long nozzles that are placed carefully down the ear canal and squeezed gently —try not to flood the ear with lotion. Massage the cat's ears gently to distribute it over the entire canal and wipe away any visible excess lotion.

A vet will prescribe different ear preparations for specific purposes, so it is safer not to use human preparations, or old ear medications that are out of date.

SKIN

The skin is a sensitive organ and disturbances cause inflammation, pain and itchiness, although the overall incidence of skin disease in cats is quite low, largely due to this species' unique cleaning and grooming habits. However, when skin diseases do occur in cats, their fastidious nature can become a problem, as excessive grooming may cause self-mutilation. As saliva stains the coat, this constant licking often becomes noticeable first as red-brown patches on the cat's fur.

Grooming also removes skin lotions rapidly, making them often quite useless in the cat, and other means of treatment, such as bathing, may be necessary. Bathing cats can be quite an experience for the un-initiated and is described on page 74.

Abscesses

Cats, particularly those that remain entire (not desexed), are strongly ter-ritorial, and both males and females fight with an awesome ferocity to protect their patches. Desexed cats tend not to wander to mark a territory, but if their home ground is intruded upon they will fight fiercely. The result of these epic battles are cats with infected fight wounds, which, if untreated, rapidly become abscesses.

The teeth and claws of cats (their main fighting weapons) carry a large number of bacteria. When they penetrate the skin, these bacteria are deposited deep in the tissues and multiply to cause an infection underneath the healing skin. Within a week after a fight, these apparently healed wounds swell and an abscess forms.

An abscess is a pool of pus, usually separated from surrounding tissues by a capsule, or wall, that is built by the body's defence mechanisms. It pre-sents as a hot, painful swelling that increases in size until it ruptures, releasing its foul-smelling contents. Abscesses can also be caused by other wounds or foreign bodies such as grass seeds that bury into the skin and muscle.

Some abscesses rupture quickly and heal. Most become quite large (it is not uncommon for a cat's whole face to swell) and the cat becomes miserable and depressed, won't eat and has a high temperature. Abscesses are usually located on the head and face, paws, or over the tail.

Obtaining medication imme-diately after a fight prevents infection, and is the best treatment for your cat. If an abscess forms, the vet will anaes-thetise the cat then open, drain and flush the abscess and prescribe antibiotics. Ruptured abscesses can be flushed once a day with a weak antiseptic. Abscesses should be kept open and draining for several days to prevent recurrence. The best way to avoid abscesses is to desex your cats, and keep them in at night (fighting time).

Flea allergy dermatitis

Fleas flourish in warm and humid climates, hence they occur over most of the populated areas of Australia, and are the major cause of allergic dermatitis in the cat.

There are several facts that must

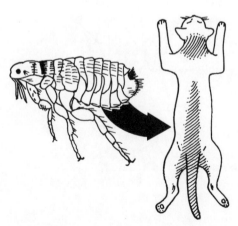

■ Common cat and dog flea: cats allergic to it develop a specific dermatitis along the lower back and tail, and around the neck.

be understood before fleas can be beaten. All cat owners must accept that *all* cats will have fleas at some time, and this does not mean that their cat is dirty or unsociable. Also, contrary to popular opinion, the flea does not live *on* the cat, but *in* the cat's environment. A flea only hops onto an animal for short periods to feed; thus the control of fleas involves equal attention to your pets and their environment.

The common variety of flea infesting cats in Australia is *Ctenocephalides felis*, a wingless, bloodsucking insect that grows to about 2 to 3 mm, its dark brown body easily visible to the naked eye. The flea lives and lays its eggs in a cat's surroundings: in dirt, cracks and crevices of buildings and in carpets. In warm, humid weather, adult fleas emerge from a pupa only three weeks after eggs are laid, and they can survive up to twelve months without a blood meal.

Only certain cats will become allergic to the flea, and they will remain so for life; the average cat can carry fleas and only have the odd scratch. Some cats overreact to substances in the flea's saliva and, each time a flea bites, an allergic reaction occurs.

Flea allergy dermatitis is intensely itchy and cats scratch and lick themselves constantly. They develop tiny red lumps and scabs over the rump, the abdomen and inside the thighs, and eventually over most of the back and neck. The skin becomes bare and thickened (this is sometimes called miliary dermatitis). In heavy infestations, flea droppings can be seen on the cat's skin, especially on the rump.

They look like small black pieces of dirt and, because they contain blood, will turn red when wet.

Treating a cat's environment involves regular washing of bedding and baskets, using 'foggers' inside the house (ask your vet about these) or, if overwhelmed, getting a professional pest controller (but put the cat into a cattery for several days while this is done).

To treat the cat itself there are flea collars, powders, rinses and sprays. Always ask a vet's advice, as many dog preparations are totally unsafe for cats, and follow the manufacturer's instructions exactly. Malathion is a safe rinse, as are powders containing carbaryl. Take care when treating nursing cats and their litters; many products are unsafe for kittens under three months of age. To use a flea powder, rub it well into the coat then wipe off any excess with a damp cloth, otherwise the cat will lick it off.

In allergic cats with skin problems, you may need medication to stop the itch-lick-itch cycle until fleas are under control. Don't rely on these products—you must get rid of the initiating cause, the flea.

Mange mites

Mange is caused by tiny, microscopic mites, or insects. The canine mange mites rarely infest cats, which have their own variety, *Notoedres cati*. These cause notoedric or 'head' mange as the mites mainly live on the head, particularly the temporal area. Contact with other cats spreads the mites.

The mite spends its entire life cycle on a host cat. Female mites burrow into the top skin layers, making tunnels. They feed off the skin tissues and lay their eggs, then the eggs hatch into larvae which burrow elsewhere, maturing into adult mites in three weeks. This burrowing and tunnelling is irritating, and cats affected with notoedric mange scratch constantly.

The symptoms of notoedric mange are redness, tiny lumps and thick, grey, crusty scales, with eventual hair loss over the temples, ears and face (note that in some cats it is normal to have only thin hair growth in the temporal area). Occasionally the mites spread elsewhere on the body. To diagnose mange, your vet will gently scrape the surface layers of affected skin and examine them under a microscope for mites.

Dog mange treatments can be dangerous for cats, so use the correct rinse or tablets dispensed by a vet. Isolate the affected cat if possible, and rinse all in-contact cats with a safe insecticide like malathion, used strictly according to instructions.

■ The microscopic notoedric mange mite infests cats in the temple area, causing hair loss and inflammation.

Ringworm

Ringworm is a fungal infection of the skin, so-called because it can cause circular hairless patches to develop. The ringworm fungus invades hair follicles, the hairs break off and the lesions spread in a circular manner. Cats are one species on which these bare, scaly 'circles' are easily recognisable. *Microsporum canis* is the common fungus infecting cats. The lesions usually begin on the head or the limbs and then the discrete, round patches join together as the infection spreads over the body.

Ringworm occurs most frequently in kittens and, as it can easily be transmitted to humans, infected kittens often mean infected children. Other animals in the household are equally at risk of infection. Isolate affected animals and preferably destroy their bedding. A four to six week course of griseofulvin tablets from a vet, combined with weekly antifungal rinses, is the best treatment. Griseofulvin can also be given to in-contact animals to prevent spread of the fungus. This drug must *never* be given to pregnant queens as it can cause deformity in kittens.

Contact dermatitis

Contact dermatitis is an inflammation caused by contact with an irritating substance, and is commonly seen, for instance, around the necks of cats allergic to flea collars. Paint, cement powder and lime are a few of the many irritants in most cats' environments. The result of contact with any of these substances is a painful, raw, weeping area over the contact site, which is often exacerbated as the cat self-mutilates the lesion by licking and scratching. The offending cause must be tracked down and removed, and medication prescribed by a vet to stop itching and allow healing.

Feline acne

Feline acne occurs most commonly on a cat's chin (where there is a complex of sweat and oil glands), usually in cats that aren't cleaning themselves properly or in those with greasy skin. The cat develops a painful and swollen chin that may prevent it from eating. Close examination reveals pustules (pimples), blackheads and, in severe cases, draining sinuses. The infection responds to antibiotics and daily cleansing with a mild antiseptic or soap and water. This may need to be done once a week to prevent recurrence.

■ Eosinophilic ulcers are lesions that occur on the cat's lip, often near the large canine teeth.

blood cell that is present in certain skin and muscle diseases, and which increase in numbers in times of stress. Eosinophilic ulcers affect cats of all ages and commonly occur on the upper lip margin and the hard and soft palates. Their cause is unknown. Lesions begin as small, reddened and eroded areas with a raised margin, then as they progress, they become larger, ulcerated and disfigure the lips. Occasionally these ulcers occur as pink, raw, well-circumscribed plaques on the abdomen, inside the thighs and on the feet.

A course of corticosteroids injected into the lesions by your vet seems to be the most successful treatment. Some are removed surgically.

Neurodermatitis

Neurodermatitis, or lick granuloma, is the result of an anxiety neurosis, in which lesions are caused by continual licking. Cats have very rough, barbed tongues, and excessive licking irritates and breaks the skin. The condition appears to be more common in short-haired pedigreed cats. The constant licking causes loss of hair, redness, inflammation and granuloma formation (a roughened, pink, raw area)

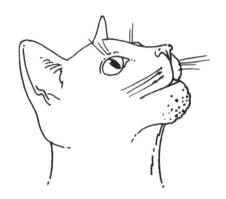

■ Feline acne is an infection of the cat's chin, causing it to swell and become painful.

Eosinophilic ulcers

Eosinophilic ulcers contain large numbers of eosinophils, a type of

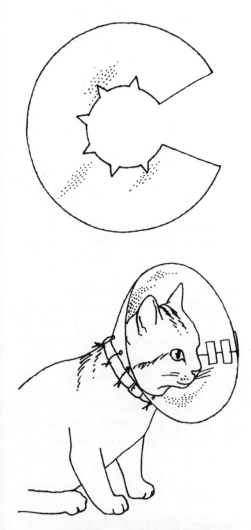

A new baby or pet, a teasing child, moving house, confinement and isolation for long periods, or just plain lack of attention can begin this syndrome.

Surgical removal or corticosteroids injected into the lesion are the most common forms of therapy. However, it is extremely hard to break cats of their licking habits. Sometimes Elizabethan collars are used, but the most important treatment is a review of the affected cat's way of life. The cat must be given lots of love and affection. Get catnip toys and spend time playing with your pet, and get a neighbour to visit and pat the cat to relieve the boredom of long hours of isolation.

Skin tumours

The most common skin tumour by far in cats is the squamous cell carcinoma, a malignant, eroding and invasive cancer that occurs mostly on the ear tips, nose and eyelids of white cats, or those with a lack of pigment in these areas. It frequently follows a condition called feline solar dermatitis (sunburn), and occurs most commonly in older cats, no doubt after years of sunshine.

Initially the ear tips are tender and red, the skin peels and they curl forward. Hair loss occurs, the ear tips thicken and each summer the inflammation becomes more severe. At some stage, the lesion changes into a carcinoma and ulcerates, and the ear tips become eroded and bleed easily when bumped. Similarly, carcinomas on the nose and eyelids begin as small raw areas that scab over but refuse to heal, eventually invading the surrounding tissues.

■ Elizabethan collars may be required for short periods if a cat is causing skin disease by licking itself constantly. The cat can still eat comfortably, but is unable to reach the skin lesion.

on the abdomen, inner thighs and near the tail, or anywhere cats can easily lick.

Almost all cats afflicted with neurodermatitis are bored, stressed and sometimes highly strung and nervous.

Even though they are malignant, if treated early enough these cancers can be cured. Don't ignore a chronic wound on the eyes, ears or nose; have your vet check the cat as soon as possible.

Treatment varies according to the lesion. As unacceptable as it sounds, the ear tips are amputated in affected cats, and once the hair grows most cat owners forget the lack of pricked ears. After all, it is the same lovable cat. Other treatments include radiation and cryosurgery (freezing).

Try to change the habits of white cats that lie in the sun for long periods. Block-out lotions for humans are excellent if easily absorbed into the skin (so the cat can't lick them off) —apply daily during sunny weather.

GASTROINTESTINAL TRACT

Cats are carnivores and have relatively simple digestive tracts. Each section of this tract, which comprises the organs that ingest and digest food, is designed to digest specific nutrients, producing enzymes that aid in their breakdown.

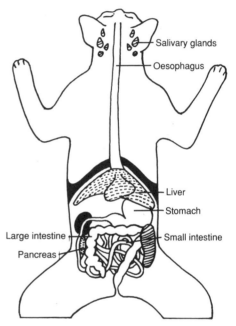

- Simplified anatomy of the cat's gastrointestinal tract.

- Prolonged exposure to sunlight commonly causes cancer in Australian cats, particularly on white ears, noses and eyes.

Mouth

Numerous diseases affect the cat's mouth, and teeth and gum problems are exceedingly common. Tumours such as carcinomas can occur on the palates, gums and tongue. The viruses of cat flu and kidney disease ulcerate the tongue, and infections of the entire oral cavity (stomatitis) are common.

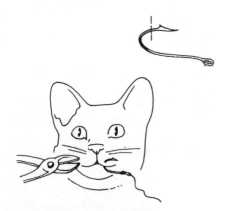

■ Cats can become attached to fishing hooks and lines. Don't try to remove the hook in one piece: cut the hook below the barb and then remove the remaining piece.

Car accidents frequently result in broken jaw bones, which are usually repaired with non-reactive wire and small pins that hold the bones in place for the six weeks required for healing. Most cats cope remarkably well, eating soft food in a matter of days.

Fish hooks are a common foreign body that gets caught in and around cats' mouths. Don't try to push or pull the hook; instead, cut the barb off with small pliers and pull the part attached to the fishing line back through. Often the cat will be distressed and it is far easier and safer for a vet to give the cat a short anaesthetic in order to remove the hook.

Most mouth problems cause similar symptoms: excessive drooling, sometimes bad breath, cats that drop food from their mouths in pain despite being hungry, and cats that resent having their mouths opened. These sort of signs indicate professional attention is needed.

Teeth

The rounded head of the cat holds only thirty permanent teeth (which are all present by the time the cat is six months old) compared to the elongated jaw of the dog, which has forty-two teeth. These teeth are specifically adapted to the cat's carnivorous habits: the four long canines hold prey, while the premolars and molars slice and cut the meat for swallowing.

Most teeth problems in cats are a direct result of their failure to adapt to soft domesticated diets. Meat and canned foods fed alone provide no chewing exercise, while imbalanced diets like an excess of liver can cause teeth to loosen and fall out.

Dental plaque and calculus

After eating, a layer of food, saliva and bacteria coat the teeth and this is plaque. Eventually, plaque becomes mineralised into a hard, yellow substance called calculus, or tartar. (See 'Home Care for Healthy Teeth' opposite for treatment of this problem.)

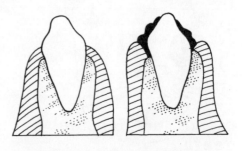

■ (Left) A healthy tooth with tightly adherent gum margins. (Right) A continually soft diet has allowed tartar to build up on the tooth surface, and the gums are receding from it.

Periodontitis

The periodontal membrane lines the tooth socket and cushions the tooth as it rests against the bone. Inflammation of this lining is thought to cause more loss of teeth in cats than any other factor.

Soft diets lead to continual plaque and calculus formation, which then provides cracks and crevices for proliferating bacteria, releasing toxins and enzymes that cause inflammation and periodontitis. Infection occurs in the tooth socket, loosening the tooth which is eventually lost. (See 'Home Care for Healthy Teeth' below).

Gingivitis

Gingivitis, an inflammation of the gums, goes hand in hand with periodontitis in cats, and is extremely common and debilitating. Gums become red and swollen, with a thickened rolled edge on the tooth margin. As with periodontitis, affected cats will drool thick saliva and sit at their food dishes, hungry but afraid to eat. (See 'Home Care for Healthy Teeth' below).

Halitosis

Any disease that disturbs the healthy balance of the mouth can cause halitosis (bad breath). It is another symptom that tells you your cat has problems and needs a check up.

Home care for healthy teeth

A balanced diet is crucial for healthy teeth. As all of the above problems can be caused by a soft diet, you should accustom your cat to eating some dry biscuits each day. The feeding of bones is contentious, but cats can cope with chicken bones and these provide good chewing exercise. Rubbing a cat's teeth at least once a week with a cloth dipped in hydrogen peroxide, sodium bicarbonate or a veterinary toothpaste helps to remove plaque. This may not be tolerated by all cats, so an anaesthetic may be required for a total teeth clean once or twice each year. This is far better than allowing gum and tooth disease to progress until your cat is miserable and unable to eat.

Stomach

Cats' stomachs are relatively small, and cats tend to eat little and often. This, combined with their careful and discriminating eating habits means that

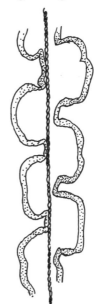

■ Playful cats may swallow sewing cotton which becomes caught in the intestine. The thread acts like a purse-string and causes the gut to pucker, necessitating life-saving surgery.

cats rarely overload their stomach with garbage and swallow far fewer foreign bodies than dogs.

However, as already mentioned, fish hooks are a common foreign body. And, as cats love to play with cotton and string, serious obstructions and infections can occur if the thread is swallowed with a needle or a toy attached. Never try pulling on the cotton—take the cat straight to your vet.

Gastritis, or stomach inflammation, can also be caused by drugs such as aspirin, by cats licking insecticides off their coats, and from the swallowing of excess groomed hair in long-haired cats.

Eating grass

Many theories have been put forward but none proven to explain why cats eat grass. Cats cannot digest vegetable fibres efficiently and they are not a normal part of their diet, so usually any ingested grass is vomited or passed in the faeces undigested, often with hair or worms. It is possible that cats use this undigestible material to remove unwanted foreign material from their gastrointestinal tracts.

Vomiting

The cat can vomit easily. This is a good form of protection if undesirable material has been inadvertently swallowed, so don't panic if your cat has the occasional vomit. However, persistent vomiting is always a symptom of underlying disease usually indicating serious problems and must never be ignored. As vomiting leads to dehydration (loss of body fluids), the cat drinks to replace the lost fluid, thus stimulating more vomiting and further dehydration.

A cat that has vomited several times but is still alert and well should be observed closely. Remove all food and water (this rests the stomach lining), and confine the cat so you know whether vomiting continues. Cats are very secretive about such things and often vomit in private. If vomiting persists over the next few hours, or the cat becomes depressed, call your vet.

Diarrhoea

Diarrhoea is the passage of loose, watery faeces. It has many causes including milk intolerance, heavy worm burdens in kittens, infectious diseases and tumours from the leukaemia virus. As with vomiting, diarrhoea is a symptom of an underlying disease and indicates that a cat needs attention.

Cats' toilet habits are a very private matter, and unless a litter tray is always used, diarrhoea, like vomiting, may be hidden in the garden. If diarrhoea is suspected but the cat is still bright, confine the cat with a litter tray handy and remove all food for a period of twelve to twenty-four hours. The cells lining the intestine are able to heal rapidly if rested from digestion.

To prevent dehydration, give the cat frequent small drinks of water, *not* milk. Add electrolyte powders such as Lectade and Vytrate from a vet to replace the body salts lost in diarrhoea. A simple test for dehydration is to pull the skin up on the back of the neck—in healthy cats, this immediately springs back into place,

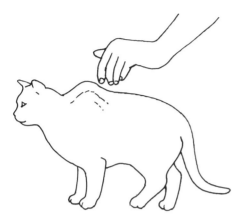

■ Persistent vomiting and/or diarrhoea can rapidly cause dehydration. Dehydrated skin remains raised when pulled up, while healthy skin springs back into place.

while in dehydrated animals, the skin remains elevated. Cats with this amount of dehydration need intravenous fluids to replace the lost fluid and to prevent shock.

If diarrhoea is persistent or contains blood, if dehydration is obvious, or if vomiting occurs with diarrhoea, take your cat to a vet as soon as possible.

Constipation

Constipation is common in old cats, when loss of muscle tone may cause the passing of droppings to be slow and ineffectual. In some cats, grooming can lead to the swallowing of large amounts of hair, which can also cause constipation.

Sometimes injury from car accidents, or poor bone development from an imbalanced diet, will affect the bones of the pelvis. The bony ring through which the intestine passes may collapse and place pressure on the rectum, preventing normal passage of faeces. A diverticulum (sac) may form in the rectum where faeces becomes impacted. Manx cats, which don't have a tail, have an inherited condition called megacolon where the intestine 'balloons' and the droppings accumulate.

Constipated cats strain continually without passing faeces, become depressed and may vomit. In the early stages, administering gentle laxatives like coloxyl (without danthron) or paraffin oil may soften the mass. If straining persists after twelve hours despite these treatments, a vet will have to administer a general anaesthetic and enemas to break up, soften and remove the faeces.

In chronic constipation, most cats can be persuaded to take bran mixed with their food each day. Oils like paraffin can be useful, but prolonged use interferes with vitamin absorption.

Liver

The liver is the largest gland in the body and has many important functions, including carbohydrate, fat, protein and fat-soluble vitamin metabolism. It inactivates many drugs and toxins, has remarkable powers of healing and regeneration, and can function on surprisingly small amounts of healthy tissue.

In cats, liver problems are usually secondary to other disease including the leukaemia virus, tumours and poisoning. Symptoms of liver disease include depression, poor appetite, vomiting and diarrhoea and jaundice (the yellow staining of tissues by excess bile pigments). Cats recovering from liver disease need a high-quality protein and low-fat diet. Cottage cheese, chicken and boiled rice are excellent substitutes if the cat is amenable to a change in diet. Vitamins A, D, E, K and the B complex should be supplemented.

HEART

Every cell in the body requires a constant supply of oxygen, which is carried by the red blood cells. The heart is the muscular organ that un-flaggingly pumps the oxygenated blood to every part of the body, every second of an animal's life. It is divided into four parts with valves separating each chamber. Veins are the blood vessels that bring the de-oxygenated blood back from the body cells into the right side of the heart. From here it is pumped to the lungs to collect fresh oxygen. This oxygenated blood returns to the left side of the heart and is pumped from here via the arteries around the body again.

Heart disease can be caused by infection, poisons, inherited factors and tumours.

Congenital heart disease

Congenital heart disease affects a kitten from birth. It is often diagnosed at the first vaccination, when abnormal heart sounds are detected. Affected kittens are often the smallest of the litter and may not join in the communal games; exercise causes laboured breathing and the kitten's gums may have a blue tinge. Other congenital problems obstruct the oeso-phagus, or food pipe, causing vomiting as soon as the kitten is weaned on to solid food.

Most congenital problems are diagnosed before a kitten reaches one year of age, and many can be cured with specialist surgery.

Cardiomyopathies

Cardiomyopathies, diseases of the heart muscle, are the most common type of heart disease in cats. These diseases occur mainly in mature male cats, at any age from eight months to fifteen years, and may be secondary to another disease, or of unknown cause. The cat may have been briefly leth-argic, but usually the onset of symptoms is very sudden. The most common sign is an acute attack of laboured and difficult breathing due to a build up of fluid in the lungs. Sometimes cats will die within minutes. Other symptoms depend on which side of the heart the muscle is affected.

There is no cure for most cardio-myopathies. The congestive form of the disease has been found to respond favourably to the amino acid taurine. If affected cats are treated immediately, cardiomyopathies may be controlled with drugs and restricted exercise for a variable length of time.

Aortic thromboembolism

Aortic thromboembolism in cats is always secondary to a cardiomyopathy, and may be the first sign that the cat has heart muscle problems.

The aorta, the major artery of the body, lies against the spinal column

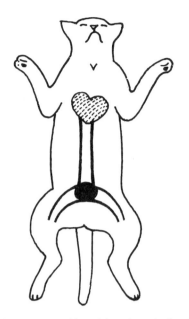

■ A common position of thromboembolism in the cat's aorta. The clot seriously affects the cat's blood supply to the hind limbs.

and branches into other smaller vessels. A thromboembolus is a piece of blood clot from damaged heart muscle that has broken away and is floating in the circulation. This clot lodges somewhere in the aorta, usually where it divides into the two main arteries that supply the hind limbs, and disturbs all circulation to these limbs.

Cats with an aortic thromboembolism suddenly become acutely distressed and develop a floppy paralysis in the back legs. The muscles here become very painful and, later, swollen and firm. The cat's legs become progressively colder to touch and the femoral artery inside the leg lacks a pulse.

This is an emergency. The condition may be treated with surgery, drugs to dissolve the clot, or a combination of both. If the cat survives, it may take weeks for the back legs to regain function. Because this aortic clot is always secondary to a heart muscle condition, the cat must be maintained on treatment continually and lead a quiet existence with freedom from stress, restricted exercise and a diet low in salt.

Treatment of feline heart disease is advancing constantly, but at this stage most affected cats have a short life expectancy.

LUNGS

The lungs are the organs of breathing. As they expand when a cat inhales, fresh oxygen is exchanged for carbon dioxide, and the carbon dioxide is then expelled from the body as the cat exhales.

Most diseases of the lungs and upper respiratory tract (windpipe, nostrils, etc.) will cause similar symptoms: coughing, lethargy and abnormal breathing patterns. Severe lung problems cause distressful breathing, and affected cats adopt a crouched position with elbows pushed out and head and neck extended. Open-mouthed breathing in cats is unusual and indicates either serious lung disease, heat stress or excessive nervousness. Unlike dogs, when cats pant they are in distress.

The viruses of the cat flu complex are the most common infectious agents of the respiratory tract in cats (see 'Feline Respiratory Disease' on page 79). Numerous other organisms, toxins, tumours and trauma can cause respiratory difficulties.

Lungworm

Aelurostrongylus abstrusus is the lungworm of cats. This small, 1 cm long worm is a common inhabitant of cat lungs, but most infections are short-lived and cause little disease; a persistent, dry cough is often the only symptom.

The worm has two intermediate hosts. Worm larvae on the ground penetrate the feet of snails and slugs. The snails and slugs plus the larvae they are carrying are then eaten by birds, frogs, rats or mice, and the larvae then encyst in the new hosts' muscle tissues. Eventually, these small creatures may be eaten by a cat, and the larvae migrate to the cat's lungs and grow to adult worms. The adult female lays her eggs in clusters in lung tissue. Newly hatched larvae travel up the windpipe, are swallowed and pass out onto the ground in faeces and the cycle begins again.

The greatest irritation to lung tissue is caused by reaction to the egg clusters and the migrating larvae six to twelve weeks after infection. Treat-ment should be prescribed by a vet. It is fortunate that most infections with lungworm cause few problems because hunting cats continually reinfect themselves.

Pleura and pyothorax

The pleura is a very fine layer of tissue that covers the lungs and inner surface of the chest cavity. It reacts to any sort of inflammation by producing excess fluid, and, as this fluid builds up, the lungs are no longer able to expand efficiently. An affected cat becomes distressed and breathes with its neck and head pushed out, chest on the

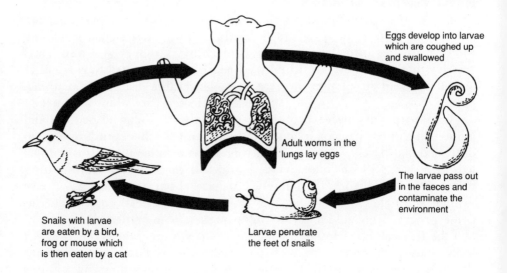

Eggs develop into larvae which are coughed up and swallowed

Adult worms in the lungs lay eggs

The larvae pass out in the faeces and contaminate the environment

Snails with larvae are eaten by a bird, frog or mouse which is then eaten by a cat

Larvae penetrate the feet of snails

■ The lungworm life cycle.

ground and its mouth open.

Pyothorax (literally, a 'chest full of pus'), is one type of pleural inflammation often caused by cat fights when teeth or claws penetrate the rib cage, depositing germs inside the chest. These cause an insidious infection, with pus slowly building up in the chest. Because cats can adapt incredibly well to reduced lung capacity, they show few symptoms until the very last stages of this disease (an affected cat may become quieter and less active, and perhaps eat a little less). When the lungs can no longer compensate, the cat suddenly becomes very depressed and has difficulty breathing.

Treatment is very difficult and cats with pyothorax have a poor prognosis. If your cat has obviously had a fight, getting prompt treatment can help prevent such secondary infections.

URINARY TRACT

The kidneys, as well as helping to manufacture red blood cells, maintain the crucial fluid balance of the body while absorbing useful salts and excreting the waste products of metabolism. Two thin tubes called ureters take urine from the kidneys to the bladder, from where it passes out of the body in another narrow tube called the urethra.

Chronic progressive renal disease

Acute renal (kidney) disease, which results from poisons such as antifreeze, from trauma and from drugs like aspirin, is uncommon in the cat.

However, chronic renal disease is perhaps the most common debilitating disease of old cats, and is the end result of different ageing and disease processes that have caused kidney inflammation.

The disease is insidious, as signs of kidney failure only appear when about two thirds of the kidney cells are not functioning. The failed kidneys cannot conserve urine or proteins, and also allow waste products to build up in the circulation. This protein loss causes malnourishment, and the result is a thin, dehydrated cat that urinates and drinks excessively. Other symptoms include anaemia, poor appetite, tongue ulceration and vomiting.

While chronic progressive renal disease cannot be cured, cats may remain quite healthy on the following regimen for considerable periods. (As little research has been done on this disease in cats most treatment is extrapolated from dogs.)

■ To maintain a good urine flow while preventing dehydration, unlimited fresh water must always be available. Depending on the condition, your vet may recommend the addition of salt to food.

■ Dogs with failing kidneys need a low protein diet, but this is unpalatable to cats, which have much higher protein requirements. The compromise is to feed as much high-quality protein as possible, such as white meats (for example chicken), cooked eggs, cottage cheese, milk, cream and small amounts of liver. Red meat is poor-quality protein.

■ A high level of animal fat is needed to supply energy for maintaining body weight and to increase diet palatability. Weigh the cat regularly to make sure the diet is adequate, and supplement with vitamins B and C.

■ Divide the cat's diet into three to four small meals a day, which will enable the kidneys to handle waste excretion more easily.

■ As much as possible avoid stress. Cats with kidney disease are usually old as well as sick. Any form of stress (for example, a new pet or a cold sleeping place) can worsen the condition. Be aware of your pet's needs and wants.

Feline urological syndrome

Feline urological syndrome, or FUS, is a group of symptoms of unknown cause that result in cystitis (inflammation of the bladder), bladder calculi ('stones') and, in male cats, obstruction by these calculi to urine flow. Most cats affected are between one and six years of age.

In female cats, FUS causes continual straining to urinate with the passage of only small, blood-tinged amounts of urine. The cat will have a cystitis, and possibly bladder stones. She may change her normally clean habits and urinate in the house.

FUS in male cats causes similar symptoms, but calculi will almost

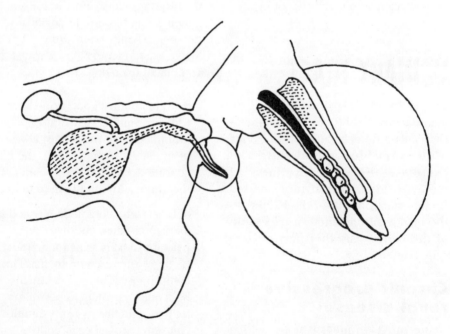

■ Feline urological syndrome in male cats: tiny 'stones' or urinary calculi block the urethra and prevent the flow of urine, causing the bladder to become dangerously swollen and very painful.

always be present and often block the urethra. The anatomy of the male urethra is different from the female. The male uretha is longer and very narrow as it passes through the penis. Even the smallest calculi can get stuck and obstruct urine flow.

An obstructing calculi is an emergency and causes acute pain. The following symptoms indicate rapid veterinary attention is required:

■ The cat will first lick his protruding penis continually, straining to pass urine without success, often in the house regardless of training.

■ He will become more agitated, crying out in pain, especially when handled.

■ If untreated, the bladder becomes tight with urine, and waste products overflow from the kidneys into the circulation; the bladder may rupture and the cat will die.

If any of these symptoms are apparent, take your cat to a vet as soon as possible.

Treatment involves anaesthetising the cat, passsing a catheter through the penis, unblocking the urethra and releasing the urine from the bladder. Sometimes the catheter is left in place to help pass other calculi that may be in the bladder. An operation called a perineal urethrostomy can be performed if FUS recurs. This removes the narrow portion of the urethra where it passes through the penis, resulting in a larger hole, like the female cat, through which most calculi can pass.

Female cats respond to simpler treatment, but in both sexes FUS has a high rate of recurrence with up to 70% of affected cats expected to have repeated bouts of FUS regardless of treatment.

As yet the cause of FUS is unknown. Theories, none of which have been proven, have blamed dry cat food, excess magnesium, a virus, inherited factors and early castration. Many affected cats are fat and lazy and live inside, having access to a litter tray only for long periods (these cats may 'hold' urine until they can go outside, thus inflaming the bladder). Research will hopefully soon provide more answers.

The following recommendations could help to prevent FUS recurrence:

■ Increase the cat's water intake as a means of continually flushing its bladder. This can be done by adding salt to the cat's diet (about one quarter of a teaspoon daily), by supplying unlimited water and by feeding canned food and moistened—not dry—biscuits.

■ Use urinary acidifying tablets (on your vet's recommendation) if the cat's urine is alkaline.

HORMONAL DISEASE

The body has intricate, well co-ordinated methods of controlling metabolism and other functions: nerves help by relaying messages as electrical impulses, while hormones relay chemical messages via the bloodstream. Each hormone is produced by a specific gland and has a specific task to perform.

Diabetes mellitus

Diabetes mellitus, the common sugar diabetes of humans, is not infrequently diagnosed in cats.

The pancreas is the gland that produces the hormone insulin, which is required to help the tissues absorb their necessary glucose from the bloodstream. If insulin is deficient, as in diabetes, then the cells can't utilise glucose, which builds up in the bloodstream to dangerous levels. Without glucose, cells starve. The body begins to break down protein and fat to supply the missing energy, causing a loss of weight even though the cat is initially hungry and will eat more than usual. The excess blood glucose also causes increased urine production, which is followed by increased drinking. Eventually, affected cats become sick and weak, stop eating and begin to vomit, while still drinking and urinating to excess.

Factors thought to trigger diabetes include obesity, genetic predisposition, stress and the overuse of drugs such as corticosteroids and female hormones. The disease often appears suddenly in old cats. It is incurable, and cats will only survive with insulin injections once or twice a day. Most cats will rapidly grow accustomed to the pricks of the tiny needle.

To begin with cats are 'stabilised' in a vet hospital. Once home, a fixed daily routine of controlled diet and exercise must begin, as any changes mean alterations in the dose of insulin. The cat's urine must be collected each day and tested for glucose levels; this can often be difficult in the average cat. Although it would appear that diabetic cats may be easier to manage than dogs, it takes a devoted owner, a patient vet and an amenable cat to cope with the disease. Determination on the part of all three will be required for successful treatment.

SKELETON

The skeleton consists of all the bones in the body and their flexible connections, the joints. Healthy bone structure is most dependent on a well-balanced diet, especially in the growing cat; imbalances of vitamins and minerals can cause permanent deformities.

Nutritional secondary hyperparathyroidism

Nutritional secondary hyperparathyroidism (sometimes incorrectly called rickets), is a disease of mineral imbalance that causes weak, thin, easily fractured bones, and is most often seen in the growing kitten.

Calcium is an essential mineral for strong bones. Low blood levels of calcium cause the parathyroid hormone to work excessively, removing calcium from the bones in an attempt to build up blood levels while replacing the lost calcium with non-bony tissues. This results in weak bones that bend and break after the smallest injury.

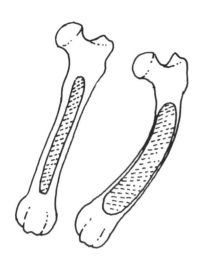

■ (Left) Normal bone has a thick, strong cortex around the marrow. (Right) A diet low in essential minerals such as calcium has resulted in a thin, bowed cortex.

Low blood levels of calcium are commonly caused by 'all-meat' diets, as discussed under 'Nutrition' on page 76. Kittens reared solely on a diet of beef heart, for example, will show symptoms of irritability in four to seven weeks along with pain and a reluctance to play and run. Jumping from a low chair can break a leg, the pelvic bones may collapse causing chronic constipation, and the cat may have trouble giving birth if allowed to become pregnant.

The diet of a cat with nutritional secondary hyperparathyroidism should be changed to a mixture of commercial products supplemented with calcium prescribed by a vet. Kittens may need to be kept in cages for several weeks until their bones become stronger.

Fractures

The term 'fracture' can be confusing, but a fractured bone simply means a broken bone (refer to 'Fractures' under 'Dogs' on page 55 for a full description).

A cat with a broken leg will walk with difficulty, resent handling, and the affected leg will be swollen and swing or hang at an odd angle. Breaks in smaller bones will be swollen and painful over a more localised area. Place the affected cat on a blanket, its good side down, for transport to a vet. Don't splint or bandage the leg as this causes further pain and is unnecessary.

An X-ray will show the extent of the damage. The best way to mend broken bones in cats is by 'internal fixation', where light, non-reactive metal pins, plates, screws or wire are attached to or inside the bone during surgery under general anaesthesia (cats resent heavy and cumbersome plaster casts). The cat must then have its exercise restricted for about six weeks until the bone heals, after which

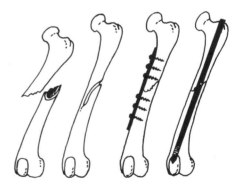

■ (Left to right) A simple fracture or broken bone; a 'greenstick' fracture; two types of internal fixation using a metal plate and screws; and a metal pin.

time the pins are then removed, although screws and plates may be left in for life.

Amputations

Occasionally a limb will be so severely damaged that amputation is the only way to save the cat. Amputation may be necessary, for example, if a cat has been caught in a rabbit trap. The leg below the trap jaws may become gangrenous (dead) due to loss of blood and nerve supply.

The entire limb must be removed at amputation as stumps are useless to a cat and merely get in the way, and are usually injured constantly. The appearance of a leg taken off neatly at the hip or shoulder is surprisingly far more acceptable and less noticeable than leaving a stump.

Cats are remarkable amputees— they will still jump fences, climb trees

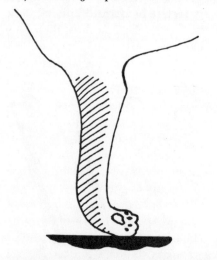

■ Radial paralysis occurs following traumatic damage to the nerves controlling the shaded muscles. The cat can no longer lift its leg to place the paw correctly, and if the paralysis is permanent, amputation may be necessary.

and generally behave like their four-legged friends. They appear not to develop the painful nerve problems that frustrate human amputees.

Septic arthritis

Arthritis, the inflammation of a joint, can result from infection, which, in the cat, often follows a cat fight in which a bite is inflicted near the joint. The affected joint will be swollen, hot and painful.

Cats' teeth carry a variety of infective bacteria that proliferate and cause abscesses once deposited under the skin. Prompt treatment with antibiotics when you know your cat has been fighting will prevent these infections forming, otherwise the infected joint will need opening and draining under anaesthetic to flush out the pus.

Hypervitaminosis A

Hypervitaminosis A, which means an excess of vitamin A in the body, occurs in cats fed a diet with a high proportion of liver, cod liver oil or vitamin supplements. It causes bony growths to develop on the spinal vertebrae of the neck, on the elbows and then on other bones in the body. The bones of growing kittens fed an all-liver diet become permanently distorted.

As vitamin A begins to build up (it is stored in the liver and can't be excreted like other vitamins), cats become inactive and resent handling. Eventually, they will walk in a crouched position with back arched and tail on the ground. As grooming becomes difficult, their coats will be rough and

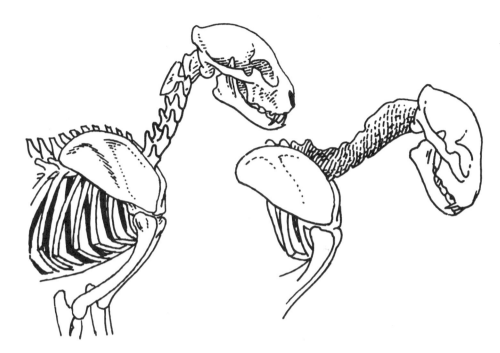

■ Cats fed large amounts of liver can absorb too much Vitamin A. (Left) A normal skeleton; (right) The fused bones of hypervitaminosis A.

dirty. Their livers may feel swollen, and their teeth may loosen and fall out.

The diet of affected cats must be corrected as soon as possible. Three months or more may be required for any improvement, and most cats are left with some permanent problems. Chronic cases never recover.

NERVOUS SYSTEM

The nervous system, which helps to co-ordinate the body, is a vast network of nerves connecting the brain and spinal cord with every part of the body, relaying messages in the form of electrical impulses.

Traumatic injuries

The motor car is a consistent cause of severe injury in the cat, and damage to the brain and spinal cord is common, resulting in many problems from paralysis to coma. A cat with spinal or brain damage may be unable to move and have pupils of unequal size. It may be rigid or relaxed, depending on the nerve supply involved. Handle these cats carefully as they are often frightened and distressed; see 'Emergencies' on page 87 for advice on handling.

Injuries to the nervous system are emergencies. Damage and swelling of the brain and spinal cord will often respond to prompt treatment, so it is vital that you take an injured cat straight to a vet.

Nerve damage can be difficult to assess: slight bruising will heal quickly, while severely injured nerves may take weeks or months to recover or may never regain full function. These injuries may require much devotion by owners who are prepared to nurse a cat for prolonged periods.

'Stretched tail' syndrome

The 'stretched tail syndrome' is a common and frustrating car accident injury in cats, and results from damage to the nerves and vertebrae (the bones of the spinal column) in the region of the tail and hip. Injured cats have floppy tails with no feeling that drag on the ground and cannot be held erect. As the nerves that co-ordinate the bladder and rectum are also located in these parts of the spinal cord, serious problems arise with urination and defaecation. The bladder is usually unable to release urine, so the cat must be catheterised (meaning the passing of a fine, soft tube through the penis and up the urethra to the bladder) at least daily. This may be required for weeks until the bladder regains nerve control. Feeding laxatives and bran helps an injured cat to pass faeces.

A floppy tail may need to be amputated if it remains paralysed, as constant dragging damages the tail tip. As the cat can no longer feel or move the tail, amputation initially worries owners more than the cat. However, the greatest problem lies with the bladder, and if nerve control is not regained in three to six weeks it is unlikely to return, and the cat may have to be euthanased.

Seizures

Epilepsy, a common cause of seizures in dogs, is uncommon in cats. Fits are more likely to occur after poisonings, or from infectious diseases such as toxoplasma, infectious peritonitis and the leukaemia virus, which quite frequently affect the brain.

A seizure, or fit, results from sudden abnormal and excessive electrical activity in the brain. In a 'typical' fit, a cat will fall to one side with limbs outstretched and head drawn back. The body will convulse, or have constant, strong muscle spasms. Most seizures last only seconds, or at the most one to two minutes.

Do not handle a cat during a seizure: you can't help and will almost certainly get scratched or bitten. Most cats recover and appear normal in a matter of minutes, then they can be gently wrapped in a thick blanket and transported to a vet immediately. Move quietly, as handling will often precipitate another fit.

Thiamine deficiency

Thiamine, or vitamin B_1, can be destroyed by heat, by certain food preservatives and by an enzyme called thiaminase. Deficiencies occur in cats after eating mince with particular preservatives, in low-grade canned fish foods where the thiamine has been destroyed by heat (this is rare today), or by eating certain varieties of fresh fish that contain thiaminase.

Symptoms, which can take over six weeks to appear, include loss of appetite and weight, dilated pupils and inco-ordination of the back legs. As

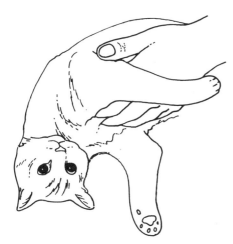

■ Thiamine (vitamin B_1), deficiency is manifested by dilated pupils and seizures; the cat adopts a peculiar pose bent forward with its head tucked into its chin.

the disease progresses the cat begins to convulse (fit) in a typical manner with legs outstretched but the head bent forward and tucked into the chin. Muscle spasms occur over the entire body and a cat may scream. Handling often precipitates these attacks.

Early treatment with vitamin B_1 gives a rapid response. If untreated, brain lesions may be permanent. Cats that have recovered must have a varied and well-balanced diet which eliminates the abovementioned foods, and which is supplemented with oral vitamin B_1.

REPRODUCTION

The female cat, more correctly called the queen, will reach puberty and enter her first heat cycle between four and twelve months of age. Most cats 'come on heat' repeatedly every three to five weeks between late winter and late summer, although there are often large variations in individual heat cycles. After a pregnancy, the queen will come on heat once the kittens are weaned (sometimes while she is still nursing).

Each oestrus cycle lasts about seven days, although some can last for several weeks. Unlike many animal species, cats will not shed their 'eggs' (ovulate) until they are mated. A queen mated by several tomcats during a heat cycle can give birth to kittens with different fathers in one litter. (This also occurs in the bitch.)

Although physical signs of heat are few (no discharge or vulval swelling), a cat makes up for this with fascinating performances: she becomes overly affectionate, arches her back, treads her feet, rolls and rubs constantly against any available object, and becomes highly vocal, miaowing continually in a loud, persistent voice. This has given rise to the common phrase for the heat cycle: to come 'on

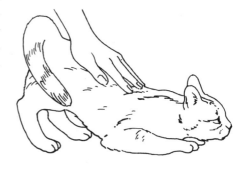

■ Cats 'on heat' become very vocal and affectionate, arch their backs when stroked, raise their tail, and often tread with their hind limbs.

call'. Living with a 'calling' cat in the house for several weeks is a convincing argument for desexing.

PREGNANCY

The length of pregnancy in the cat is about sixty-five days, with a range of sixty to seventy days possible. Foetuses can be palpated by a vet between twenty and thirty days after mating, when they feel like individual walnuts. After forty-two days the kittens' bones are mature enough to show up on an X-ray.

The average litter size of the queen is four kittens. In cats, as in dogs, this litter may comprise kittens with several different fathers; if several matings occur with different males, the female's eggs may be fertilised by each male.

The pregnant queen must have a balanced diet, which can be increased in the last three weeks to enable her to feed both herself and her rapidly growing unborn kittens. Rather than giving the pregnant cat one or two huge meals, offer her three or four small feeds each day; with her full abdomen, she will be unable to eat large amounts at each sitting. Let her nibble as she pleases, without letting her become fat—obese queens will usually have trouble kittening. Moderate exercise throughout pregnancy is important to keep the queen fit and strong for the task ahead.

To reduce the numbers of worms that may contaminate the kittens' environment, cats should be wormed every three weeks throughout pregnancy and lactation. Always tell your vet the cat is pregnant, as pregnant cats and their unborn kittens are extremely sensitive to many drugs.

Your cat may already have her own basket in which she feels secure and happy to give birth. If not, try to introduce her to a kittening spot several weeks beforehand. Cats like to kitten in safe, quiet, warm and dark places; for example, a large cardboard box with one side cut down to allow the queen easy access can be placed in the bottom of a large cupboard. Line it with the cat's normal bedding, newspaper or warm rugs. Don't expect her to settle down in the middle of a brightly lit kitchen.

Trimming the hair away from teats and vulva on long-haired cats helps to keep them clean during birth. You should notice teat development in the last few weeks; milk will usually be present two to three days before the birth.

BIRTH

As birth approaches, a cat will become restless. A day or two before, she will begin to nest and scratch around in rugs or newspapers. Hopefully this will be in your carefully prepared box, but if it is not try to prevent her from settling into inaccessible places, especially under the house. If the cat chooses to ignore your spot, you may be able to move the kittens after birth.

Cats are generally very adept at giving birth, but maiden (first-time pregnant) or very nervous queens may have difficulty. Try to observe the kittening, but do so quietly and from a good distance. Queens can interrupt the birth process if disturbed or upset and may not start again for a day or more, or may hide the kittens.

As birth begins the cat will have strong contractions as the first kitten

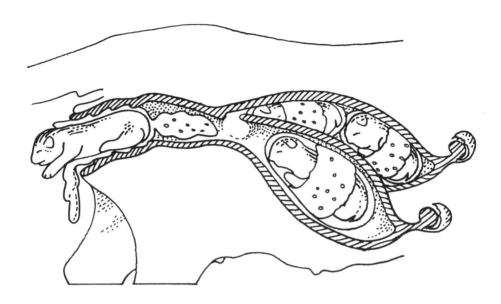

■ The birth process: kittens in the uterus are still inside their placental membranes. The membranes of the kitten appearing at the vulva have already ruptured, although the placenta will remain attached at the umbilicus until severed by the queen.

moves into the pelvis and vagina. A membrane will rupture, releasing clear fluid, and a kitten should be seen at the vulva (a tail and back legs or head will be seen as both backward and forward deliveries are normal in cats). Expulsion is rapid, and each kitten will be born inside another membranous sac called the amnion. As the kittens are born a black-green discharge will be seen. The queen will break the amniotic sac, clean the membranes from the kitten, chew through the umbilical cord, and begin licking the kitten firmly, her tongue stimulating the newborn's breathing. At some stage she will usually eat the accompanying placenta, which is thought to be a protective mechanism, to hide all signs of recent birth from predators in natural situations.

On occasion, a cat will be slow to break the sac containing a kitten, and if this happens you can do it for her. With clean hands, break the sac and clear the kitten's nose and mouth. If the mother cat doesn't then take over, gently but firmly rub the kitten's chest with a towel to stimulate respiration while holding it upside down (this drains any fluids that are present from the nose and mouth). If the queen won't bite through the cord, tie it about 2 cm below the abdomen with clean cotton, then cut below this. Encourage the cat to proceed by herself.

The process of kittening varies enormously, with kittens usually being born at intervals of thirty minutes or less. However, there may be an hour or even many hours between kittens, but if the cat is contented and nursing her kittens then she is probably just resting between births.

LACTATING QUEENS

Nursing cats must have as much food as they desire, as feeding a litter of kittens requires enormous amounts of energy. Dry food can be left without spoiling, allowing the cat to help herself. Otherwise, feed the cat frequent small feeds of a variety of commercial foods throughout the day, together with plenty of milk and extra protein such as cooked eggs and small quantities of liver.

Continue worming every three weeks throughout lactation.

BIRTH PROBLEMS

Birth problems can result from kittens that are too large, because the queen is inexperienced, or in queens that are tired and weak.

The attitude of your cat should tell you if help is required. Any queen that has strained for one hour without producing a kitten is having difficulties. Distress or pain, a kitten stuck at the vulva, or membrane rupture without a kitten following are all signs that should never be ignored, and you should call your vet immediately. A caesarian may need to be performed to save the cat and kittens. **A queen in difficulty tires and weakens very easily, so don't delay getting professional help.**

Retained membranes

As each kitten is born try to count the placentas as they pass during birth: they should equal the number of kittens. Retained membranes are uncommon in cats, but if any placentas are not passed they will cause a brown, foul-smelling discharge and serious infection. If you suspect a retained membrane, your vet can administer an injection to help it pass soon after birth.

Mastitis

Mastitis is an inflammation of the mammary tissues, causing affected cats to become listless and stop eating, and to resent their kittens suckling. One or more mammary glands will be swollen, hot and painful, and the milk will often be discoloured. The condition is treated with antibiotics, and you may have to feed the kittens for several days until their mother improves. It is a good idea to check the mammary glands daily for signs of mastitis.

KITTENS

Warmth is essential for kittens, as newborn kittens are unable to shiver, an important regulator of temperature, and so become cold very easily. Heating pads are excellent, but the kittens must have room to move away from the heat if desired. They also need frequent feeding and a clean, dry environment. A healthy litter will be peaceful, with the kittens drinking often and then sleeping.

Kittens that cry incessantly and are restless are probably cold, hungry or sick. Warm cold kittens carefully near a well-wrapped hot water bottle before placing them back with their mother. Weak kittens may need feeding with an eye dropper until strong enough to

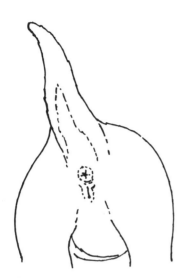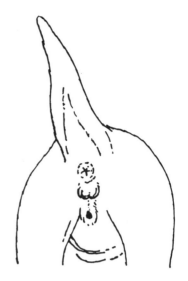

■ Sexing kittens. Male kittens (right) have a greater distance between their urogenital openings and their anuses than female kittens (left). This is because in the male, the testicles sit between the penis and the anus. In very young kittens the testicles will not be obvious.

clamber onto a teat. Get early treatment for sick kittens that don't respond to warmth and feeding; they can weaken, dehydrate and die rapidly.

Always ensure all kittens drink from the teat within the first few hours to get colostrum, which is the high protein milk excreted by the queen in the first twenty-four hours after birth, and which contains protective antibodies that help kittens combat disease. After twelve to twenty-four hours the kittens' intestines alter and can no longer absorb colostrum.

Sexing kittens

The idea of sexing kittens may sound silly, but it is remarkable how many adult cats have been presumed by their owners to be a member of the opposite sex!

Sexing new kittens is difficult. Hold the kitten and lift the tail to enable a good view of the anus and genitalia. In the female, the vulva (external opening of the genital organs) has a narrow vertical opening and is located below and quite close to the anus. The male genital opening is a tiny round hole. Because the testicles (which are usually too small to feel at this stage) sit between this opening and the anus, there is a longer distance between the anus and the genitalia in the male than there is in the female. Comparing several kittens when possible makes it easier to pick the difference.

Weaning

For the first week or so kittens spend all of their time drinking and sleeping. Their eyes will open at eight to ten days, and by the third week they begin to play and explore. The mother cat then starts to teach them to defaecate and urinate out of the kittening area, so provide a low litter tray nearby and clean it frequently (this is important because cats dislike dirty trays). The kittens will have good toilet manners from an early age.

Start offering kittens solid food at four weeks of age—soft canned food is easiest and is well-balanced nutritionally (avoid using cereals such as Farex, which do little for kittens).

Introduce milk, watered down at first. If the kittens don't develop diarrhoea, gradually increase the milk to full strength. Start kittens on a *varied* diet from the very beginning. Don't let them develop a preference for one particular brand or type of food, as eating habits formed early are almost impossible to change.

The kittens should be weaned by six to eight weeks of age. During this time, gradually reduce the queen's food and fluid intake, which helps to dry up the teats and make her more comfortable.

As hookworms and roundworms are dangerous to kittens, worming must begin at one to two weeks of age (refer to 'Protecting Your Cat With Worming' on page 80).

The period between six to twelve weeks of age, when kittens learn good, and bad habits, is crucial for socialisation. Lots of affection, attention to house training and gentle handling will help them become friendly, clean and well-behaved kittens.

Orphan kittens

Nursing queens are often very accommodating to an introduced kitten, accepting it with minimal fuss. Always try to find a feline foster mother for your orphaned kitten, before resorting to fostering it yourself.

Orphan kittens require constant warmth, frequent small feeds, absolute cleanliness (which means sterilising bottles and teats after every use) and freedom from stress. Warmth is *essential*—kittens must be kept very warm (in an ambient temperature up to 30°C) for the first few weeks until they are able to warm themselves. Heating pads are more reliable than hot water bottles, which must be refilled frequently to maintain an even temperature. But be careful not to overheat the kittens.

Whether the adoptive mother is feline or human, try to ensure that orphan kittens get some colostrum from their own mother in the first twelve hours after birth; this will provide them with some protection against disease. Then start on the replacement formula at half strength and work up to full strength over a few days to allow the kittens to adjust.

There are excellent commercial formulations available for rearing kittens, such as the Wombaroo formula, that are correctly balanced and need no supplementing; ask a vet for advice. Cow's milk is not adequate as kittens require at least twice the amount of protein it offers. Small nurser bottles and teats are also available. Always warm the formula to body temperature before feeding. For the first week, feed every two to three hours, cutting this back gradually to four to six feeds a day by the third week. It is best to feed small amounts often. Commercial formulas give a guide to feeding volumes; adjust this to individual kittens and their weight gains.

Mother cats stimulate their kittens to defaecate and urinate after each meal by licking and cleaning them. You can take over this task for the first week or so by gently rubbing the lower abdomen with a lubricated finger or tissue.

If diarrhoea is a problem, obtain a good electrolyte powder from your vet, mix this with water and halve the formula strength for twelve hours, feeding extra water in between. Don't neglect persistent diarrhoea, as kittens can dehydrate in hours.

Start kittens on solid food as early as possible, certainly by the third week, to encourage early weaning.

A daily weighing session is important. Kittens weigh between 90 and 140 g at birth, and after the first few days they should put on weight continuously.

REPRODUCTIVE TRACT

Problems can arise in the reproductive organs of both the queen and the tomcat. Complications of kittening and lactation are discussed under 'Birth Problems' on page 124.

False pregnancy

Following an unsuccessful mating or an unmated heat cycle, a cat's hormones frequently behave as if she were pregnant. Fortunately, this is not very noticeable and ends within forty to forty-five days. Unlike dogs, only rarely will cats make milk. Desexing is the only permanent cure for repeated false pregnancy.

Pyometra

Pyometra, meaning a 'uterus filled with pus', is a very serious infection usually seen in non-desexed female cats over five years of age. It usually follows a heat cycle, a false pregnancy, the continual use of oral or injectable contraceptives, or a hormone injection for mismating. Hormonal influences alter the cells that line the uterus, allowing bacteria to cause infection.

In open pyometra the pus can drain through the cervix (the outer opening of the uterus), but the queen will clean herself more frequently so the discharge from the vulva is often not noticed and this infection can become a chronic problem. If the cervix is closed, the pus continues to build up inside the uterus and the cat becomes extremely sick. She will often drink and urinate excessively, become very depressed, stop eating and may begin to vomit. Secondary damage can also occur to the kidneys.

Treatment of both open and closed pyometra involves the surgical removal of the uterus and ovaries and usually intensive care with intravenous fluids and antibiotics. Desexing at an early age prevents pyometra. Desexing (which can be performed at any age) should also be considered for those breeding queens that are no longer producing kittens.

Cryptorchidism

Normal male cats are born with both testicles in the scrotum, but in some tomcats, one or both testicles will fail to descend into the scrotum. These cats are called cryptorchids. If this condition occurs in breeding tomcats, they should not be so used as the condition can be inherited.

In the pet tom, the condition will be noticed at the time of castration. As retained testicles can be anywhere from the kidneys to just above the scrotum, abdominal surgery is needed. It is important that *both* testicles be removed.

CANCER

The thought that your cat may have cancer is understandably alarming and distressful, but bear in mind that many types of cancer are treatable and veterinary cancer therapy is continually being advanced. Early attention to any suspicious lumps or bumps will often cure skin cancers.

Cancer is also referred to as a tumour and benign tumours, or those that don't invade other parts of the body, usually grow slowly and are easiest to remove surgically. They don't often recur after treatment. Malignant tumours are more aggressive and grow rapidly, usually invading surrounding tissues or other organs in the body. They are not as easily treated and often recur. Treatment of cancer varies with each tumour, but can include surgery, radiation therapy, chemotherapy and cryosurgery (freezing).

The incidence of cancer increases in frequency as cats age. Every cell type in the body has its own cancer;

the most common ones occurring in cats are described below.

Squamous cell carcinoma

Squamous cell carcinoma is described in detail in the section on 'Skin' on page 99. It is often seen as a sequel to chronic sunburn in cats with non-pigmented (white) ear tips, eyelids nose and lips, and it can also occur inside the mouth.

Mammary tumours

In female cats mammary tumours are almost always malignant and must be treated as early as possible. They begin as firm, irregular lumps around the teats in the mammary (milk-producing) tissue and should be removed at this stage. If left untreated they grow rapidly, spreading to other organs like the lungs. Usually a vet would take an X-ray of the lungs to see if any tumours were evident before operating.

■ Mammary tumours appear as a series of firm nodular lumps around the nipples of female cats.

Feline leukaemia virus

Feline leukaemia virus (FeLV), the most common and serious cancer in cats, is caused by a virus that is contagious, spreading from cat to cat. All cats can be affected, although kittens are the most susceptible. As this fragile virus is easily destroyed outside the body, prolonged, close contact is needed for it to spread. It is therefore most common in catteries, breeding colonies and households with several cats. The virus is spread in the saliva, urine, faeces and sneezing discharges of infected cats. It can also pass in the mother's colostrum and across the placenta, causing abortion or the birth of weak kittens.

It is important to realise that the virus is not necessarily fatal and that most cats do not develop the disease. A small number of cats, less than 10%, succumb to the virus quite quickly, developing signs of disease and usually dying within two to three months. Others remain healthy for variable periods of time, but as they never develop an immunity they pass the virus on to other cats and eventually

■ Less than 10% of cats succumb and die quickly to feline leukaemia virus. A small number carry the virus for long periods, but the vast majority of cats safely develop an immunity to the virus.

develop symptoms. However, the vast majority of cats rapidly develop an immunity to the virus and remain healthy.

The symptoms of this disease are extremely variable, as the virus affects most tissues in the body. Most common are effects on the gastrointestinal tract, such as vomiting, diarrhoea and a loss of appetite and weight. In younger cats it often invades the thymus gland, an organ in the chest, putting pressure on the lungs and heart. The virus also causes anaemia, and suppresses a cat's immune system (the body's defence), making the cat vulnerable to a whole range of other diseases.

FeLV is diagnosed with blood tests. In seriously infected catteries, new cats can be tested and those virus-positive isolated until they become immune or develop the disease. The manufacture of a vaccine is being researched. At present treatment is almost uniformly unsuccessful and is not often recommended because of the contagious nature of the disease. Sick cats in multi-cat households must be isolated, and given their own feed bowls, bedding and litter trays.

There have been no known cases of human infection by this virus, and the situation seems safe for those people with blood-test positive cats. Nevertheless, a possible public health risk should be borne in mind.

OLD AGE

Cats, on average, live longer than dogs: fifteen to eighteen-year-old cats are not uncommon. Cats that have been part of a family for this length of time are usually much loved. However, as they age they require even more attention, with an environment as caring, peaceful and free of stress as possible.

Cats become less able to cope with illness and injury with age; healing is slower, and the well-organised systems that keep the body functioning don't work quite as efficiently. Older cats are also more resistant to change: they may resent a new kitten, or cope poorly with a house move. Deaf or blind cats will cope as long as their surroundings remain unchanged and familiar.

Kidney failure is probably the most common illness of ageing cats. Your vet may suggest a diet that contains small amounts of high-quality protein, so you may have to tempt your cat with cottage cheese, chicken or liver. A vitamin and mineral supplement may be recommended by your vet.

Don't neglect routine vaccinations and worming: older animals become more susceptible to disease and parasites. Regular attention should also be paid to your cat's teeth—any signs of calculus, bad breath or dropping of food when eating should mean a trip to a vet for teeth cleaning. Many old cats become fussy eaters, and painful teeth will only worsen this problem.

Ageing cats spend their days happily sleeping. This lack of exercise can mean the growth of long claws that tangle in carpet. These can be cut safely: ask your vet to give you a lesson and show you the correct nail clippers to use.

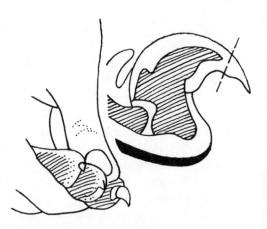

■ Old or underexercised cats often have long claws. Clip these nails regularly by cutting just below the blood vessel that runs down the centre of each nail and appears as a pink line. By putting gentle pressure on each toe, the claw will extend.

Cats are clean and fastidious creatures, but as they grow older they may not be able to maintain their high levels of personal hygiene. Long-haired cats may need extra grooming, and even sleek, short-haired cats will appreciate a daily comb. If fleas become a problem, talk to a vet about insecticides for aged cats.

Inevitably, the question of euthanasia arises, that is putting the cat to sleep with a fast-acting, painless overdose of anaesthetic. Euthanasia is a kind way to prevent prolonged suffering in a cat with a fatal disease. Your vet can discuss this sensitive issue with you. Most cat owners instinctively know when their pet's life is no longer enjoyable.

CHAPTER 3

HORSES

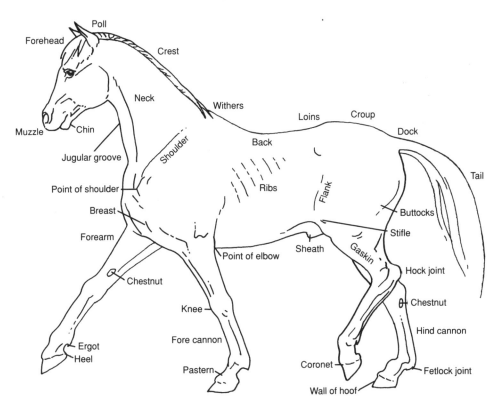

Poll
Forehead
Crest
Neck
Withers
Loins
Croup
Dock
Muzzle
Chin
Back
Tail
Jugular groove
Shoulder
Ribs
Flank
Point of shoulder
Buttocks
Breast
Stifle
Forearm
Sheath
Gaskin
Point of elbow
Hock joint
Chestnut
Chestnut
Knee
Hind cannon
Ergot
Fore cannon
Heel
Coronet
Pastern
Fetlock joint
Wall of hoof

■ The points of the horse.

Sixty million years ago the ancestor of today's horse, the eohippus, or 'dawn horse', roamed North America. Fossils depict a creature the size of a small dog, with several toes on each foot and teeth that were adapted for browsing on trees and shrubs rather than grass. This tiny 2.2 hands high horse adapted over many millions of years to climatic and vegetative changes as ancient swamps and rainforests became grasslands and plains. The animal we recognise as the horse, *Equus caballus*, had evolved by the time *Homo sapiens* was present on earth, and domestication was thought to occur around 5000 years BC. After this, horses rapidly spread over the settled world.

Australia has never had an indigenous horse. The first of the species to enter our country (three mares and a stallion) arrived with Governor Phillip in 1788 after a long sea journey from the Cape of Good Hope. A mere two hundred years later, it is the dream of most Australian children to own a horse. Before you fulfil this dream, it is wise to consider the basic requirements of horse ownership:

Can I afford a horse? Before you assume you can afford a horse, be aware that horses are expensive in both time and monetary terms. You will need to provide adequate space and shelter, a balanced diet, medication in the form of vaccinations and drenches, veterinary attention for those unplanned illnesses and accidents, as well as regular visits to a farrier, and equipment for both horse and rider.

Do I have the time? Having adequate time to be a good horse owner is also important: time to spend riding, regularly exercising, grooming, feeding and just being a friend to your horse.

What type of horse do I want? The size and type of horse must suit the new owner's age and riding ability. While mares and geldings are equally suitable, never be persuaded to buy a stallion, as they require expert handling, special lodgings and can be quite dangerous.

What do I look for? Take your time over the initial inspection. Horse buyers with experience will notice obvious abnormalities of gait, condition and temperament, but if you are in doubt, always ask a vet to inspect the prospective purchase before making a final decision. A veterinary inspection will include an examination of the animal's vital signs (pulse and temperature), general body condition, signs of lameness, the state of limbs from the hooves up and the condition of mouth and teeth. The behaviour of the horse during this inspection will provide useful clues to the horse's temperament, a factor of paramount importance. A harmonious relationship between horse and rider will depend on the horse amiably accepting handling from head to toe.

BASIC CARE

Before you take your new companion home, suitable space and shelter must be provided. A minimum of one hectare with supplementary feeding and the shelter of a simple three-sided, spacious shed is adequate for horses at pasture. This is the healthiest way to keep a horse—allowing freedom for exercise and sunshine while providing access to cover.

The shed or stall should measure at least 4 m x 4 m with a wide door opening to the north away from prevailing weather. Solid feedbins attached to the wall will enable the horse to eat under shelter.

Where space is not available and a horse must be stabled continually, creating a safe and comfortable environment is more crucial. If at all possible you should provide a small

■ All paddocked horses should have a solid and warm shelter shed with a wide doorway opening away from the prevailing winds, and a high ceiling.

yard off the stall to allow some freedom of movement. A permanent stable must be safe, warm, draught-free, easy to clean and have good drainage. A minimum area of 4.5 m by 4.5 m allows a horse to stretch out comfortably without the danger of being cast (an animal is cast when it is down in a difficult position and unable to get up). Contrary to popular legend, horses do not always sleep on their feet.

A wide doorway (at least 1.5 m wide) allows easy use by both horse and owner. The traditional stable door is excellent, allowing your horse a view of the world as well as some sunshine. Floors can be of well-compacted dirt or concrete; if they are concrete, thick bedding such as straw or sawdust or an overlay of rubber matting is required. Ceilings should be at least 2.5 m high to prevent injury to rearing horses.

Hay racks and feedbins are best attached to the walls, at a height comfortable for the individual animal. These should preferably be cons-tructed of metal, as bored horses will chew wood after they have finished feeding (see 'You and Your Horse's Behaviour' overleaf). Free access to water at all times is essential as adult horses will consume 20 to 50 litres of water a day.

If space permits, include an extra room for storing feed, riding tack and grooming gear. The closer equipment is to the horse, the more likely it will be used for its benefit!

Cleaning stables is at least a once a day chore. Horses left standing in wet, dirty bedding develop a variety of problems, usually related to bacterial infections of the lower limbs. Daily mucking out is also essential to remove worm eggs in faeces: in such warm moist conditions, bloodworm eggs can hatch and infect a horse in less than one week.

Fences are also an important consideration. Horses have a prop-ensity for self-inflicted injury and no fence is ever totally horse-proof, but **barbed wire in particular should** always be avoided. Post and rail wooden fences are excellent but they can be rather expensive. Several companies now manufacture a strong, white, plastic horse fencing which can be used to construct the entire fence, or as a top 'sight' wire to improve the visibility of plain wire fences. Whatever materials are used, the fence should be sturdy, smooth with no protruding obstacles and, above all, visible. A galloping horse will be unable to avoid a fence in time if it is not highly obvious.

Regular grooming is a pleasant way for horse and owner to communicate and develop a good rapport. Most horses love being groomed, and for those unable to roll outside it helps to remove scurf and loose coat. Basic grooming gear in order of use includes a rubber curry comb, stiff body brush and soft body brush. The latter promotes shine and is better tolerated on sensitive areas such as the face. An important part of grooming is the cleaning out of a horse's hooves using a hoof pick (see 'Hoof Care' on page 147).

Daily exercise for a horse is essential, whether it is taking it riding, giving it the freedom of a paddock, or merely a walk in the sunshine while a stable is being cleaned. Horses in the wild roam over a considerable area daily in search of fodder, while horses that are continually stabled can rapidly become bored and develop behavioural problems.

Finally, all horses that are stabled even for part of the year should have a rug for cold and inclement weather. Aged horses in particular will appreciate this extra warmth.

YOU AND YOUR HORSE'S BEHAVIOUR

The domestication of animals, and the insistence that their behaviour conform conveniently to human lifestyles, creates problems in all species. Horses that are unable to happily adjust to their routine or environment may develop any of a number of common vices or bad habits.

In small yards or paddocks the most frequent vices are fence running, pawing and digging and crib-biting. When horses are confined to stalls, their behaviour worsens and can include weaving, stall kicking, biting, digging and cribbing.

Such bad habits point to a horse that is bored and unhappy. Correcting vices can be difficult, but the first step is to examine the horse's surroundings. Where possible, allow for greater access to pasture, social contact with other horses and more attention from the humans responsible for its care. Always put yourself in the horse's position and imagine life as it sees life; correcting a problem will be easier if you understand that the needs of animals are remarkably similar to you own.

Cribbing or crib-biting is one of the worst vices a horse can develop. A crib-biting horse grasps a solid object such as a fence rail or a stable door then, holding on with its incisor teeth, it flexes the lower neck muscles and pulls backwards. Apart from excessive wear to the front teeth and enlarge-

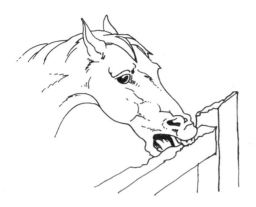

■ Crib-biting is a bad habit that is difficult to break.

ment of the neck muscles the horse is generally unaffected, and the condition is strictly a bad habit only. Cribbing, nevertheless, may progress to 'windsucking', which will cause a horse to become unthrifty and develop flatulence and colic. Windsuckers actually grunt, inhale, and then swallow air when holding on to the fence post with their teeth.

Closely stabled horses can learn cribbing from each other, and foals will learn from cribbing mothers. Aim to prevent this problem by providing a happy and interesting environment for your horse. If environmental changes don't alleviate its boredom, isolation and the cribbing, wood repellents can help, as can electric fences, cutting down on pelleted feeds and increasing the available roughage. You can also use cribbing straps, which are wide collars that fit around the horse's upper neck and prevent the contraction of the neck muscles. As a last resort several surgical procedures can be utilised, but their success rates vary.

NUTRITION

Horses are herbivores, surviving in the wild by grazing on natural pastures. They eat small amounts frequently, travelling over considerable areas in search of fodder. This continual exercise combined with small feeds means that the horse's stomach, with its relatively restricted capacity, is never overloaded.

Domesticated horses often have little exercise in comparison and must consume entire daily rations in one sitting. It is much healthier for your horse if you adopt a regular routine of frequent small feeds (at least two to three feeds daily), avoiding sudden changes in diet and feeding patterns. Where possible, allow the horse free access to pasture; it is well known that horses contented with their physical environment have the best appetites and the most efficient food utilisation.

Domestication has also meant that horses are often expected to perform considerable work, leading to greater dietary energy requirements. This need for energy rises as the workload increases, but the overfeeding of energy foods, especially grain, is a common cause of obesity and founder (see 'Founder' on page 161).

Grains and good quality hay are the most common sources of energy. Although grain is not an essential part of the average horse's ration, hay and other sources of fibre and roughage provide the bulk necessary for efficient digestion. Legume hays made of clover and lucerne also have a high energy content, as well as good levels of protein, vitamins and calcium. Good quality hay can make up a large proportion of a maintenance diet. As a simple rule, horses deprived of natural grazing should be fed 1 to 2% of their body weight as roughage daily. For an 'average' fourteen hand horse, this means at least 7 kg of hay.

Protein is provided in young green pastures and good quality hay. Foals, weanlings, pregnant and lactating mares, and sick horses have the greatest need for protein. Soyabean meal is a good protein source often used in commercial rations. Vitamins and minerals are also essential for a balanced diet, but many horse owners oversupplement with these nutrients. Extra vitamins are required only by those horses deprived of sunshine and green fodder. The need for mineral supplementation too is generally uncommon. The two minerals, calcium and phosphorus, are crucial for foals and their growing bones, however, they rarely need to be supplemented, and there is growing evidence that the overfeeding of energy foods to growing horses can adversely affect these two minerals and lead to abnormal bone growth.

Common salt, sodium chloride, should be available to horses on rations, by either adding it to the feed or as a salt-mineral block. Free access to water is essential, as adult horses drink at least 20 litres a day.

Commercial feedstuffs such as horse pellets are becoming a popular substitute for all portions of a diet except the roughage. Pellets are usually formulated for a particular period in the horse's life—weaner foals, pregnant and lactating mares, or mature horses—and they supply the specific levels of nutrients required. For the inexperienced horseperson they can be an invaluable aid for providing the correct diet. However, commercial rations are not *complete* diets and *must* be supplemented with roughage in the form of good quality hay, or provided by free access to pasture.

Adult horses

The following sample rations are simplified suggestions for horses in varied situations. The grain portion of these diets can be substituted with commercial rations in the volumes recommended by the manufacturer. It is impossible to recommend specific diets for horses as each animal must be fed on an individual basis according to its breed, age, rate of growth, state of pregnancy, work output, temperament and overall condition.

Maintenance ration for the average horse not on pasture ('average' being a mature, fourteen hand specimen): 7 to 8 kg of good quality hay; free access to fresh water; and trace mineralised salt.

Horses in medium work (several hours daily): 8 kg of good quality hay; 2 kg of grain (or the equivalent commercial ration); and fresh water and salt.

Horses in very heavy work (for example, a polo horse in full training): 6 to 8 kg of good quality hay; 5 to 7 kg of grain (or the equivalent commercial ration); and fresh water and salt.

Horses used for endurance work and vigorous sporting events sweat profusely and may require supplementation with electrolytes (body salts) to counter dehydration. Discuss this with a vet.

Weanling foals and lactating mares

Weanling foals and late pregnancy or lactating mares have a particular need for high-protein diets. Pasture quality as well as the individual horse's condition will determine whether supplementation with, for example, the specific commercial pellets, is required. Young, green pastures are high in protein and other nutrients, while old and dry pastures become largely fibrous, providing roughage but little else.

Sick or aged horses

The sick or aged horse needs a diet that is highly digestible, palatable and rich in nutrients, especially protein. You may need to use your imagination, offering a variety of foodstuffs to stimulate these horses' jaded appetites. Molasses, which is also a useful source of energy, may be added to grains to increase their palatability and fresh green grass or leafy young hay should be offered frequently. If the convalescent's appetite is poor, supplement the diet with vitamins and minerals from your vet or produce store. Aged horses with missing teeth may also benefit from a diet that includes crushed or rolled (rather than whole) grain.

Bran mash is a useful food for sick and old horses. It can also prevent constipation in foundered horses that are locked up and dieting. Mix together 1½ kg of bran and 30 g of salt and add to 1½ litres of boiling water, stir well, cover and allow to stand and cool before feeding.

AGEING BY A HORSE'S TEETH

Teeth are the most accurate tool for determining the age of a horse. Overleaf is a summary of the horse's dentition as it changes with age to give

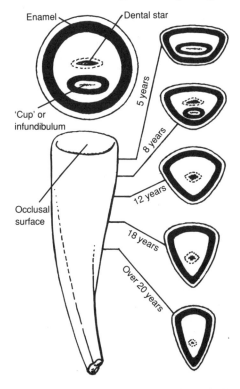

■ Ageing by a horse's teeth using the occlusal table (upper surface) of a horse's incisors. As the horse ages, the shape of the teeth becomes triangular.

you a basic understanding of how to calculate a horse's age, bearing in mind that environmental and genetic factors can cause variation.

All temporary teeth in the foal have erupted by the age of six months. The incisors and canines are then a guide to the age of five years. After this time, various hooks and grooves develop and disappear. The angle of the teeth in profile becomes sharper with age, and the wearing surface of the teeth changes from an oval shape to a definite triangle as horses age.

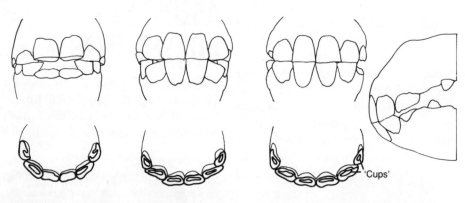

■ 2½ years: The central or first incisors have erupted.

■ 3½ years: The intermediate or second incisors have erupted.

■ 4½ years: The corner or third incisors have erupted. Most incisors have definite 'cups' (visible infundibulum). The canines are erupting and are small and sharp. By 5 years, all permanent teeth have erupted and are in wear.

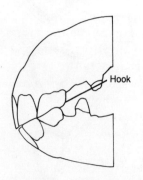

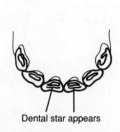

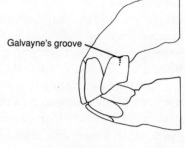

■ 7 years: The upper corner incisor has a hook, being wider than the lower incisor.

■ 8 years: The dental star appears in the central incisors. This is a yellow-brown line on the outer edge of the cups, which by now are disappearing in the lower teeth.

■ 10 years: By 9 years the seven year hook has disappeared. At 10 years Galvayne's Groove has appeared at the gum margin of the upper corner incisor.

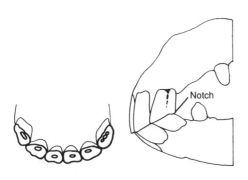

■ 12 years: Another notch has appeared, like the seven year hook, on the upper corner incisor.

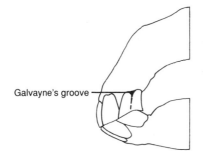

■ 15 years: Galvayne's Groove is halfway down the upper corner incisor.

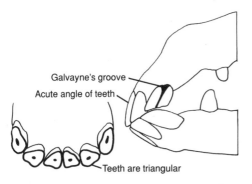

■ 20 years: Galvayne's Groove extends the entire length of the upper corner incisor. The teeth have a very acute angle in profile.

ROUTINE HEALTH CARE

As with all animal species, horses require regular preventative treatment against certain diseases and parasites. Care of the teeth and hooves should also be part of this health programme.

PROTECTING YOUR HORSE WITH VACCINATION

Vaccination is a means of stimulating the body's defence mechanisms into producing antibodies against specific diseases. It is the safest way to protect your horse against serious diseases such as tetanus and strangles.

Tetanus

Vaccination of horses against tetanus, a highly fatal disease, should be given top priority by all horse owners. The spores of the tetanus organism are commonly found in soil and horse faeces, and as horses are the most susceptible of all animals to this disease protection is essential.

Tetanus is caused by the bacterium *Clostridium tetani*, which produces a neurotoxin that spreads along nerve trunks to affect the central nervous system. The organism thrives best where there is little oxygen, for instance, in deep puncture wounds such as those caused by nails driven into the sole of the hoof. The lesion may have healed or been missed by the time symptoms appear, usually after seven to twenty-one days.

The neurotoxin causes frequent, then constant, muscle spasms of the entire body. The horse will be very stiff: the tail will stick out rigidly, the third eyelids move across the inner corners of both eyes and eating, drinking and walking will be difficult (the common name for tetanus, lockjaw, is very apt). The horse eventually dies from fixation of the respiratory muscles.

Treatment of tetanus is difficult, and the survival rate is less than 50%. A vet must supervise treatment, which primarily involves the continuous sedation of the affected horse to control the muscle spasms. A quiet, dark location and gentle, calm nursing are essential, as any sudden noise or movement will initiate more spasms.

Tetanus vaccination procedure

The following regimen must be followed to ensure good immunity to tetanus.

Foals: The first vaccination should be given at six to eight weeks of age, followed by a second vaccination four weeks later which gives protection for twelve months. A third vaccination is then required.

Adult horses: Vaccination may be given at any age with two vaccinations four weeks apart and a follow-up booster twelve months later.

Pregnant mares: A vaccination should be given in the last month of pregnancy to pass on protection to their new foals.

All adult horses: Boosters *must* be given every five years.

Injured horses: Tetanus anti-toxin is an injection that provides fast but temporary protection, and should be given after every injury.

Strangles

Strangles occurred in large-scale epidemics amongst military horses in both world wars, and in working draught horse stables of times past. Today, improved treatment and vaccination has reduced the severity and incidence of the disease, but it still occurs whenever horses congregate or are kept together in large numbers.

Strangles is caused by the bacterium *Streptococcus equi*. It affects only horses, especially those under five years of age, and causes inflammation of the upper respiratory tract. Horses with strangles rapidly become depressed and stop eating, develop a high temperature, sore throat, painful cough and a thick, yellow pus discharge from the nostrils. The lymph nodes in the throat region may swell, abscess and burst.

The infectious bacteria are passed out in the discharges from the nostrils and abscesses, contaminating feed and water troughs and creating a highly contagious environment. Both sick horses and inanimate objects can carry the organism for at least four weeks, infecting any horses that come in contact with the bacteria. As the disease needs only one week to incubate, a major outbreak occurs readily.

Treatment with antibiotics is usually very successful, and with proper care and nursing deaths are rare. Affected animals must be isolated, and their stable, food and water troughs, and grooming gear must all be disinfected.

Strangles vaccination procedure

There is much controversy about the usefulness of the strangles vaccine. It is not always totally effective, but most vaccinated horses will still have a less severe attack of strangles if a breakdown does occur. Painful reactions and swelling can occur at the injection site, especially if the horse has previously come in contact with the disease.

Each horse should be assessed on an individual basis when considering strangles vaccination. Any horse that is taken regularly to shows, pony clubs or riding schools should be considered a candidate for vaccination. Ask your vet for advice.

The following is the vaccination regimen for strangles.

Foals: The first vaccination should be given at three months of age, followed by a further two vaccinations two weeks apart.

Adult horses: A course of three vaccinations two weeks apart is required.

All vaccinated horses: Annual boosters should be given to maintain immunity.

PROTECTING YOUR HORSE WITH WORMING

Regular drenching must become part of any horse-care programme to decrease the incidence of internal parasites—all worms can reduce body weight and performance, and certain equine worms may be fatal. The following are the most common.

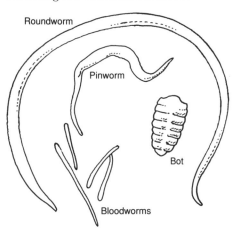

■ Important worms of the horse (not drawn to scale).

Bloodworms

Bloodworms, or large strongyles, are without doubt the most dangerous of all parasites occurring in horses. Some authorities estimate these worms may be responsible for 90% of all horse colics, many of which become fatal.

The most damaging of the three common large strongyles is *Strongylus vulgaris*, a pink-grey worm growing to only 2 cm in length. The infective larvae are picked up and swallowed with pasture, burrowing through the large intestinal wall into arteries (blood vessels), where they develop into adults over the next four months. The young adult worms then migrate back to the large intestine, where they attach themselves to the walls causing ulceration, bleeding and bouts of colic. The females lay eggs that pass out with the horse's droppings and, if the weather is warm and humid, these eggs can develop into infective larvae within one week. The entire cycle takes about six months.

Adult female worms in the large intestine lay five thousand eggs daily. In a horse with an 'average' worm burden this means the deposition on pasture of *fifteen million* eggs each day, and overcrowded paddocks rapidly become heavily contaminated with bloodworm eggs.

The bloodworm larvae are the real killers. During their time within the arteries they inflame, weaken and injure the vessel lining, causing blood clots and clusters of larvae to form. Intermittent bouts of colic result, or the larvae may totally block the blood vessel preventing crucial blood supply from reaching sections of intestine. The damaged intestine must be removed surgically, but often the inflammation is so great that treatment is not possible.

Foals are born without blood-worms, but quickly begin to pick up worm eggs once they are nibbling pasture. Damaging larvae can be migrating through a foal's blood vessels for six months before worm eggs will be detected in their faeces. The majority of foals can be assumed to have some arterial injury by the time they are seven years of age. (See 'Drenching Procedure' on page 145.)

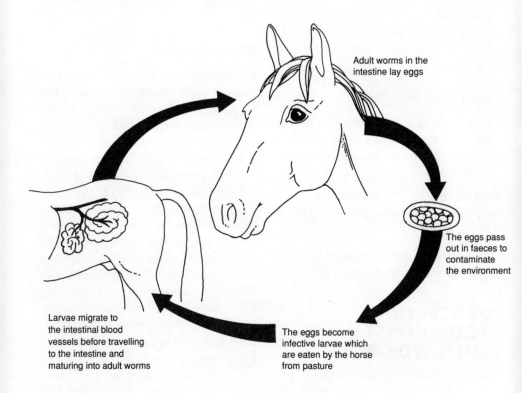

Adult worms in the intestine lay eggs

The eggs pass out in faeces to contaminate the environment

Larvae migrate to the intestinal blood vessels before travelling to the intestine and maturing into adult worms

The eggs become infective larvae which are eaten by the horse from pasture

■ The bloodworm life cycle.

Redworms

Redworms, or small strongyles, are red-coloured worms just visible to the naked eye. They are very common, but not as damaging as their larger relatives, remaining in nodules in the intestinal wall rather than migrating through the body. Large numbers can cause weight loss, diarrhoea and colic. (See 'Drenching Procedure' on page 145.)

Roundworms

The roundworm of horses, *Parascaris equorum*, is largely a parasite of foals. After six to twelve months of age, foals develop a strong immunity to these worms, often spontaneously expelling them in their faeces. Pregnant and lactating mares are the only adult horses continually affected, and they act as reservoirs for the worms, ensuring their survival as they pass them on to their foals.

Adult roundworms are white, cylindrical and easily observed in the faeces (occasionally, these worms can grow to 50 cm). The outer shell of the roundworm egg is thick, tough and sticky, adhering to feedbins, stables and even the mare's udder. The worm can remain viable for years, making control of the environment difficult especially as the female adult worm lays 200 000 eggs per day.

Foals become infected by swallowing eggs that have passed out in faeces. The worm larvae now in the intestine burrow through the gut wall and pass via the bloodstream to the liver, heart and lungs. Eventually the larvae reach the windpipe, where they are coughed up, swallowed and grow into adult worms in the intestine. The cycle takes ten to twelve weeks.

Heavy roundworm burdens cause irritation to organs from larval migration, and the adults interfere with nutrient absorption and may even tear or block the intestine. A roundworm infested foal will have a poor growth rate, rough coat, a potbelly and may scour (have diarrhoea). (See 'Drenching Procedure' on page 145.)

Pinworms

The pinworm, *Oxyuris equi*, is a common horse parasite that lives in the lower end of the large intestine. It is greyish-white, with a round body and a sharply pointed tail, and as the adults can grow to 10 cm, they are easily recognisable in manure.

Female worms travel to the rectum and anus where they lay their eggs on the skin. The eggs are attached by a sticky, irritating substance, causing the horse to rub its tail constantly against any available object. The eggs then drop off onto feedbins or water troughs, where they are picked up with food or water. The entire cycle takes over five months.

The pinworm is seen mostly in stabled horses, as once they are in the outside environment the fragile eggs cannot survive under dry conditions. The worm causes little damage apart from itchiness around the anus and the resultant scruffy, rubbed tail. (See 'Drenching Procedure' on page 145)

Bot flies

Bots are not worms—they are flies that use the horse as an intermediate host in their life cycle. There are three common bot flies in Australia, all of them *Gastrophilus* species.

The adult flies are dark yellow, hairy and rather like bees, and are most active in summer and autumn. They don't bite horses, but do cause annoyance while laying their eggs on the coat hairs of the legs, neck, chest or face (depending on which fly). Removing these eggs is tedious and difficult and can be done using a special bot knife, by thorough and regular grooming, or by vigorously scrubbing the area carrying the eggs with hot water. The heat causes the eggs to hatch and the larvae die prematurely. Drenching at the correct time is the most useful method of control.

Before developing into larvae, the eggs have to be licked from the legs or chest into the horse's mouth. Those laid on the face burrow through the skin and facial muscles until they enter the mouth. The larvae then migrate in the mouth tissues and down the oesophagus to the stomach where they grow into the 1 cm 'grub' called the bot. These bots remain attached to the stomach lining for ten months where, contrary to popular opinion, they

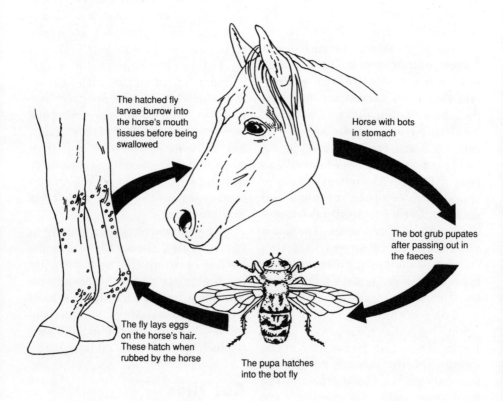

The hatched fly larvae burrow into the horse's mouth tissues before being swallowed

Horse with bots in stomach

The bot grub pupates after passing out in the faeces

The fly lays eggs on the horse's hair. These hatch when rubbed by the horse

The pupa hatches into the bot fly

■ The bot fly life cycle.

rarely cause injury unless present in very large numbers. After this period of attachment the bots drop off and pass out in the droppings at the end of winter, burrowing into the ground and pupating until the warmer months when the adult fly emerges.

Tapeworms

The usual tapeworm affecting Australian horses is *Anoplocephala perfoliata*, which is mainly a problem in young adults. In large numbers, the worm causes loss of weight, a rough shaggy coat and digestive disturbances, however, tapeworms are not as common as other internal parasites.

A particular grass mite is the necessary intermediate host for *Anoplocephala* tapeworms. A worm egg is eaten by and encysts inside a mite, which is then eaten by a horse. The cyst ruptures and the tapeworm completes its life cycle in the horse's intestine. This cycle takes three to four months.

Tapeworms are not susceptible to many horse drenches and require specific treatment. Your vet can diagnose an infection by detecting worm eggs in the droppings under a microscope.

Drenching procedure

The following drenching regimen applies to bloodworms, redworms, roundworms, pinworms and bot flies.

Foals: Treat from six weeks of age for roundworms, then continue treatment every six to eight weeks until the foal is six months of age. Foals should be drenched against bloodworms, red-worms and pinworms from six months of age, and this treatment repeated every six to eight weeks thereafter.

Adult horses: Treat against bloodworms, redworms and pinworms every eight to twelve weeks for life. In crowded situations, it may be necessary to drench at least every six weeks. All adult horses should be treated for bot flies twice yearly. The most effective times are during winter (in cold climate areas, start after the first frost). All the common paste drenches are also available with a boticide included.

Pregnant mares: Treat every six to eight weeks against roundworms, blood-worms, redworms, and pinworms during pregnancy and lactation.

Internal parasite control

Most individual horse drenches contain drugs that treat the most common worms with one dose. Tube drenching must be performed by a vet and involves the passing of a stomach tube via the nostrils. This method ensures the drugs are delivered at the correct dose rate.

Paste drenches are an excellent way to deworm your horse as long as you keep in touch with your vet regarding the newest and most effective products. For horse owners with one or two horses in spacious paddocks, paste drenching with faecal examinations is usually sufficient. Including a once or twice a year tube drench would ensure a very efficient worming programme.

For those with large numbers of horses, drenching must be not only

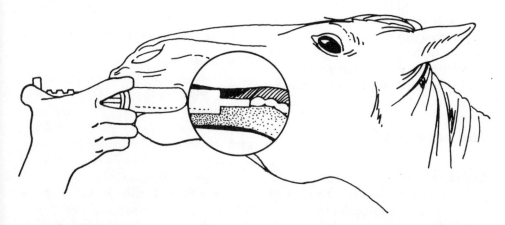

■ When paste drenching, always aim to deposit the paste on the back of the tongue to ensure the entire dose is swallowed.

more frequent, but very efficient. Depending on the stocking rate, tube drenching up to six times a year may be necessary to maintain healthy horses and low environmental contamination.

Worm resistance occurs when a small number of worms inside a horse have survived a drenching. These worms lay eggs and build up their numbers unaffected by the drugs being used. Eventually, a large proportion of worms on the property will be resistant to the usual drenches. To avoid this problem, it is recommended that one particular drench be used for twelve months, then another for the next twelve months. Make sure the actual chemical group is different, not just the brand name; ask a vet for advice. Using one drug continually or changing drugs with each drench may lead to resistance.

Controlling worm-egg contamination of the environment is just as important as treating the worms inside the horse. **Never assume you can eradicate horse worms; you can only control them and this requires constant vigilance.**

All new horses should be drenched before being introduced to a property, and *every* horse on a property must be included in a drenching programme to prevent continual pasture contamination.

Manure should be removed once a day from stables and small yards, and stables cleaned completely at least once a week. In larger yards and small paddocks, remove the droppings at least twice a week—this is necessary to prevent the eggs in these droppings developing into larvae infective to horses.

On a larger scale, rest paddocks for at least three to four months, or practise rotational grazing with sheep and cattle (the worms of these species will not affect horses and vice versa). A good time to do this is during warm and humid weather when worm larvae become infective quickly and the pastures are most dangerous for horses.

Treat pregnant and lactating mares to decrease the amount of worm eggs that will be picked up by their foals.

Ask your vet to perform regular faecal examinations (twice a year) to check for worm eggs. This is a useful guide to the efficiency of your drenching programme. Buy drenches from a vet, and ask for advice on the best products as drenches are constantly being improved.

HOOF CARE

Horse's hooves grow at a rate of around 1 cm each month, giving a horse a totally new hoof every six months. Regular hoof trimming and care is therefore an essential part of horse care, and you should equip yourself with a hoof pick and a good farrier. Unshod horses should have their hooves trimmed and shod horses their shoes replaced every six to eight weeks.

Shoeing is required only when a horse is working hard daily, racing, competing regularly, or is ridden over hard surfaces. Horses that are turned out to pasture should always have their shoes removed.

Before and after every ride you should clean out your horse's hooves. The best instrument for this is a hoof pick, which will remove stones, compacted dirt and vegetable matter lodged in the sole. Doing this regularly ensures you will notice any sole abnormalities and prevents conditions such as 'thrush'.

Thrush is a bacterial infection of the frog that occurs when horses spend time standing in wet and

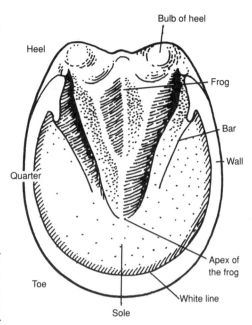

■ Anatomy of the sole of the hoof.

unhygienic conditions, causing the frog to develop a foul odour and blackish discharge. Early treatment involving trimming, cleaning and packing the frog with medicated preparations helps to prevent the infection spreading into the sensitive tissues of the hoof.

Dry and brittle hooves often develop cracks and splits; blacksmiths or vets are best equipped to deal with these problems as they occur. Oil-based hoof conditioners, daily fresh green feed and specific dietary additives can help keep hooves in a supple and healthy state.

Regular hoof cleaning will teach your horse good manners—all horses should be happy to have their hooves and limbs handled properly. Such horses are popular with vets and farriers!

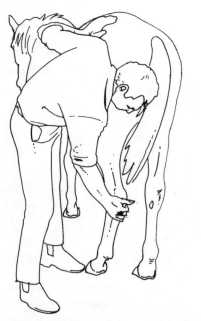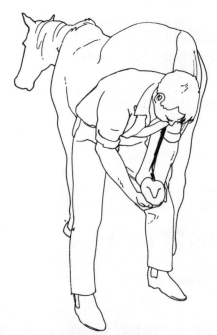

■ Picking up a back hoof: always stand close to the horse and with one hand resting on the rump, run the other hand gently but firmly down the horse's leg right to the fetlock; the raised leg should rest comfortably on your thigh.

■ Picking up a front hoof.

CASTRATION

The castration of stallions is probably the most common routine surgery performed in the horse. The result, the gelding, is a much more pliable animal for the average horse owner; stallions can be dangerous and require special facilities. Castration involves the removal of both testicles, an operation usually performed under general anaesthesia. It can be done at any age, but most colts are castrated around twelve months of age.

Castration is an act of veterinary science and, legally, can only be carried out by a qualified veterinary surgeon.

ANAESTHETICS, SURGERY AND MEDICATION

Because of size and convenience, most minor surgery in the average, well-behaved horse is performed under local anaesthetic. Such minor surgery includes the stitching of wounds and the removal of small tumours.

General anaesthesia is essential for major operations. As in smaller animal species, a rubber or plastic tube is passed down the windpipe and connected to a source of anaesthetic gas and oxygen. Depending on the length of the surgery, most horses will be on their feet within one hour after an anaesthetic. The horse should be kept in a warm and dry place until fully recovered from the anaesthetic (several hours at least). If the horse is in a paddock, stay with it to prevent any injury from fences or other objects nearby until it is walking normally. Food and water can then be provided.

All skin sutures in horses should remain in place for fourteen days unless specified otherwise by your vet. After any surgery, exercise should be restricted until the sutures have been removed and the wound has healed.

Medication for sick horses must often be administered as an injection. Never attempt injections unless you are under veterinary supervision, as the wrong injection technique frequently causes large and painful abscesses. Medication may also be dispensed as powders in the feed, but unless your horse is a greedy eater it may be necessary to disguise the taste of the powder with molasses. Always mix oral medication with a *small* amount of food; and only when this is entirely eaten should you give your horse the remainder of its meal. Powders can also be mixed to a paste and administered as per a paste worm drench if they are rejected when given with food.

Sick horses need good nursing. They should be rugged if outside or, better still, kept in a warm, dry stable with plenty of clean bedding, and isolated from other horses. Tempting food such as fresh green pick, bran mashes and soaked grains should be offered to an ailing horse.

EMERGENCIES

Described below are the most common emergencies occurring in horses. In any urgent situation, remember that vets are there to help you and always telephone for advice.

WOUNDS

Horses are particularly adept at causing themselves injury, and the average horse owner must expect, sometime, to be confronted by a wounded horse. The correct care of horse wounds is aimed at:

■ minimising infection by keeping any injuries clean and by using antibacterial drugs;

■ having wounds sutured within six hours of the injury;

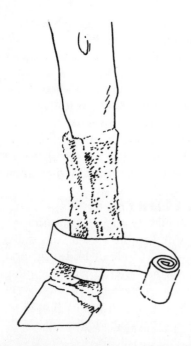

■ Bandaging the lower limb. After a padding of cotton wool, the crepe and elastoplast layers should begin at the hoof end: this produces a firmer bandage.

■ restricting the movement of the wound edges on the lower limbs with pressure bandaging;

■ ensuring that all deep wounds have good drainage; and

■ protecting horses against tetanus.

If you are confronted with a large, deep tear and possibly a lot of bleeding, don't panic. Telephone a vet immediately, keep yourself and the horse calm and reach for the hose. Running cold water gently over it cleans a wound of debris and hair, helps to constrict bleeding vessels and minimises swelling. Keep hosing until the vet arrives. If the horse has not learnt to tolerate water, begin by

trickling the water onto its hooves. Slowly work your way up the limb to the site of the injury. Haemorrhage (bleeding) will rarely continue after fifteen minutes of hosing, but if it persists pack the wound tightly with cotton wool or a clean towel and apply pressure. Don't allow the horse to move as this may stimulate further bleeding.

Stitching a wound is a task for a vet. Don't expect a successful job if you leave it until the next day—it is a proven fact that all wounds are infected within twelve hours and infection is the major cause of wound breakdown. Antibiotics are essential to minimise infection in serious wounds and should be given by injection or orally for at least five days. *Never* use old remedies such as stockholm tar and kerosene; they are extremely irritating to a wound and can cause further damage. Even disinfectant powders packed onto a wound surface can retard healing.

Daily hosing with cold water after the wound has been treated is a useful way of keeping wounds clean. The regular application of water has also been shown to stimulate the growth of new, healing tissues.

Horse wounds have a peculiarity: the production of 'proud flesh' or exuberant granulation tissue. Granulation tissue is normal in all healing wounds, but in horses it can grow into large, pink, grape-like masses that prevent wound edges from moving inwards. This occurs most often on the lower limbs where high skin tension causes constant movement of the wound edges. Avoid old-fashioned irritant remedies for proud flesh. The tissue should be trimmed back to the correct level by a vet, then a veterinary ointment used to control the tissue. The most satisfactory way to immobilise wound edges and therefore encourage healing and discourage proud flesh is to apply pressure bandaging. Bandaging also helps to control swelling and reduces wound contamination.

Before dressing, a wound should be clean and dry. Apply medication first if necessary and then paraffin gauze, and wrap a thick layer of cotton wool around the entire limb over the injury site. A crepe bandage should be wrapped around the cotton wool and the dressing completed with a sticky elastoplast. Begin your placement of the crepe and elastoplast from the bottom of the cotton wool up; this holds the dressing in place effectively. Pressure bandages should be firm but not too tight. Always check several hours after bandaging for any swelling, which may indicate that the dressing is too tight.

Cleaning and dressing a wound daily may be required for at least a week. Once the wound looks clean and has little discharge, dressings may be left on for several days. Persevering with bandaging until a wound is healed will result in faster healing and minimal scarring. Restricting a horse's exercise while a wound heals is also important. Horses that are worked or gallop around a large paddock will rupture suture lines and disrupt dressings.

Puncture wounds and large lacerations that cannot be stitched must have good drainage. Wounds must heal from the inside out, so keep the lower part of the wound open so any debris can escape or can be flushed out every day if required. Open wounds can become fly-struck; in hot weather, spray once a day with a fly repellent wound dressing.

All injured horses must be protected against tetanus. Anti-toxin should always be given in particular to unvaccinated horses.

FRACTURES

Advances in veterinary science have meant that many types of broken bones in horses can now be successfully mended. Internal fixation using metal pins, plates and screws has largely replaced the heavy and often unsatisfactory plaster cast.

Horses with broken legs are obvious: the limb may hang at an odd angle, the foot may be dragged, often massive swelling is present over the fracture site and the horse will move with great difficulty using only three legs. Smaller fractures of minor bones will still cause horses to limp severely, although swelling may not be as obvious. **A suspected fracture is an emergency** and immediate veterinary attention is required to assess the injury and possible treatment and, importantly, to relieve the horse of pain.

CHOKE

Obstruction of the oesophagus with food or other ingested material is known as 'choke', and it is most commonly seen in horses that have eaten quickly or eaten while travelling. The oesophagus, or the 'food pipe', is a narrow cylindrical organ that begins at the back of the throat, travels down

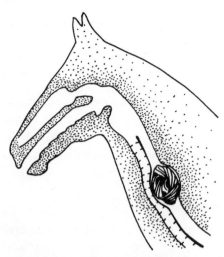

■ Choke is an emergency. It occurs when a bolus of food becomes stuck at some point in the oesophagus, or food pipe.

the neck, then passes through the diaphragm to join the stomach. Obstruction can occur at any point. As swallowing is impaired, regurgitated material may pass on to a horse's lungs causing pneumonia. This condition should always be treated as an emergency and the obstruction relieved as soon as possible. Fast treatment helps to prevent complications such as pneumonia.

A choked horse will look distressed, drool and swallow excessively, stand with head and neck stretched forward and have a profuse greenish discharge from both nostrils. If your horse is showing these symptoms, contact a vet immediately and remove all food, water and bedding from the horse's reach. The horse will be treated initially with medication that relaxes the muscles of the oesophagus and by then passing a tube down the oesophagus via the nostrils to try to budge the obstructing mass. Some

chokes will respond dramatically, while others may require repeated treatments. The most severe cases need surgery to remove the obstruction.

COLIC

Horses with severe colic should always be regarded as emergencies. Some horses will require intensive treatment and possibly surgery, which should begin as soon as possible. Refer to 'Gastrointestinal Tract' on page 157 for more details.

FOALING MARES

Problems of foaling mares present some of the true emergencies in veterinary practice. Unlike other large animals such as the cow, which can take its time producing a calf, giving birth for the mare is almost explosive. A normal equine birth begins and finishes within fifteen to thirty minutes, so any problems that occur must be corrected quickly if a foal is to be saved.

In a normal birth, the foal appears at the vulva front feet first, with its head resting on its front legs. Any changes from this pattern will almost always mean problems for the mare and foal, so never hesitate to call a vet at the first sign of trouble. Refer to 'Birth' on page 166 for further details.

EYES

In the wild, horses needed to locate their predators quickly in order to flee danger, so a horse's eye is designed to provide wide vision and the ability to see behind and to both sides.

While the human lens changes to focus, a horse's lens is fixed, and focusing is achieved by raising or lowering the head. Our eyes work together to focus on one scene; a horse's eyes work independently to see two different pictures. When grazing, horses can focus on both far objects and those under their noses at the same time. This wide range of vision does have the disadvantage of making horses unable to see to the front very effectively. For this reason you should always approach horses from the side, and you will be more easily recognised and accepted.

Conjunctivitis

Inflammation of the conjunctiva can result from windy conditions, flies, injury and from feed that is excessively dusty. Affected eyes become red and swollen and they should be bathed with clean, warm water and a veterinary ointment applied to them at least two to three times a day.

As well as causing conjunctivitis, flies spread diseases such as habronemiasis (see opposite). Fly veils and the twice daily application of a veterinary fly repellent ointment around the eyelids will help.

Ulcers

Injuries such as puncture wounds or grass seeds embedded in the conjunctiva can rub and tear the fine, sensitive eye covering, the cornea. Any break in the cornea is termed an ulcer, and without prompt treatment in-

fection may cause rapid, irreparable damage.

Horses with eye ulcers will blink continually and affected eyes will be very red and swollen with a copious discharge. Ulcers are very painful and *must* receive veterinary attention. The correct ointment is essential, and if the ulcer is severe the vet may stitch the eyelids together to protect the eye and allow faster healing. If left unstitched, the horse should be kept out of bright light.

Habronemiasis

Habronemiasis occurs mainly in warm climates and is caused by the horse stomach worm, *Habronema*. These worms develop inside flies that deposit the worm larvae in the inner corners of the eyes, in wounds, or on the prepuce of male horses. The larvae penetrate the skin causing irritation, and raised, raw nodules form, which in the eye can look like cancer. Eventually, the larvae in the nodules migrate to the stomach to grow into adult, egg-laying worms.

A vet will need to dispense the specific treatment required. As well as controlling flies around your horse, its manure must be removed regularly to prevent the habronema worm eggs hatching.

SKIN

The skin is a large and very sensitive organ that reacts quickly to any irritant, and in the horse, as in all other animal species, it frequently becomes diseased.

Viral papillomas

Viral papillomas, or warts, in horses are caused by the equine papilloma virus. Occurring usually on the muzzle and face of young animals, the virus can be spread by grooming gear or close contact. Although they may reduce the aesthetic appeal of your horse, they rarely cause problems and the majority of warts will disappear within three to six months. Surgical removal of large, single lesions is possible, but treatment is usually neither recommended or necessary.

Lice

Two types of horse lice are common throughout Australia: a sucking louse and a biting louse. Both cause intense irritation, scruffiness of the coat, mane and tail from constant rubbing, and poor condition and weight loss when present in heavy numbers. The sucking louse also causes anaemia.

All lice are 'host specific', meaning that horse lice only infest horses.

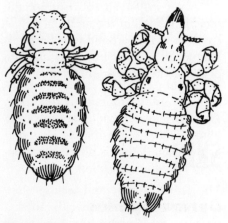

■ Horse lice. (Left) The biting louse, *Damalinia equi.* (Right) The sucking louse, *Haematopinus asini.*

Off the horse itself, they can only survive for several days, but this is often enough for them to spread to other horses via grooming gear and rugs.

Lice infestation is largely a problem of winter and early spring, as hot temperatures kill the nits (eggs) and slow down egg laying.

The eggs are attached to hairs as they are laid, where they remain while maturing into adults over the following three weeks. Female lice then lay about one hundred eggs over the succeeding few weeks.

Horses that rub and scratch themselves on fence posts and stables should always be examined for lice. To do this, part the long hairs of the mane, or look carefully on the skin along the horse's back. Both the eggs and the small, flat wingless bodies of the lice are visible to the naked eye.

Effective insecticidal washes such as Asuntol and Nucidol are widely available; take care to mix these preparations exactly as instructed. Horses should be washed at least twice at fourteen-day intervals to kill the newly hatched adult lice before they begin egg laying. Pour-on lice preparations, commonly used in cattle, should *never* be used on horses, as serious side effects can occur.

Queensland itch

Queensland itch, caused by sandflies of the *Culicoides* genus, occurs mainly in the hot and humid areas of Australia.

Only a small percentage of horses develop an allergy to the sandfly bite, and these horses are affected for life. They spend the hot months of the year

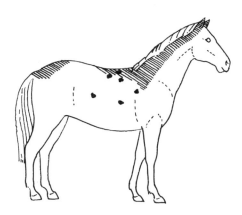

■ The shading indicates the areas most affected by Queensland itch, an allergy to the bite of the sandfly. The black patches approximate the location of vitiligo.

scratching, rubbing and biting until the areas around their ears, mane, back and tail become hairless and thickened. Each year the itchiness returns with the sandflies.

Treatment and prevention is very difficult. Basically, affected horses must be kept away from sandflies. Insecticidal washes applied twice a week offer some relief, while lotions and anti-itch injections are at best only very temporary treatments. The best solution is to hood and rug the horse when sandflies are most active at dawn and dusk, or to stable them at these times in fly-proof stables.

Ringworm

Ringworm is caused by several types of fungi that invade the hair fibres and surrounding skin tissues, usually over the girth, shoulders and loins.

The condition begins with many small, raised and painful lumps. Scabs form, then drop off, leaving small hairless patches (in the horse the classical, round, hairless patches may not occur). In severe cases horses will look quite moth-eaten.

Ringworm is easily spread to other parts of the body, or to other horses, by the careless use of grooming gear and saddlery, so these objects should always be disinfected. As in other animal species, younger animals are the most susceptible to ringworm. The fungi also spread easily to humans, so care should be taken when treating infected horses.

There are many anti-fungal horse shampoos and washes available, and preparations containing iodine are very useful. Shampoo the horse, rubbing the wash well into the affected areas. This should be done twice a week until hair regrowth is obvious and the lesions are no longer spreading. Contact your vet if the lesions persist.

Vitiligo

Vitiligo is that frustrating and as yet unexplained condition whereby mature horses develop patches of depigmentation, or white hair. The most common type occurs as white spots along the back or on the body, and is possibly an inherited condition. The other form of vitiligo results from injuries that destroy the pigment cells in the skin. There is no known treatment for either condition.

Dermatophilus

Dermatophilus, or 'rain scald', is a very common skin disease in horses, often occurring after warm, overcast and rainy weather. It is caused by a bacterium, *Dermatophilus congolensis* that thrives in moist conditions and is spread by flies and close contact. The organism affects horses of all ages, but is most severe on white skin. The lesions are usually seen on the face, back and lower limbs, and begin as areas of matted hairs with a crusty scab underneath. This falls off to leave a bare, raw area.

Rain scald will often heal spontaneously if weather conditions become dry. Chronic and severe lesions will develop if horses are kept in long, wet grass or rain continues for prolonged periods.

Several washes with a medicated horse shampoo are usually sufficient to control the infection. Severe cases will need antibiotics.

Greasy heel

Greasy heel was a prevalent disease in the days of working draught horses with their long-haired pasterns. The disease is still seen today in horses kept in constantly wet and dirty conditions. Usually scratches and abrasions above the heels initiate the disease, then the skin becomes inflamed, deep cracks occur, an excessive greasy discharge develops, the horse becomes lame and, eventually, thickened, grape-like skin growths form above the heels. The reason for the sudden oily discharge is unknown, but after this occurs the area becomes vulnerable to secondary bacterial and fungal infection.

Poor management often plays a part in this disease and is something that can be corrected. Affected horses should be moved to clean and dry surroundings, their 'feathers' (the long hair above the heels) clipped and the greasy area washed with a mild soap then dried thoroughly. An astringent medication such as white lotion, which is a mix of 30 g of zinc sulphate, 15 g of lead acetate, and 500 mL of water, is useful. It is available from your vet or chemist, but always consult a vet regarding treatment, as antibiotics may be required.

Girth galls

Girth galls are raw, ulcerated areas that often occur beneath saddles and under girth straps. They are caused by any form of friction, for example, from loose and mobile or dirty and unpliable girths.

Rest horses with girth galls if possible, or use a thick, soft saddle rug (for example, sheepskin) and padding under the girth. The lesions must be kept clean and dry. Obtain the correct ointment from a vet, or white lotion as described under 'Greasy Heel' opposite is also useful.

Photosensitisation

Plants such as St John's Wart, or particular fungi on plants, contain photodynamic substances that sensitise the lightly pigmented areas of a horse's skin to ultraviolet light. Piebalds with their large patches of non-pigmented skin are especially vulnerable. Photosensitisation may also be secondary to liver damage caused by certain plants.

Photosensitised horses will develop 'sunburn', with the skin becoming red and thickened with crusty scabs. In the acute stage, affected areas will swell and may be intensely itchy. Eventually, the skin will dry up, die and peel off in large sheets.

Affected horses must be moved immediately into shade, preferably into a stable, and kept off the original pasture. Call your vet, as often these horses become very sick.

Melanomas

Melanomas are skin tumours that occur specifically in grey and dappled horses. Seen commonly under the tail, around the anus, or as isolated lumps anywhere on the body, melanomas are firm, often black, painless swellings of variable size.

The older the horse the more frequently these tumours are observed. Although they are classed as malignant, their growth is very slow and many melanomas will never require treatment. Observe the size of the lump and if it is obviously increasing in size, consult a vet; some melanomas can be removed surgically.

Sarcoids

Sarcoids have for many years been the subject of research to determine their cause and successful treatment. Thought now to be initiated by a virus, they are the most common skin tumour in all horses.

All breeds, ages, sexes and types of horse and donkey are susceptible. Sarcoids occur mainly on the head, legs and lower abdomen and are extremely variable in appearance. They can be small, flat and wart-like,

remaining the same size for years, or they can grow to over 20 cm in diameter, have a raw, ulcerated surface and invade the surrounding tissues aggressively. Microscopically, they all have the same tissue components and patterns.

There are numerous forms of treatment, none of which is always successful, and a large percentage of sarcoids recur after treatment. Treatment for sarcoids includes anti-cancer drugs, implants of radioactive material and surgical removal combined with electrocautery or cryosurgery. The latter is the freezing of affected tissues, and is perhaps the most successful form of treatment.

GASTROINTESTINAL TRACT

The gastrointestinal tract, or digestive system, consists of the organs concerned with food: its ingestion, digestion and passage through the body. These organs include the teeth, stomach, liver and small and large intestines which, in the horse, have a length of approximately 30 m.

Teeth

Horses do require dental care at certain periods in their lives, and specific behaviour can alert the horse owner to a possible problem. Abnormal eating habits are the most common symptom: the drooling of excessive saliva, tilting of the head and the dropping of semi-chewed balls of food from the mouth while eating (called quidding). A slow, prolonged weight loss or poor performance when a bit is used can also indicate a tooth problem.

The sloping anatomy of a horse's teeth creates an overlap, and points can develop on the outer edges of the upper teeth and the inner edges of the lower teeth that can be sharp enough to cut and abrade the cheeks or tongue. Obvious external swellings of the jaws indicate more serious problems such as a tooth infection.

To properly inspect a horse's mouth, a vet will use a metal gag, which prevents the horse closing its mouth, protects fingers and hands and allows a thorough examination. Any sharp points can be rubbed off using a tooth rasp or float.

Diarrhoea

Diarrhoea is a symptom of an underlying problem in the horse which can be a bacterial infection, parasites, incorrect feeding (sudden changes in feed patterns, excess lush green feed or grain), mouldy food and poisonous or irritant plants. It can also occur in stressed or nervous horses.

Diarrhoea is normal in foals suckling mares going through their first heat cycle after foaling. In orphan foals it may be caused by incorrect mixing of formula (see 'Orphan Foals' on page 169).

Bacterial infections frequently cause profuse, watery diarrhoea in both foals and adults. The affected horse can rapidly become weak, dehydrated and refuse to suck or eat. Dehydrated horses have sunken eyes and skin that loses its elasticity—pinch the skin on the neck of a healthy horse and it springs back into place; but on a horse that is dehydrated, the skin remains elevated.

Isolate a horse with diarrhoea and place it in a warm, frequently cleaned stable. Simple diarrhoea in horses that are still bright can often be controlled by allowing only small amounts of good quality hay and no green feed. Electrolyte powders from your vet should be mixed with fresh water and the horse encouraged to drink as much as possible.

Any horse or foal with persistent and severe diarrhoea that is obviously weakened and dehydrated must have immediate veterinary attention.

Colic

The *Oxford Dictionary* defines colic as 'severe griping pains in belly', and horses affected with colic are restless, paw the ground, kick their abdomens and frequently glance at their flanks. If the pain is severe enough they will go down and roll, often quite violently. A horse in this state is a distressing sight and indicates that immediate veterinary attention is required. While waiting for help to arrive, walk the horse to prevent rolling and further injury and keep it calm and quiet.

Colic is a symptom of underlying disease, and can be caused by a multitude of problems, usually disturbances of the gastrointestinal tract. Mild colic can result from the excitement of a thunderstorm, or from a simple change in diet causing the intestinal movement to increase and the intestinal muscles to contract painfully.

These spasmodic colics usually respond quickly to veterinary treatment. The feeding of large amounts of lush green pastures or mouldy hay can cause excessive gas production and a flatulent colic. Impaction colic can occur if horses eat large amounts of sand or dirt with their food (this is common in times of drought), or eat their dry straw bedding. Colic can also result from infections in organs such as the liver, uterus and spleen.

Certain types of colic can be fatal—bloodworms are suspected of causing up to 90% of all colics. They damage and sometimes obstruct blood vessels, preventing blood from reaching sections of the intestine. Another potentially fatal form of colic is caused by the 'twisted bowel'. For reasons usually not understood, the intestine will twist around itself blocking the passage of food. Fatty tumours attached to the bowel by stalks can also strangulate the intestine by twisting around a loop of bowel, again preventing the passage of food. All these colics cause severe pain and can lead to peritonitis (infection of the abdomen), shock and eventual death.

Because these serious causes of colic can be ultimately fatal, medical and surgical treatment must be provided early in the course of the disease. Even then, success is not guaranteed as abdominal surgery in the horse is very difficult.

Old-fashioned colic remedies are occasionally still forced down a horse's neck, although they will rarely be effective. Due to the variety of diseases that can cause colic, the correct diagnosis is essential before any treatment can be initiated. Many bouts of abdominal pain in horses are caused by serious disease, so **always call your vet in the early stages of any bout of colic.**

■ One of the most serious causes of colic is the 'twisted bowel'.

RESPIRATORY TRACT

One of the most common respiratory diseases in horses is caused by a *Herpes* virus and is similar to the human cold and flu. The virus is very contagious, and is spread in droplets from coughing or in nasal discharge, therefore, close contact with other horses quickly spreads the disease. Affected horses will have a brief temperature rise, a poor appetite and will develop a clear nasal discharge that may become thick and yellow if secondary bacterial infection occurs. After a few days, the horse begins to cough. Uncomplicated cases resolve in seven to fourteen days.

This disease is best treated with good nursing: keep the horse isolated, rugged and in a warm, dry environment. Provide fresh green pick and bran mashes to stimulate appetite and, most importantly, allow the horse to rest. If forced to continue to work a chronic cough will result, which will be very difficult to cure and may progress to bronchitis and pneumonia.

The most useful treatments are those that break down respiratory mucous, clear the airways and alleviate coughing, for which you should see your vet.

Foal rattles

Foal rattles primarily affects young foals under six months of age. It is caused by the bacterium *Rhodococcus equi* and is particularly common in situations such as horse studs where large numbers of horses are kept together. The organism remains in the environment, causing disease in each crop of foals.

Affected foals become lethargic, stop sucking, develop a very high temperature, an increased rate of breathing and a cough. The bacteria form abscesses in the lungs, and the foal's chest develops a rattling sound. The infection can also spread to the joints. Older foals may develop a chronic pneumonia and gradually lose weight despite continuing to suckle.

Foal rattles is a problem disease that requires early and aggressive veterinary treatment if foals are to survive.

LAMENESS

One of the most frequent problems encountered by horse owners is lameness, attributable to numerous possible factors: inherited poor conformation, injury and trauma, infection, incorrect diets and the overworking of young, immature horses. The following commonly diagnosed conditions are only a sample of the possible diseases that can cause lameness. Diagnosis often requires X-rays, and is definitely a task for a vet. **Minor limps can progress to major lameness quickly and should never be ignored.**

Splints

A splint is a bony swelling caused by periostitis of the second or fourth metacarpals, the splint bones which lie on either side of the cannon bone of the front leg. They are held tightly to the cannon by a ligament. The periosteum is the outer, very fine covering of all bones. Any disturbance of the splint bone ligaments irritates the periosteum, causing it to produce an excess of new bone. This can occur after kicks or falls, from poor conformation, or from heavy training schedules in young horses.

Initially a hot and painful swelling forms over the splint bone and the horse becomes lame, especially when trotting on hard ground. Initially, the swelling is soft and quite large, but as this fibrous tissue changes to bone the lump shrinks, becoming hard and painless. At this stage, lameness is rare unless the splint interferes with the horse's joints or ligaments.

Treatment is necessary only if a splint is causing lameness, or if the lump is unacceptable to the horse's owner. Surgical removal is the only successful treatment.

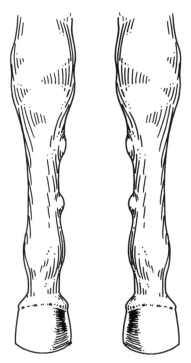

■ Splints are small bony lumps that are most commonly seen on the inner surface of the cannon of the front leg.

Navicular disease

The navicular bone is a long, flat bone that lies behind the joint just above the hoof. Horses that are worked hard, such as show jumpers and stock horses, have constant concussion of their front limbs causing an inflammation of the tissues between the bone and its closest tendon. The navicular bone progressively degenerates and erodes

where the tendon has torn away; these show up on X-ray as 'holes' on the bone surface.

Lameness is intermittent at first and improves temporarily with rest. Eventually, both front feet are affected and horses are constantly lame from pain in the heel and frog area. A shuffling gait with shortened forward stride results and the heels contract.

The best treatment for navicular disease is a medication available from your vet that is administered in the horse's feed and that increases the blood supply to the extremities, slowing down the degeneration of the navicular bone. Horses can often remain pain free and in work for prolonged periods.

Founder

Inside the solid hoof wall are layers of very sensitive tissue called laminae. Inflammation of these tissues results in an extremely painful and crippling lameness called founder or laminitis. The condition, which can affect one or more feet, requires immediate veterinary attention.

With the onset of founder, the laminae inside the hoof become inflamed, deprived of blood supply, and may separate from the outer hoof wall. This separation leads to rotation of the pedal bone within the hoof towards the sole. The bone may actually penetrate the sole, making treatment and recovery difficult to impossible.

Fat ponies that are allowed access to rich pasture while having no exercise are commonly affected by founder, and for all horses any

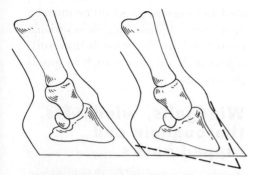

■ (Left) The bone inside the healthy hoof sits approximately parallel with the outer hoof wall. (Right) Founder causes the bone to rotate downwards where it may penetrate the sole. The correct method of trimming foundered hooves is demonstrated by the slashed line: the heel is lowered and the toe shortened in an effort to realign the bone to the hoof wall.

increase in carbohydrate intake is dangerous, which can occur if horses find their way into grain bins or poultry food. Even maintenance diets high in grain can be dangerous for susceptible horses.

Founder can also be caused by acute infections (for example in mares that retain their afterbirth longer than eight hours after foaling), from overexercising horses on hard surfaces and from allowing horses unlimited access to cold water after vigorous activity.

The symptoms of founder are characteristic of an animal in pain: the horse stands with feet apart and leans backward in an attempt to take weight from the toes. The feet are hot and the horse is very reluctant to move and may lie down continually. Pain causes an increase in temperature, pulse and respiration rates.

Founder must always be regarded as an emergency, as the pedal bone can irreversibly rotate within the hoof

in twelve to eighteen hours. Anti-inflammatory medication from a vet is essential and the most important part of treatment. Forced exercise is not recommended unless gentle walking appears to relieve the horse. Standing the horse in cold water may help to relieve pain and inflammation.

Fat ponies should be shut away from pasture and fed only small amounts of hay daily (and some bran to prevent constipation) until their weight has decreased considerably. The provision of fresh water is essential.

Hoof trimming is an important part of aftercare but must be performed correctly, that is, the heel must be lowered and the toe shortened. *Never* lower the toe, as this exposes the rotated bone to further pain and pressure. Correct trimming realigns the bone to the hoof wall. Different types of padded and raised shoes (for example, the heart bar shoe) are also available that can take pressure off a painful sole.

Prevention of founder or laminitis is easier than treating the disease and, once foundered, horses are thereafter susceptible to further bouts. Don't allow ponies to become fat—give them regular exercise and keep horses away from feedbins and excess grain.

Tying-up

'Monday morning disease', tying-up and azoturia are all terms that describe a serious lameness correctly called exertional myopathy. The term 'Monday morning disease' was popular in the days of working horses, when, after labouring for five days and resting for the weekend, these horses 'tied-up' on Monday if their high energy working diet was continued on their days of rest.

The disease is most commonly seen in very fit, highly trained animals that are kept on a high intake of grain and other energy foods. Sometimes a horse is maintained on the same high energy diet while being rested for several days, and tying-up follows after the horse returns to training. Tying-up also occurs in unfit, overweight and overfed horses that are suddenly expected to perform heavy work. Nervous fillies and mares also appear to be more susceptible.

The muscles most affected are those of the rump, back and hind limbs, which become hard and painful. Affected horses suddenly develop a stiff, stilted gait, may refuse to move and appear to be in pain. If muscle cells break down, a muscle pigment called myoglobin will pass out via the kidneys making the urine a dark red-brown colour (this is azoturia). Fatal kidney failure can then occur.

Tying-up is always serious and a vet should be called immediately. Warmth is very important: rug horses immediately, rub them down and walk them gently until the vet arrives. Do *not* force exercise. After the initial treatment, house tied-up horses in warm, dry stables and allow them to rest. Rest and a low energy diet may be required for four weeks or more, after which normal exercise and diet should be slowly reintroduced.

Horses that have tied-up once are thereafter susceptible to repeated bouts, so a regular, closely monitored feed and exercise programme must be maintained. If daily exercise is variable then food intake must follow suit, especially if the diet is high in grains and cereals.

Windgalls, windpuffs, thoroughpin and capped hocks

Windgalls, windpuffs, thoroughpin and capped hocks are common names that describe swellings of the joints or tendon sheaths, usually occurring in the knees, hocks or fetlock joints. Thoroughpin is a swelling of a specific tendon sheath of the hock. A capped hock is the fluid-filled swelling of a bursa that runs over the point or back of the hock which may result from a blow or be self-inflicted in horses that kick their stables.

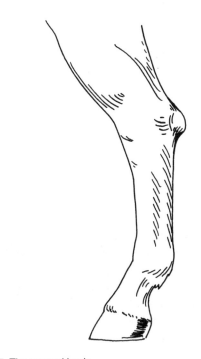

■ The capped hock.

Heavy work or training causes windgalls to appear, and although they will decrease in size with rest they rarely disappear. Treatment to drain the fluid is only temporary and generally unnecessary as all these conditions rarely cause lameness. Any painful swellings should be checked by a vet.

Stringhalt

Stringhalt is a poorly understood disease that causes horses to walk with a peculiar hind limb gait: as they move forward, their fetlocks are suddenly jerked upwards towards their abdomens. Horses of any age and breed can be affected.

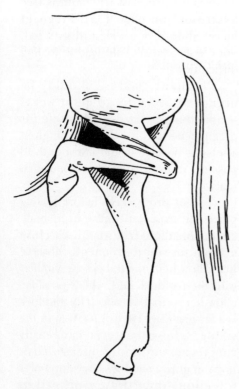

■ Horses affected by stringhalt jerk their fetlocks sharply towards their abdomens as they move forward.

Australian stringhalt is thought to be caused by horses grazing on pastures rich in dandelions. Affected horses should be moved to another paddock.

The condition will sometimes disappear with time, but for some horses it may become more pronounced. There is no medical treatment, but the surgical removal of a portion of a particular hind limb tendon, the lateral digital extensor, can provide partial to complete relief.

Sole punctures and abscesses

Penetration of the sole with a foreign body such as a nail or piece of wire or wood is a common cause of lameness. The initial wound may heal over rapidly, leaving bacteria within the sole that multiply to form a very painful abscess. A horse will often refuse to bear weight on the affected foot.

Sole abscesses must be opened and drained by your vet, a search made for the foreign body and the wound dressed daily with a poultice bandage. Antibiotics and protection against tetanus will be necessary.

Corns

A corn is bruising of the sole that affects the underlying sensitive tissues inside the hoof, usually of the front feet. Horses with corns are often quite lame, especially if the corns become infected and develop into abscesses. Corns can result from concussion to poorly shaped flat feet, from stone bruises if horses are ridden on rough ground and from incorrect shoeing techniques.

Treat horses by removing their shoes and, if possible, allowing them to rest. Otherwise reshoe with a raised shoe that will take pressure off the corn. As with sole abscesses, antibiotics (if infection is present) and protection against tetanus are necessary.

Seedy toe

Seedy toe is a separation between the inner and outer parts of the hoof wall, usually in the region of the toe. Horses with chronic laminitis or those with brittle, cracking hooves are susceptible to seedy toe. The resultant cavity becomes packed with dirt, stones and vegetable matter and secondary infection develops.

The affected area should be cleaned out, pared down to normal, healthy tissue and the cavity packed with medicated dressing such as cotton wool soaked in iodine. Waterproof boots are an excellent means of keeping the area dry and clean until healing is complete.

REPRODUCTION

Many horse owners will wish to enjoy the pleasures of watching their mare rear a foal. However, careful management is required to keep both the mare and her foal in good health and condition.

PREGNANCY

The length of pregnancy in the mare averages 330 to 340 days, or eleven months. This varies considerably, however, and colt foals are usually carried longer than fillies. Mares can produce twins but rarely rear them successfully, and the incidence of twinning is very low, around $1/2$ to $1^{1}/_2\%$. Pregnancy is best diagnosed by a vet around the 42-day mark by rectal palpation. Blood tests and ultra sound can also be used.

Care of pregnant mares revolves around good feeding, which will allow them to maintain their own body condition while providing additional nutrients for their growing foetuses. Unless they are on very good pasture, daily supplementation of the diet is important in the last few months (see 'Nutrition' on page 135). Pregnant mares should be sleek and well fed, not obese, as this could lead to foaling difficulties.

Pregnant mares should be drenched every six to eight weeks —ask your vet for drenches safe for pregnancy—and they should be given a tetanus booster in the last month to pass on immunity to their newborn foals.

Two or three weeks before foaling place the expectant mare in a small, clean, obstacle-free paddock close enough for you to frequently observe her. Allow her time to become familiar with the paddock and, where possible, allow her to foal outside. The paddock is a far healthier environment than the stable, where bacteria can easily congregate and cause disease. Foals born in grassy paddocks develop fewer infections than those confined to stables.

BIRTH

In the last few weeks of pregnancy, a mare's vulva will become flaccid and slightly swollen. The udder develops noticeably and then distends a few days before foaling. Closer to the event the ligaments of the pelvis relax and the abdomen may drop, and in the last few days the mare will 'wax up' as colostrum oozes onto the udder surface and forms a plug at the teat.

Most mares foal at night or very early in the morning. As foaling becomes imminent, mares will stand alone and appear restless, switching their tails, looking at their flanks and lying down frequently. They may also sweat over the shoulders and flanks. As foaling begins the first membranes will appear, rupture and release fluid. The birth process then becomes rapid and almost explosive: the whole event is often completed within fifteen minutes. The mare lies out flat to foal, and rests briefly at each stage between vigorous efforts. Foals should be born front feet first with their heads lying on the forearms. As the hips of the foal are expelled mares will remain down and rest, with the umbilical cord still attached.

Towards the end of the birth process, a mare will remain resting with the foal's feet in her vagina and the umbilical cord still attached. This is normal and it is important *not* to interfere and break the cord as during this time a considerable amount of blood is passing along the cord to the foal. The cord will break naturally when the mare rises. It is important that the mare's placenta is passed after the foal see 'Retained Membranes' on page 170.

Although the vast majority of mares foal alone and successfully, you

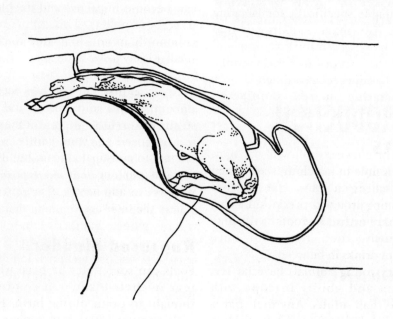

■ During birth, the foal should enter the world front feet first, with the head resting on the forelegs.

may wish to observe the birth. Do this quietly and from a distance because, like many animal species, mares are capable of temporarily postponing the event if they are unduly disturbed.

Problems usually arise when a foal is presented incorrectly, with perhaps a leg curled back, or the forehead presented rather than the muzzle. **This constitutes a real emergency and every minute counts.** Due to the rapidity of birth in the mare, a vet has a very short time in which to correct such problems and save the foal.

LACTATING MARES

Mares suckling foals require a far greater intake of food than normal. An inadequate diet will mean either the mare will lose weight, or the foal will not receive enough milk. A diet high in protein is very important, and properly balanced commercial rations are available specifically for lactating mares. Any mare suckling a foal should be observed for loss of weight, and if this occurs her food intake should be adjusted accordingly.

Lactating mares should be wormed every six weeks.

FOALS

There is little to match the excitement of watching a new, gangly foal gambolling around a paddock. Like all newborn animals foals will play vigorously, then rest, and have frequent drinks in between.

Very young animals have far less stamina and ability to cope with disease than adults. Any foal that is depressed, lethargic and not suckling should receive prompt treatment.

Colostrum

Colostrum is secreted by all female mammals and is the thick, high-protein milk produced by the mare in the first twelve to twenty-four hours after birth. It is vital for the health of the foal as it contains antibodies from the mare that provide immunity against disease for a considerable time after birth. After the initial twelve to twenty-four hours, a foal's intestine can no longer absorb colostrum. Foals that have been born weak and are slow to get to their feet must still get colostrum within the first twelve hours of life, even if you have to milk the mare and feed the foal yourself.

Retained meconium

Meconium is the waste product inside a newborn foal's intestine. It is the first faeces or droppings to be passed. Foals can become impacted and unable to pass these pellets. This occurs most commonly in colt foals due to their smaller bony pelvic diameter.

Impacted foals will suckle normally at first, but will then become uncomfortable and colicky and will strain frequently. Many studmasters are practised at giving gentle, warm enemas to constipated foals, but if you are inexperienced it is safer to call your vet to administer treatment and relieve the blockage.

Ruptured bladder

Foals can sometimes be born with a tear in their bladder, a condition thought to occur during birth. Foals with ruptured bladders appear and behave normally for the first twenty-four hours, after which they become progressively depressed and refuse to suck, crouching and straining frequently. Their abdomens swell and little to no urine is passed. Careful observation of the normal passage of urine and faeces is very important in newborn foals, especially in the first week of life.

Surgery to correct the tear is straightforward, but *must* be performed before the foal becomes too sick.

Umbilical problems

Foals born in dirty conditions should always have their umbilical cords swabbed with a dilute iodine solution for several days to prevent the entry of bacteria that may cause diarrhoea, infections at the umbilicus and in the joints (these conditions are known as navel and joint ill).

As well as navel ill, hernias of the umbilicus are common in newborn foals. They are characterised by a visible swelling of variable size and a definite ring of muscle (the hernial ring) that can be felt. It is important to observe foals suffering hernias, as sometimes a loop of bowel may slip through the opening and become twisted. The hernia will become hot, painful and swollen. Small umbilical hernias may disappear in the first twelve months of life, while larger hernias require surgical correction. This is best done in the weanling foal.

Pervious urachus

The urachus is a small tube within the umbilical cord that has carried urine from the developing foetus during pregnancy. After birth it should immediately close off, but sometimes this does not occur and foals will dribble urine from their umbilicus. Most close naturally in two to three days, however, if dribbling persists, a vet will need to cauterise the umbilical stump or perform surgery. Do *not* tie the cord.

Scrotal hernias

The scrotum is the sac that holds each testicle. These hernias almost always require surgery and, as with umbilical hernias, foals with scrotal hernias should be carefully observed as a section of bowel may slip through the opening, causing the scrotum to be obviously swollen and painful.

Both umbilical and scrotal hernias are inherited, a factor which must be borne in mind when selecting breeding stock.

Limb deformities

Quite often foals are born with weak flexor tendons, usually in the region of the fetlock and pastern, and will be unable to hold their legs straight 'sitting back' on their fetlocks. Most cases of weak flexor tendons improve dramatically within the first week provided foals have enforced rest. This means keeping mare and foal confined in a stable or small yard until the limbs strengthen.

A more serious condition, contracted tendons, occurs when the tendons are too tight and the foal knuckles over. Rest is again important, and a vet may need to splint the foal's

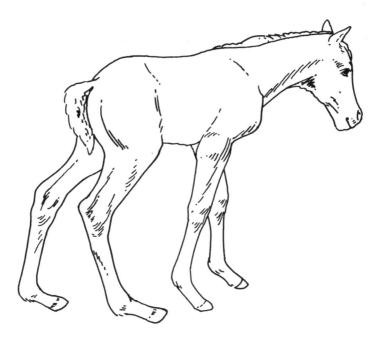

■ Some newborn foals have very weak tendons, here in the lower hind limbs. Enforced rest in a stable allows the tendons to strengthen over one to two weeks.

legs for support. Surgery can be performed in severe cases.

Diarrhoea

Diarrhoea in foals is common, especially foals in dirty stables and orphan foals (refer to 'Gastrointestinal Tract' on page 157).

Orphan foals with diarrhoea should be treated by decreasing the formula concentration and feeding extra water mixed with electrolyte powders until the diarrhoea is under control. **Any foal with severe diarrhoea must have veterinary attention.**

ORPHAN FOALS

Always try to find a surrogate mother for an orphaned foal. This is the best course even though it can be very

difficult to foster a foal. Mares do not take kindly to strange foals and a successful fostering may take weeks of perseverance. Your vet may need to assist by sedating the mare at first to protect the foal.

The immediate concern in a foal's first twenty-four hours of life is to find another source of colostrum if the mare has died. Many horse studs keep frozen colostrum for this type of emergency and are usually happy to help. Three hundred to 500 mL of colostrum will be sufficient before you begin to feed the orphan formula.

If a surrogate mother cannot be found, you must decide on a diet for the orphan. Mare's milk contains less fat and more sugar than cow's milk, so a combination of skim milk and added lactose (milk sugar from a chemist) is usually the best. Goat's milk has the composition closest to mare's milk, but it is difficult to obtain in large quantities and dairy replacers are usually used instead. The following two formulas have been used to rear healthy foals:

1. Mix together 1 litre of skim milk (powdered is adequate), 500 mL of cow's milk and add nine level tablespoons of lactose. Add a total of one level tablespoon of dicalcium phosphate per day and one vitamin ADE sachet per week for the first month only.

2. Mix 250 g of Denkavite with 2 litres of water, and add ten level tablespoons of lactose. Add one level tablespoon of dicalcium phosphate per day.

Always dilute any formula for the first two to three days to allow the foal to adjust to its new diet. Feed the formula at room temperature. For the first week, feed the foal every hour (or at the very least every two hours) around the clock. A foal of average size (Arab, stock horse etc.) should be consuming about 500 mL per feed. Increase this amount until three weeks of age when the foal should be drinking about 2 litres every two to three hours. After a month, feeding frequency can be decreased to every six hours. Foals should not be weaned before six months of age.

Foals learn rapidly to drink from a bucket, so bottle feeding is generally not necessary. Hygiene is essential, and all food utensils must be washed thoroughly with a solution such as Milton between every feed. Mix the formula fresh daily.

As well as a milk diet, the orphan foal should have free access to fresh water, a grazing paddock, hay and a balanced commercial feed. Specific rations for orphan foals are available and worth seeking out; ask your vet to help. Otherwise, use a weaner diet and slowly introduce foals to this as soon as possible. The best of these are based on extruded soya bean meal, an excellent source of protein.

Orphans must be housed in dry, clean stables and, to prevent loneliness and behavioural problems, it is a good idea to find the foal a companion. If a quiet horse is not available, foals will often be happy with a sheep or goat.

Hand-reared foals can be notoriously spoilt and can become dangerous— as they grow they begin to play with their human family as they would with other foals. Treat your foal as a horse from the beginning and it will grow into a well-disciplined adult.

REPRODUCTIVE TRACT

Several problems can commonly arise either during the reproductive process or in the reproductive organs of the mare and stallion.

Retained membranes

Following the birth of the foal it is essential that the passing of the membranes be confirmed. As a mare has two horns to her uterus, there should be two elongated sections of placenta. Check these for missing patches or tears, particularly at the tips. Usually if a mare retains membranes they will be easily seen hanging out of the vulva. Never tug or pull: removing them requires professional skill and patience.

Always call a vet if the membranes are still present six to eight hours after birth. Serious infections, tetanus or founder can result if the membranes are not removed quickly.

Cryptorchidism

Puberty in the colt usually occurs between twelve and twenty-four months of age. Testicles almost always descend into the scrotum before twelve months of age and it is usual for both to be present at birth. Not uncommonly, only one testicle will descend correctly—this is called cryptorchidism, or retained testicles, and such horses are often called 'rigs'. The castration operation in these horses involves abdominal surgery to find the retained testicle, which can be anywhere from the kidneys to just above the scrotum.

DONKEYS

Domesticated in Africa over 5000 years ago (a history older than that of the horse), donkeys have always been used as pack animals in warm, dry areas on all continents. Today, these sturdy creatures are bred competitively, taken to shows and can be found as children's pets all over the world.

A donkey's basic health care is very similar to that of horses and ponies, however, donkey owners should be aware of the few differences that exist. Flourishing naturally in hot, dry countries, donkeys are now kept in a variety of climates. Shelter should always be provided for those that live in cold areas of Australia.

Working donkeys' hooves are normally small and neat, kept that way from constant work on the hard and stony ground of their natural habitats. Brought to lush, wet climates and living in long, green pastures their hooves become overgrown and misshapen. **Any donkey that lives on soft ground should have its hooves trimmed every eight weeks by a farrier.** Shoeing is not necessary unless the donkey is performing regular harness work on hard surfaces.

Donkeys carry the same internal parasites as horses and require a regular drenching programme. They are also common carriers of the horse lungworm, *Dictyocaulus arnfieldi*, and are thought to be the reservoir of infection for horses, which show more serious symptoms when infected. The lungworm adult is a threadlike worm up to 10 cm long that lives in the air spaces of the lungs. In donkeys, infections are extremely common but usually have little effect, whereas in horses these worms have a retarded life cycle where the worm larvae live for long periods in the lungs before becoming egg-laying adults in the intestine. These immature worms irritate the lungs, resulting in a persistent, long-standing cough.

Chronic coughing in donkeys, or horses that graze with them, should alert their owner to the possibility of lungworm. A vet will need to be consulted as the usual horse drenches have little effect on this parasite.

Donkey reproduction is similar to the reproduction of horses except that females, or jennies, have a longer gestation period —up to twelve and a half months is required to produce a donkey foal.

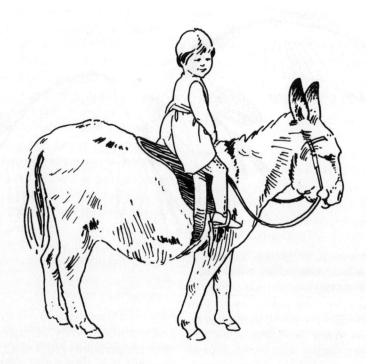

CHAPTER 4

BIRDS

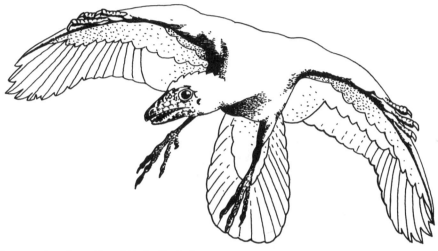

■ The archeopteryx, thought to be the first bird-like creature, showing clearly the remnants of a reptilian ancestory.

The close reptilian ancestry of birds is evident in so much of their anatomy: birds have similar egg-laying reproductive tracts, skeletal structure and kidney function; they have retained scales on their legs; and even their power of flight is not unique, as some of the earliest reptiles were able to glide and fly.

The plumage of birds, however, is unique, as feathers are structures shared by no other vertebrate. Thought to be derived from reptilian scales, feathers are composed of the same protein, called keratin. Extremely efficient insulators, their most important function is to conserve heat and maintain birds' relatively high body temperatures (40°5 to 42.5°C) by trapping air pockets against the skin. Feathers are also necessary for repelling water and, of course, for flight. They are used in courtship rituals, in defence and for nest building.

Constant preening and grooming is essential for the preservation of perfect feather-to-feather connections. Each feather is tipped by barbs that interlock with those of the adjoining feathers. As birds groom, feathers are passed through the beak to 're-zip'

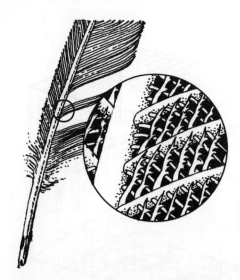

■ Preening ensures the correct position of the tiny interlocking barbs that maintain the perfect feather-to-feather contact required for effective insulation.

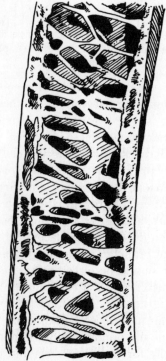

■ Birds' bones are extremely light, as much of their bone marrow is replaced by air sacs; the bones are stabilised by light, bony struts.

these barbs. In those species with a uropygial gland (the 'Pope's nose' of chickens!), preening is thought to spread oil from this gland to help with repelling water.

Many birds bathe, either in water or in dust, to help the grooming process, and meticulous preening is a way of life for all birds. Those that are dishevelled and unkempt are either sick or moulting.

Birds' skeletons are extremely light. The bones are very hard, but are thin-walled and many of the larger bones have hollow areas filled with air sacs rather than bone marrow. These air sacs or air-filled pockets are covered by fine, transparent membranes. They are located throughout the body, in the abdomen, the chest, inside certain bones and between the shoulder blades. Connected to the lungs, they function as part of the avian breathing apparatus and lighten the body for flight.

Birds are creatures of fascinating structure and habits. When kept as pets, they are deprived of escape by flight, so attention to the physical and emotional needs of all pet birds is essential to compensate for this loss of freedom.

BUDGERIGARS

One of the most popular pet birds worldwide, the budgerigar's natural habitat extends over the dry, inland plains of Australia. The naturalist John Gould introduced the bird into England in 1840, and huge numbers were sent overseas until their export

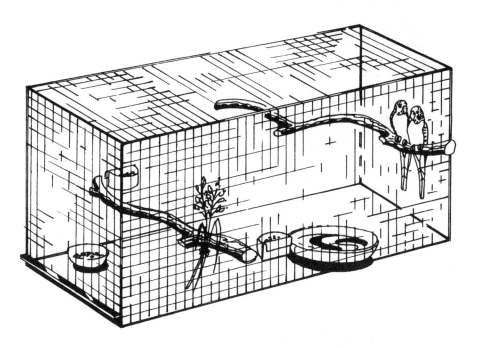

■ An excellent budgerigar cage, with adequate length for flying and natural branches for perches. Each of these fortunate budgies also has the company of a mate.

was banned in the 1950s. Today, the native grass-green budgie has been bred into a multitude of different colour mutations.

Budgerigars are intelligent and very sociable; in the wild they live in flocks of many thousands. One of their most important requirements therefore is attention from their new flock, the family. Spend time talking to your bird and you will be repaid with displays of affection and personality. If you have little time to devote to your budgie, start out with two birds and a larger cage.

Caging any bird causes stress, so purchase the largest cage you can possibly afford. Unless your budgie is fortunate to have an aviary or be allowed supervised flying time at home, the cage should be long enough to allow flying between the perches. As flying space should be provided horizontally, tall cages are useless.

All cages must be easy to clean and have practical feed and water dispensers. Perches are a neglected item: avoid using plastic or metal perches, and throw away those boring wooden dowels and replace them with several branches of varying diameter. These should be placed so the budgie can turn around at each end without damaging any feathers. Natural perches have several advantages: they provide the opportunity for important exercise for your bird's feet and beak as well as being a source of entertainment, especially if covered with a little bark.

Sandpaper rolls to cover perches should be avoided: they abrade and inflame the feet of all species of bird and do little for claw growth. Also be wary of synthetic cage covers, as budgies love to peck and swallow pieces of thread, or tangle them around their claws. Avoid the tendency to fill cages with toys—it is better to develop a strong human–bird bond than to rely on toys to prevent boredom.

Locate cages away from household fumes (see 'Poisons' on page 181), draughts and excessive noise. Hanging cages outside for short periods is fine if birds are observed constantly (dangerous predators include wild birds, cats and dogs) and provided the cage is in half sun and half shade. Daily sunshine is the best source of vitamin D, but never hang a budgie's cage in full sun all day.

Cages should be cleaned at least once a day, as infections can result from dirty perches and fouled water and food. Exercise is also important. Flying time outside the cage is great for morale as well as good exercise, but always observe your budgie in the house: too many birds have been injured on hot stoves and by flying into windows and falling into cooking pots. Budgies are exceedingly inquisitive!

A bath once or twice a week is often appreciated. Provide a dish of water that is wide enough for your bird to have a good splash in.

SEXING

Budgies are sexed by their cere, the featherless area above the beak. In adult males the cere is blue, in females it is brown. The cere of juvenile birds is a pale pink-blue colour in both sexes.

NUTRITION

Budgerigars are seed eaters, but providing the correct diet involves more than purchasing a packet of seed from the supermarket. Variety is the key to complete nutrition and budgie mix is a good dietary basis. It should contain mainly millet (panicum) and canary seed (phalaris) and often has rape, niger, wheat, sesame seeds, and other grains added. Make sure the seed is not dusty; buying from a produce store or good pet shop may ensure fresh seed.

A budgie will eat the seed whole after removing the husk with its beak. Never assume an overflowing seed dish is still full of seed—it may be all husks. Empty and refill dishes at least once a day.

Seed needs to be supplemented with vegetables and fruit. Start your bird on a changing variety of fruit to avoid dependence on a single item; you could include spinach, apples, thistles, chickweed, sprouting grasses and dandelions. Feed only a little each day, as overloading a bird with unaccustomed 'greens' will cause diarrhoea.

Cuttlefish is an important source of calcium and provides exercise for the beak. Grit is also essential. Birds have no teeth and seed eaters rely on their muscular stomach, the gizzard, to grind seed. Grit is stored in the gizzard and helps this grinding process. Try to obtain mineralised grit as it is a good source of essential minerals and place it in a small dish in the cage. Vitamins should also be added—sunlight provides vitamin D, and Ornithon and Avi-Drops available from vets and pet shops are good avian supplements. All vitamin and mineral supplements are labelled with the correct dosages.

Tonic seed bells and other treats provide extra nutrition and prevent boredom, but should never be used as the complete diet.

Birds eat constantly and a budgerigar can starve to death in forty-eight hours if deprived of food. Water is just as essential and must always be available and freshly changed each day.

■ Budgerigars (and other small birds) should be held very gently, resting in the palm of the hand with the head between index finger and thumb to prevent biting.

HANDLING

Always handle birds gently—patient owners will be rewarded by budgies that obligingly sit on a finger. To handle new or nervous birds for examination or treatment, grasp the budgie from behind, and cradle it in your palm, keeping the head (and therefore the biting beak) under control between the thumb and first finger.

CANARIES

Canaries originated in Europe and, like budgerigars, have been bred for many years to produce birds with a wide range of shapes, colours, feathering, and whistling ability. Male canaries are the renowned whistlers, and must be kept out of sight of other canaries to produce the best song. Moulting, a stressful time for all birds that may last six to eight weeks, will cause a temporary cessation of whistling.

Unlike budgies, canaries rarely become attached to humans; they are prized more for their song than their companionship. Nevertheless, a single canary in a cage requires as much attention and care, and has similar basic requirements to the more outgoing budgerigar

A canary's cage must be as large as possible, allowing flight between perches. Canaries require perches that are oval rather than round. Natural branches that provide a variety of diameters are the most satisfactory. Be careful where you locate the cage. Avoid draughts and sudden changes in temperature, and be wary of toxic fumes and predators such as cats and native birds.

Canaries love a bath and many will happily submerge several times a week if water is offered in a suitable, shallow dish such as the bird baths available from pet shops. Grooming and feather care is also enhanced by bathing.

Canaries and budgerigars have life spans averaging six to seven years, although there are many reports of birds that are ten years and older.

NUTRITION

Canaries, seed eaters like budgies, are usually fed a greater proportion of canary seed to millet than budgies. Basically they have similar dietary requirements to budgies and as great a need for variety.

Fresh water and a daily offering of greens and/or fruit is essential, as is the provision of cuttlefish and grit. Mineralised grit and Avi-Drops provide vitamins and minerals. 'Egg and biscuit' is a favourite supplement for canaries, providing extra protein in particular. A commercial product is available, but you can make your own by mashing hard-boiled egg yolks with crushed arrowroot biscuits and moistening with water. This mixture is especially useful during moulting (and for breeding birds).

HANDLING

Canaries can be held in a similar manner to budgerigars. Always hold them lightly and gently, as canaries are easily stressed, especially when sick.

PARROTS, GALAHS AND COCKATOOS

Peachfaces (African lovebirds) make excellent pets when kept in pairs. Single birds, however, can become aggressive and neurotic. Cages must be large enough for two birds, with natural branch perches. Include a nest box (available from pet shops), as these parrots seem to like a cosy retreat in their environment.

Peachface parrots are seed eaters, preferring a mixture of both budgie and parrot seed mixes. Greens and fruits are essential, as is grit, cuttlefish and fresh water. Small amounts of wholemeal bread is relished by some birds.

Rosellas rarely make good pets as single specimens, often becoming very aggressive and cranky when isolated. They should be kept in an aviary with a compatible rosella companion.

Galahs and **sulphur-crested cockatoos** can make wonderful and amusing companions, but so many are left to languish in small bare cages, isolated for long periods from their owners. Don't even consider owning one of these birds unless you can provide a large, spacious cage (preferably an aviary), and devote time and energy to the bird's care. These creatures are very intelligent and are prone to the development of the chronic depression and similar neuroses that afflict bored, lonely and isolated humans.

Always use large, natural branches as perches as these will provide entertainment and chewing exercise, although you will need to replace them regularly. Offer other branches of native shrubs such as banksias, with leaves, flowers and any berries or fruit intact. Where possible, allow galahs and cockatoos some freedom to explore the backyard, first ensuring security from neighbouring animals.

Diet is based on a high-quality parrot seed supplemented with fruits and vegetables daily. Tonic seed bells, wholemeal bread and crackers are useful treats. Always supply mineralised grit, cuttlefish, vitamins and fresh water. Vitamin supplements such as Avi-Drops are available from vets and pet shops and are easily administered in the bird's drinking water. Supplements are labelled with suggested dosages. Parrots will also often enjoy chewing on left-over cooked bones.

Many of these larger seed-eating birds become obsessed with sunflower seeds and will eat little else, resulting in obesity and possible nutritional deficiencies. Refuse to cater to this addiction by making birds eat all the seeds in a mix if possible.

HANDLING

Unless these larger parrots are tame, immobilise them by wrapping them in a towel before examining them. Hold the head in the way described for budgies, always trying to keep their beaks under control as they can inflict rather painful bites.

COMMON HEALTH PROBLEMS

A sick bird appears lethargic and sleepy, with feathers fluffed (indicating chilling) and eyes closed, huddling often on the floor of its cage with little interest in food or its surroundings. This so-called 'sick bird look' indicates prompt veterinary attention is needed—birds weaken rapidly once they are diseased.

Before you take your bird to a vet, remove the water container but don't clean the cage as examination of recent droppings is very important. Cover the cage and heat the car for the trip.

Apart from any prescribed medication, sick birds need warmth, freedom from noise and other stress, rest in the form of twelve hours sleep each day (cover and darken the cage), and a highly palatable diet or vitamins if they are not eating. Remove grit from the cage as some sick birds over-eat grit, impacting the gizzard.

Warmth is the most important requirement of any sick bird; ambient temperatures should reach 27 to 32°C. Aviculturists have hospital cages that have a light bulb under the cage to provide heat, or you can create the correct environment by partially covering the cage and sitting it on a heating pad or electric blanket. *Always* monitor the temperature with a thermometer and vary it by altering the distance between the cage and the

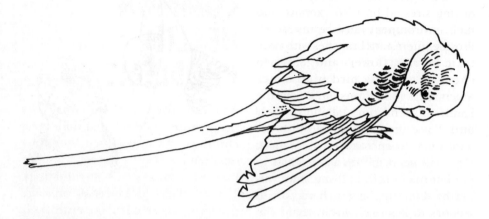

■ Sick birds are lethargic, with feathers fluffed for extra warmth; they will often sit huddled on the floors of their cages.

heat source. A properly warmed bird's feathers should return to a sleek appearance—overheating will cause birds to pant and hold their wings out. A moist atmosphere prevents birds from dehydrating, so place a pan of water near the cage and heat source.

Unnecessary handling is not recommended, but if a bird is eating little, small amounts of a glucose solution every few hours will provide energy (mix one teaspoon of glucose per cup of warm water). If a bird refuses to eat, your vet will need to provide feed via a tube. Birds can survive only a short time without food.

STRESS

Birds in the wild use their intelligence in hunting or searching for food. They exercise constantly and many are very gregarious and social creatures, living in well-defined groups or in flocks of many thousands of birds. Birds gain their sense of safety by being able to fly away from perceived danger, and caging them immediately introduces a feeling of insecurity and deprives them of mental and physical exercise. Unless this is replaced by good care and attention most birds become lethargic and apathetic.

Other sources of stress to birds include constant noise, fluctuating temperatures and a lack of eight to twelve hours' darkness each day. Be alert to these possibilities and locate your bird's cage appropriately, covering the cage each night to ensure adequate sleeping time.

Many stressed birds become neurotic and develop vices, preening excessively and eventually pulling out their own feathers, bobbing and weaving in the cage, or becoming aggressive. Others retreat from any contact with humans. Neurotic, bored and stressed cage birds are frequent veterinary problems. (The birds most commonly affected are the larger parrots and cockatoos.)

A programme of slowly reintro-
ducing stressed birds to exercise and
their environment must be instituted.
Provide interesting branches with non-
toxic berries, flowers and leaves to
chew, or give the bird pine cones
which are a good diversion. Roster the
family to spend time talking to their
bird. Place the cage outside with the
door open to encourage exploration.
(You will need to clip a wing first to
prevent the bird from flying away; this
can be done by using a sharp pair of
scissors to remove two-thirds of the
length of the flight feathers on one
wing only.) Stay with the bird to
provide reassurance and protection
from cats, dogs and snail baits.

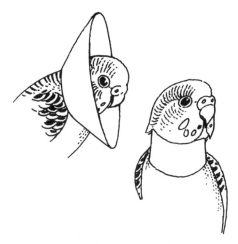

■ Elizabethan collars are a useful means of
preventing feather pulling in sick birds, enabling
them to eat easily but preventing them from
chewing their feathers.

Smaller birds like budgies may
appreciate the introduction of a mate.
This must be done carefully by placing
the second bird in another cage
alongside the first and waiting until
signs of friendship are established.
Many budgies refuse to tolerate
another bird in their cage.

In severe cases of stress, a course
of female hormone injections can
have a calming effect until improvement of the bird's lifestyle leads to a
permanent solution. Always remember
that birds are intelligent, living
creatures that require mental stimulation and caring attention.

Feather plucking

Feather plucking is a vice or bad habit
occurring in birds that are bored, kept
in small cages, fed inadequate diets,
and that are generally neglected by
their human family. The feathers are
continually pulled from the breast
area or over the rump, leaving bare,
inflamed areas. (This differs from the
irritation caused by mites and lice, but
always check for these first.)

Improving an affected bird's
environment is essential, but determined feather pluckers are difficult
to cure. An Elizabethan collar (see
above) may be necessary—this should
be fitted by a vet—or a course of
hormone injections may need to be
followed.

POISONS

**Birds are exceedingly sensitive to any
toxins in their environment.** Always
avoid using aerosols such as insect or
starch sprays near the cage, and be
aware that the fumes from overheated
teflon frypans or oils including butter
and margarine will kill caged birds, as
will nicotine from heavy smokers.

Heavy metal poisoning from
excessive zinc ingestion can occur with
new galvanised wire in aviaries or from

the chewing of old lead paint. Wire should be weathered, or brushed with weak acetic acid (vinegar) before use. Phenol disinfectants are dangerous; you should use the quaternary ammonium group, which are safer. Most fruits are safe, but avoid avocados—they can be fatal. Make sure your indoor plants are not poisonous if your bird explores the house. Finally, *never* give alcohol to birds: the well-intentioned 'sip of brandy' can do more harm than good.

NUTRITIONAL PROBLEMS

For specific birds, see the nutrition sections under 'Budgerigars' (page 176), 'Canaries' (page 178) and 'Parrots' (page 179), and the diet section under 'Native and Introduced Wild Birds' (page 198).

Obesity

Obesity is common amongst pet birds, many of which are overfed and underexercised. Budgerigars frequently lay down excessive fat over their chests, giving them a puffed-out appearance, and this extra layer of fat can lead to the formation of benign fatty tumours.

Feeling the sternum or keel bone of birds gives a good idea of correct weight. The keel lies down the centre of the bird's chest: if it is prominent it means that the bird is too thin; if it is undetectable it usually means that the bird is overweight.

If you have an overweight budgie, you should allow it only two teaspoons of mixed millet and canary seed a day

■ Overfed and underexercised budgies quickly become overweight. Fat tends to be deposited heavily over the chest, giving birds a pouted appearance.

supplemented with vitamins and minerals and unlimited greens. Slowly reintroduce exercise if possible, but don't expect a caged budgie to be able to fly across the room as wing muscles atrophy or shrink quickly when not in use. Monitor the bird's weight loss and condition closely.

If you have an overweight galah, you need to give it only two dessertspoons of an equal mix of canary and millet seeds and a maximum of six sunflower seeds a day. Cut out the sunflower if the bird is very fat. Add vitamins and minerals and unlimited greens, and encourage exercise.

Backyard wild bird feeding

Many people enjoy attracting native birds to their gardens by feeding them daily. However, this is creating problems as wild birds become too dependent on this easily obtained food, much of which is nutritionally unsound. Zoos and vets are seeing a growing number of these birds, and several syndromes are becoming apparent.

Nutritional secondary hyperparathyroidism is a common dietary disease discussed under 'Dogs' (page 54) and 'Cats' (page 116). It is also seen in carnivorous birds fed an 'all-meat' diet and is caused by a calcium deficiency and imbalance. Carnivorous birds eat all of their prey which can include small mice, birds, lizards, etc., and this provides them with a balanced diet. Meat alone (meaning here only the muscle or flesh) is totally unbalanced, being too low in calcium, too high in phosphorus and lacking many vitamins. Young kookaburras, magpies and currawongs are growing up with bone deformities because they are fed pieces of meat by well-meaning humans.

Vitamin B deficiencies occur in meat-fed magpies causing convulsions, inco-ordination, inability to walk and eventually death. Vitamin A deficiencies from an all-meat diet can lead to blindness, skin disorders and cheesy growths inside the mouth and pharynx.

The practice of feeding parrots with mixtures of bread soaked in sugar and water is causing feather deformities, especially in young birds. These birds normally consume large quantities of pollen and insects in the wild, which provide them with essential protein.

If you must feed birds, the Wombaroo company manufactures insectivore, granivore, and honeyeater and lorikeet foods that are complete diets (ask a vet about obtaining these). Alternatively, avian mineral and vitamin powders from a vet or pet shop can be mixed at the suggested dose rates into the food you offer. Refer to the diet section under 'Native and Introduced Birds' (page 198) for examples of the correct foods to offer.

The best method of attracting birds is to plan your garden sympathetically. Several excellent books are now available on the subject, but all flowering native shrubs will immediately draw native birds.

INTERNAL PARASITES

Worms

A variety of worms can infest birds, but most problems with worms occur in overcrowded aviaries. The individual pet bird is rarely affected, although diarrhoea and weight loss should be investigated. If your bird shows signs of these, have a vet examine its droppings for worm eggs. Ascarids, or roundworms, are long, cylindrical, white parasites, and are very common and easily seen in droppings.

Canker

Trichomonas gallinae is a protozoan, a microscopic organism that invades the gastrointestinal tract of birds. In acute cases birds die suddenly, or may vomit from infection of the crop, develop diarrhoea and generally become weak and depressed. More chronic cases develop thick, cheesy deposits inside the mouth.

Canker, which is also known as frounce or by its scientific name trichomoniasis, has always been a very common disease of pigeons, but it is now seen quite often in a large variety of pet birds. Any budgerigar that is vomiting should always be examined for canker.

Material from affected birds' crops is examined under a microscope to detect the highly mobile organisms. Spartrix tablets, Emtryl or Flagyl are anti-canker treatments, obtainable from a vet.

Air sac mites

Certain species of mites invade the air sacs of birds, causing loss of weight, loss of voice (canaries stop whistling), lethargy and respiratory disease. Crackling and wheezing noises may be heard with each breath and breathing may be laboured. Canaries, budgies and finches are often affected.

Treatment consists of hanging a mini pest strip in the vicinity of (but outside) the cage every alternate week; the vapours are absorbed by the birds, thus killing the mites. The chemical Ivermectin, administered by a vet, is also effective.

BACTERIAL INFECTIONS

A very wide range of bacteria causes disease in birds, with most resulting in similar and non-specific symptoms such as diarrhoea, depression and lethargy, decreased appetite and fluffed feathers. These infections are more common in aviary birds than caged pets, but can affect any bird under stress or those living with dirty surroundings and contaminated food or water dishes. As the organisms can spread rapidly and affected birds weaken and die rapidly, professional help should always be sought immediately.

Chlamydiosis (psittacosis)

Chlamydia psittaci is an organism that causes a highly contagious disease called chlamydiosis or psittacosis. Rarely a problem for individual caged birds, this disease is very common in both wild flocks and aviary-bred birds.

Chlamydiosis is contagious to humans, and can cause serious respiratory disease. The organism is usually inhaled during close contact with sick or healthy carrier birds, so strict hygiene must be observed after handling birds, and any outbreaks of the disease investigated.

Most birds carry the organism without showing symptoms of disease, spreading it via their droppings or nasal discharges. Stressful situations such as overcrowded and dirty pet shops or aviaries, unsatisfactory transport methods and poor nutrition will initiate outbreaks of illness with a high fatality rate. The non-specific symptoms as described for bacterial infection, may also include conjunctivitis or a chronic weight loss.

There is no simple test for chlamydiosis, and the disease is usually diagnosed post-mortem.

SKIN AND FEATHERS

The skin is the largest and one of the most sensitive organs of an animal's body, reacting quickly to irritation or inflammation.

Moulting

Moulting, the normal shedding and replacement of feathers that usually occurs once each year, is an extremely stressful time for all birds. Protein and energy requirements increase, and birds become more vulnerable to chilling. Pay extra attention to your bird's diet during this period, adding supplements like egg and biscuit (especially for canaries) and vitamin seed bells. Keep moulting birds in a warm environment and in darkness for eight to twelve hours each day. Baths several times a week encourage extra grooming and aid the moulting process.

The artificial conditions of lighting and warmth that occur in nearly all homes can cause birds to become 'stuck in the moult'. This is a continuous, partial moult during which canaries often stop whistling for prolonged periods. Try to ensure that your bird's hours of daylight and darkness follow nature's patterns, not your own.

Psittacine feather and beak syndrome

Psittacine feather and beak syndrome is one of the most serious problems of Australian parrots. The virus that causes the disease has not long been isolated, and it appears to be widespread in both wild and captive bird populations. Numerous species of birds can be affected, but the virus is especially common in sulphur-crested cockatoos, galahs, Major Mitchell cockatoos, corellas, peachface parrots and cockatiels.

The disease strikes young birds under three years of age, often becoming noticeable at their first juvenile moult between six and twelve months of age. Acute cases occur in which birds die quickly with enlarged livers. However, the virus normally takes a chronic course, slowly affecting the growth of feathers and beak until the bird is unable to eat or fly. The disease is nearly always fatal.

The virus causes a progressive loss of normal feathers, which are replaced by deformed, twisted and short quills. The yellow crest of cockatoos and the area over the hips and thighs are usually first affected (you will need to lift up the wings to detect this). The feather loss progresses to the lower legs and across and down the back to the tail in a roughly symmetrical manner. The first sign may be stress or fault lines across otherwise normal feathers. Later, affected feathers are narrowed or pinched-off at the base, with the shafts often retained (sometimes with blood inside), and new growth is often twisted. There is no regrowth of normal feathers. Some-

■ The psittacine feather and beak rot syndrome commonly begins as patches of abnormal feather growth over the hips and thighs.

times the feathers develop a dirty, pale brown colour, and in certain birds chronic sores develop on the elbows. Peachfaces may show multiple small skin nodules near the feather follicles.

Both upper and lower beaks are slowly and progressively deformed by the virus. Initially, the upper beak becomes very long and overgrown, and the beak colour changes from grey to a dark brown-black. This overgrowth usually breaks off and a type of 'rot' begins to under-run the beak with a build-up of dead tissue. The rot continues, causing both beaks to become more brittle, broken, shorter and deformed. Eventually the bird can eat only soft food, usually being too uncomfortable and in too much pain to eat at all.

This disease follows a long, debilitating course, often taking months or even one to two years before

affected birds eventually die. There is at present no cure. Any parrot that demonstrates a progressive deformed feather growth should be examined by a vet.

In the early stages, supply affected birds with soft food and keep them in warm, draught-free places. Once a bird's quality of life is obviously diminishing and pain is evident, the kindest solution is euthanasia.

■ As psittacine feather and beak syndrome progresses, the crest feathers are lost and the beak becomes brittle, crumbly and deformed.

External parasites

A multitude of insects infect caged and wild birds. If you have an infected pet, always use insecticides recommended for birds. Products that contain carbaryl and pyrethrin are amongst the safest to use.

Scaly face and leg mite

The microscopic scaly face and leg mite, *Cnemidocoptes pilae* occurs in most avian species, but it is an extremely common parasite of budgies in particular. Individual pet birds are affected as frequently as aviary-bred specimens.

The mite spends its entire life cycle on the bird, burrowing into the featherless skin of the cere and legs. As mites disturb the germinal or growing layer of the skin (which is rather like human nail cuticle), the result is an excessive and deformed production of skin and horny beak material. Extra layers of scaly material also develop on the legs. In canaries the legs are most often affected by these horny growths, thus earning the common name of 'tassle foot'.

As birds use their beaks to groom and clean their feet, both beak and cere *and* the legs should always be treated. Paraffin oil 'drowns' the mites but is not as efficient as insecticidal preparations. Obtain ear drops from your vet that are used to treat ear mites in dogs and cats. In an aviary situation, mini pest strips hung above the cage can help to control a widespread infes-

tation, and Ivermectin is useful in very difficult cases.

Whatever treatment is used it must be applied carefully—never allow oily preparations to contaminate the feathers. Use cotton buds to place the treatment only on the unfeathered areas; the smallest amount of oil can destroy feather water repellancy. Apply twice a week until the affected areas appear normal, which may take six to eight weeks.

Feather and red mites

Feather mites are frequently found on birds but most are harmless. Tiny brown stripes along the feather barbs are actually collections of these mites. They can be treated using an avian insecticidal powder available from your vet or pet shop.

The red mite, *Dermanyssus gallinae*, is a dangerous, blood-sucking insect and in favourable conditions of warmth and high humidity its life cycle may be less than one week. Eggs are laid in cracks and crevices of cages and nest boxes, and when hatched the adult mites spend only short periods on the bird, usually at night. Place a white sheet under and over the cage at night and the tiny bright red mites will be visible the next morning. They cause irritability and restlessness and, in heavy infestations, the birds die of anaemia.

Treatment must involve cages as well as birds. Treat birds with any safe avian mite powder (obtainable from your vet or pet shop), remove them to another cage, then thoroughly clean and spray the original cage with safe insecticide.

■ The microscopic mite *Cnemidocoptes* invades the featherless skin of the cere, causing excess tissue growth.

Lice

Lice are small but visible wingless insects that are common inhabitants of birds, especially of the wild population. Numerous species exist and many are biting lice, which in large numbers cause irritation and debilitation, and excessive preening in affected birds. They need close contact to be transferred.

Louse powders for birds are easily obtainable from your vet, pet shop or produce store. Shake the powder under the wings and allow the bird to fluff and ruffle its feathers—this usually distributes the powder—but don't apply it excessively. This treatment must be repeated fortnightly several times.

Broken feathers

Occasionally a bright, healthy bird will suddenly appear to be covered in blood. This usually indicates a broken feather. Catch the bird and search carefully for the site of the bleeding, which will be the remains of a quill. Grasp the quill with tweezers and pull it out quickly and firmly, then keep gentle pressure on the area for a minute or so. The bleeding usually stops quickly.

Pox virus

Pox viruses are common in pigeons, canaries and wild birds, and are spread by mosquitoes and possibly other insects, particularly in summer. The virus affects unfeathered skin, causing the development of numerous wart-like growths on the cere, around the eyes, inside the mouth and on the lower legs and feet. Applying a weak iodine solution may 'dry' the growths, but there is no curative treatment and the lesions tend to spontaneously disappear within three weeks.

Beak problems

Birds' beaks grow continually, and unless they oppose properly one or both beaks continues to grow into a long, deformed shape, eventually making it difficult for affected birds to eat. Over or undershot beaks occur when the upper or lower beak is too long or short to meet correctly; scissor beaks are set at an angle and criss-cross; and the scaly face mite also causes beak deformities. Whatever the particular problem, affected pet birds must have their beaks trimmed into a normal shape regularly to enable them to eat properly. Your vet can show you how to clip a beak correctly.

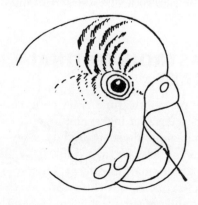

■ Incorrectly opposed beaks can become overgrown and misshapen. Regular trimming is necessary to enable seed to be picked up normally.

Brown cere hypertrophy

Brown cere hypertrophy occurs particularly in older female budgies, possibly caused by hormonal imbalances. Ceres become dark brown, overgrown and very thickened, and may obscure a bird's sight, although birds are usually healthy in other respects. Your vet can soften the excess tissue and gently pare it down, but the condition may recur.

■ The hypertrophic brown cere of female budgerigars.

GASTROINTESTINAL TRACT

The gastrointestinal tract comprises the organs that ingest and digest food and pass the finished product, such as the crop and gizzard, as well as the liver and small and large intestines. The crop is a dilatation of the oesophagus (or food tube), which is located in the lower neck and which acts as a temporary storage chamber. It is present in most seed eating birds and certain other species.

Regurgitation and vomiting

Bored, hypersexed or neurotic budgerigars may begin regurgitating their food to 'feed' a mirror, or any other shiny object in their cages. Some may try to mate their perches, or their owner's finger. Remove the object of affection, give the bird more attention and consider getting a female bird as a mate. Female hormone injections may help refractory cases.

Vomiting differs from and is more serious than simple regurgitation in that the vomiting bird will be ill and the feathers of its head and face will be covered with food and saliva. Vomiting may result from infections in the crop caused by bacteria, candida (a yeast), or protozoa.

Faeces

As birds eat continually, they therefore defaecate and urinate continually, and healthy budgies should pass about forty droppings every twenty-four hours. The black-green part of each dropping is the faeces, and the white part is uric acid which birds pass as urine. Diarrhoea is a common symptom of almost any bird disease and should never be ignored.

Candidiasis

The yeast *Candida albicans* causes small, pale lesions to develop in the mouth, oesophagus and crop, spreading to other organs in severe cases. Vomiting results from crop inflammation, and the feathers on the bird's head will be covered with flecks of food. The disease, called candidiasis (or thrush), is common in hand-reared orphan birds and is caused by stress or conditions of poor hygiene. A course of Nystatin, available from a vet, is the usual treatment.

SKELETON

Bones and joints form the solid framework of an animal's body. A strong and healthy skeleton is largely dependent on a healthy diet.

Fractures

Broken wing and leg bones are common in all birds, both wild and caged. Birds have a very high metabolic rate, so their bones heal quickly. Broken legs that would take six weeks to heal in dogs, will mend in three weeks in birds.

Within several days it becomes difficult to manipulate and reset fractures that have begun to mend incorrectly. Thus the early and correct treatment of all broken bones is essential, and particularly important for wild birds as they must have near perfect flight to survive afterwards. Always take birds with broken bones to a vet immediately. Great advances have been made in the veterinary treatment of birds, not the least in anaesthetics and surgery. Many vets now routinely perform surgery on both caged and wild birds with good success.

X-rays should always be taken initially, as a hanging wing may have only damaged ligaments and just need support from a light splint, as well as rest. If the X-ray shows a broken bone, then one of the numerous methods

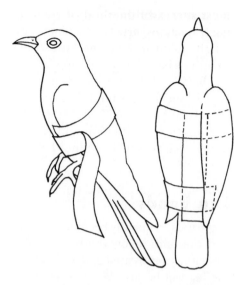

■ Simple wing injuries can be rested by taping injured wings to the body.

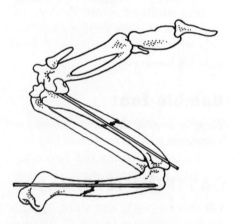

■ Complicated fractures are often best repaired by a vet using internal pinning. Intensive rehabilitation will be required, especially for wild birds.

for treating fractures in birds can be used. Simple breaks may be splinted using light materials such as sticky-tape and masking tape as birds cannot tolerate heavy bandages. Internal fixation using lightweight pins, the most successful method of treating many fractures, may be combined with a light splint to hold the bird's wing against its body for added support.

Birds with broken bones must be kept in small cages until their pins or splints are removed. Refer to the section on rehabilitation and release under 'Native and Introduced Birds' (page 206).

Leg bands

Leg bands frequently become too tight and the limb below the band swells. This must be treated immediately or the leg will be lost. Vets use jeweller's ring cutters to remove these bands; the task is difficult as even the slightest movement may fracture the leg, and because of this the bird is sometimes anaesthetised. Never try to remove tight leg bands yourself.

Bumble foot

Bumble foot is the term for infected swellings of the undersurface of a bird's foot. Usually the bacterium involved is a *Staphylococcus*, and poor blood supply to this part of the body combined with constant weight-bearing and contact with dirt and faeces makes healing slow and difficult.

Unhygienic and sharp flooring materials, chronic trauma and dirty, unsatisfactory perches predispose a bird to the disease. Any wound in the pads allows the bacteria to become established, and untreated the infection can invade the joints of the foot. Bird species most affected include ducks and raptors, or birds of prey. Raptors have long, sharp talons

that can puncture their own feet if perching materials are too small in diameter.

Affected birds have obvious swellings on their pads, are lame and have trouble perching. The lesions must be opened, drained, treated with antibiotics, and the foot bandaged if necessary. Padding the bird's perches will lessen the pressure on the feet. As vitamin A deficiency is also incriminated, feed your bird some carrots, spinach and egg yolk.

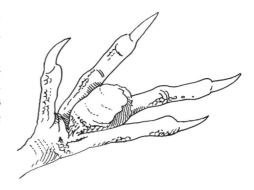

■ Bumble foot is a serious, chronic infection of the soles of the feet of birds such as ducks and raptors.

Gout

Birds, like reptiles, pass uric acid as a large proportion of their urine. Under certain poorly understood situations, these uric acid crystals are laid down as white deposits on the surface of a variety of organs including the kidneys, liver, the pericardial sac that surrounds the heart and the air sacs. This form of gout is insidious and is almost always diagnosed post-mortem.

Articular gout is very painful and occurs when the uric acid crystals are deposited in the joints. Creamy-white swellings are obvious under the skin especially over the joints of the feet.

Dehydration and water deprivation, or any other factors that cause kidney disease, are thought to cause gout. High-protein diets leading to obesity also appear to be involved. There is at present no treatment for either form of gout, with the correct diet being the best prevention.

REPRODUCTIVE TRACT

The egg-laying process frequently causes problems in pet birds, often complicated by their interesting anatomy—unlike most animals, birds have a single opening for both the reproductive and gastrointestinal tracts called the cloaca.

Egg binding

Egg binding refers to an egg that is 'stuck' in the oviduct, making it impossible, despite constant efforts, for the affected female bird to lay the egg. This occurs in breeding birds and isolated pet birds that suddenly start to lay. Affected hens are often overweight, old, or tired at the end of a breeding season; alternatively the egg may be oversized or misshapen causing problems of delivery. The bird's diet may also be calcium deficient.

An egg-bound hen will be found sitting on the floor of her cage straining with her tail moving up and down. Her cloaca will be swollen and she will quickly become weak and exhausted. The constant straining may lead to cloacal prolapse, whereby a dark pink mass will be seen protruding from the bird's vent. **This is an emergency and requires immediate attention from a vet.**

Treatment of an egg-bound bird involves keeping her in a warm, quiet cage and providing calcium, which may be injected or given orally. If the egg is not passed in six to eight hours, a vet may need to remove it by manual manipulation.

Excessive egg laying

Occasionally, caged female budgerigars will begin to lay eggs continually. Because the birds will usually be unfit and perhaps over-weight, the process is exhausting and egg binding may also occur.

Unless recently separated from a male the eggs will be infertile, and the continual egg laying becomes a problem for both bird and owner. If it continues, a course of the male hormone testosterone, prescribed by a vet, in the drinking water for seven to ten days will suppress the hen's ovarian activity.

Egg peritonitis

Sometimes a developing egg may not enter the oviduct, and falls instead into the abdominal cavity causing infection. The abdomen swells and affected hen birds become very sick. Surgery under general anaesthesia is required to open and flush the infected abdominal cavity, but the prognosis for this condition is poor.

CANCER

Cancers, or tumours, are common occurrences in most birds, but are observed more in budgerigars than in any other species of animal or bird. The cancers occur in most body tissues, including the bones of the wing or legs or the ovaries of female budgies. In overweight birds, benign lipomas or fatty tumours are common on the chest. These are obvious, distinct round swellings which may be covered by a featherless, yellow patch of skin. Dieting reduces the size of the tumour, and may be all that is required, but persistant lipomas must be surgically removed.

NATIVE AND INTRODUCED WILD BIRDS

We, the general public, must learn to take responsibility for injured or orphaned birds found in the wild. This section is aimed at those people who may find such birds and who are prepared to care for them during their rehabilitation. As with all our fauna, native birds belong to the Crown. The aim must be to always release these birds back into the wild, and special licences are required to keep native birds for any purpose.

Most vets will examine and treat native fauna on an emergency basis, and excellent organisations exist such as WIRES that will take on the aftercare of these birds if required.

INITIAL TREATMENT

Any wild bird that has obvious injuries should be placed into a darkened, softly padded box and taken immediately to a vet. Injuries can be assessed professionally and shock and dehydration effectively counteracted with subcutaneous or intravenous fluids. Birds that are not eating can be tube-fed to provide a rapid intake of energy. (This should be done by a vet as it involves passing a fine tube down the oesophagus.)

Once birds are stabilised (which may take several days), wounds can be sutured or any fractures repaired. Vets are then often grateful if the original discoverer of the bird can undertake any aftercare.

On your own

If you are unable to present an injured bird immediately for professional attention, place the bird in a secure box or cage with soft padding such as old, clean towels, cover the box totally and place it away from noise in a warm location. **Stressed birds need rest, quiet, warmth, darkness and minimal handling.** Try not to disturb the bird for one to two hours.

Shocked and injured birds are usually chilled and need an ambient temperature of about 30°C (the smaller the bird, the higher the temperature required: honeyeaters need 30 to 32°C; seagulls 30°C; kites 25 to 27°C). Use a thermometer to check the temperature (refer to 'Common Health Problems' on page 179 for methods of providing this heat).

Most injured birds are also dehydrated and may be hypoglycaemic (low in blood sugars). After a suitable rest period, prepare a solution of one teaspoon of glucose in 100 mL of warm water. Include electrolytes (Lectade, Vytrate) if you have them. Give the bird a small amount of this solution using an eye dropper or small syringe—if the bird drinks voluntarily, leave some in a flat dish in the cage. Very weak birds may need small, repeated doses of this solution hourly until they are strong enough to eat. Allow the bird another rest period after the initial liquid feeding, then food may be offered. (See 'Nutrition' on page 198 for the diets of different species).

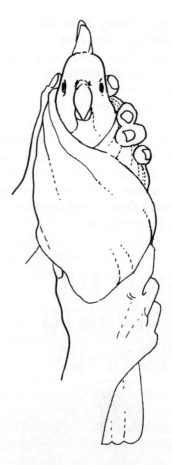

■ Cockatoos and other parrots inflict injury with their beaks. Wrap these birds in towels, keeping control of the head and beak with the thumb and index finger.

■ Small birds can be held in the palm of the hand when administering medication. Larger birds may need wrapping in soft towels.

HANDLING INJURED BIRDS

All birds must be handled as gently, quickly and confidently as possible. Rough handling can have fatal consequences in an already stressed bird. Approach an injured bird quietly and slowly. Use a towel or other piece of soft fabric to wrap around the entire bird, holding the wings firmly against the body to prevent flapping and struggling. Keep the bird wrapped in the towel and, where possible, place into a dark, covered box for transport.

Avoid the beak, keeping in mind that parrots, magpies and currawongs have very sharp beaks. Make sure if you are picking up one of these birds that its head is well covered by the towel. If necessary, control the head by holding it between your thumb and first finger. Water birds like herons and storks have very long, fast-moving and sharp bills which you should always keep away from your face.

The claws should also be avoided. Magpie claws are very long and needle-sharp, and raptors such as hawks and owls have very dangerous talons which inflict far more severe injuries than their beaks. Cover these birds entirely with a towel and hold them down until you can feel the legs through the material. Try to hold both legs, wing tips and tail together, but above all do not relax your grip on the legs. Keep the head covered, as this seems to have a settling effect. By allowing these birds to grasp a roll of soft bandage in their talons they appear to feel more secure and their talons are kept under control.

Emus belong to the family of flightless birds called ratites. These birds can be aggressive and inflict serious wounds with their powerful legs and claws, so they should only be handled by experts.

Take care if you are handling birds such as water birds or geese as rough handling can easily fracture or injure their long, fine legs or long necks.

To examine an injured wild bird, use a towel or similar drape to keep the claws and head under control before attempting to expose any part of the bird for examination. Two people can be more effective at this than one.

COMMON INJURIES AND TREATMENT

Weak and injured native birds may be suffering a variety of problems, some requiring treatment by a vet, others needing only home care and nursing. Where possible, a vet should examine the bird first to determine the problem. Below are some common ailments seen in wild birds.

■ Raptors have very sharp and dangerous talons; give these birds a roll of material to grasp, and keep their feet under control at all times.

■ Small species of birds can become weak and waterlogged after a long period of rain. These birds can often be treated at home by providing warmth, rehydration as described above, rest, and preferably some food before being released as soon as possible. A good indication of a bird's nutritional status is the muscle cover over the sternum or keel bone. If there is a good cover of muscle over the bone the bird is healthy.

■ Birds that fly into closed windows should be placed immediately into a warm, softly padded and darkened box. If the injured bird is not showing signs of recovery in one to two hours, a vet may be required to administer additional treatment. The drugs used for concussion in dogs and cats can also be useful for birds.

■ The state of a bird's plumage can indicate a problem: fluffed feathers usually mean birds are chilled and need warmth; oily feathers need to be cleaned (see 'Oil-contaminated Birds' on opposite page); and unkempt feathers indicate birds that are too weak or sick to groom.

■ Birds that are bright and alert yet are hanging one wing or balancing on one leg usually have a fracture. These birds must always be examined by a vet as X-rays are necessary to determine whether a fracture or dislocation is present or whether damaged ligaments are causing the wing to hang. (Refer to 'Skeleton' on page 190). The finder of the bird may often wish to undertake its aftercare while the fracture heals.

■ Obvious skin wounds from cat bites or gunshot will need veterinary attention as the injuries must be properly sutured and the bird treated with antibiotics. These wounds often need to be cleaned of feathers and dirt that have been dragged into the tear, and any maggots infecting the wound can be killed with a prescribed weak insecticide.

■ Birds that have lost their tail or flight feathers will need to be kept captive until the feathers have regrown. A procedure called 'imping', which has long been practised by falconers and involves the grafting of one feather on to another, enables birds to be released early. Your vet or the local bird club may be able to direct you to such an experienced bird handler.

■ Bumble foot, (which is described in more detail on page 191) and is common in raptors and water birds, can prevent birds of prey from catching food with their talons. These birds will be weak and starved and will need to be fed in captivity while affected feet heal. The bird will need to be treated with antibiotics by a vet.

■ Heavy infestations of parasites may weaken some young birds. External parasites such as lice are usually easily detected running amongst the feathers (particularly under the wings) during the initial examination. Once the bird is stronger and stabilised after rest, rehydration and feeding, it should be treated using safe avian insecticidal powder from your vet or pet shop. Very thin birds or those with loose droppings may have heavy burdens of internal parasites. Have the bird's droppings examined by a vet for worm or protozoal eggs and the correct medication can then be given.

■ Poisonings are not uncommon in wild birds, especially cockatoos and galahs which may feed on illegally poisoned grain. Affected birds will convulse or be inco-ordinated, and these symptoms indicate prompt veterinary treatment with the correct antidote is required for any chance of survival.

■ Seabirds frequently swallow fish hooks. If there is a length of fishing line hanging from the beak, make sure the bird does not swallow the line while you get it to a vet. Never pull on the line.

Sometimes a fishing line becomes tangled around the bird's legs; in these cases, have a friend hold the bird wrapped in a towel while you carefully undo the knots.

■ Botulism ('limber neck') is a disease of the nervous system caused by a *Clostridial* bacterium, and it is usually observed in water birds such as ducks that are forced to rely on stagnant and infected pools of water during prolonged dry weather. Birds that eat carrion may also develop this disease. The organism causes paralysis: the neck and wings droop and the gait becomes staggery. Antibiotics from a vet are the best treatment.

Oil-contaminated birds

Oil-contamination is a specialist area, and when large numbers of birds are affected by an oil slick, experts should control the situation.

By destroying the crucial air pockets that insulate birds, and by removing their own natural oils (causing the feathers to lose water repellancy) oil contamination makes birds very vulnerable to chilling. Most stressed birds in this state are found shocked, weak, chilled, starving, and possibly poisoned by oil they may have ingested.

If you find an oil-contaminated bird it must be immediately wrapped closely (except for the head) in a soft, absorbent material such as flannel or cotton. Make a 'poncho' if possible (see above), as this helps to warm and dry the bird, and prevents it from swallowing more oil. Transport the bird to a vet for evaluation and treatment as soon as possible. Toxic oils can cause breathing difficulties, convulsions and gastroenteritis, so antibiotics and other drugs will usually need to be administered.

■ Oiled seabirds should be wrapped immediately in a piece of soft, absorbent material made into a poncho, which provides warmth and prevents the birds ingesting oil as they try to preen.

On your own

Remember that you should still always telephone for veterinary advice even if you are unable to get to professional help immediately. In these cases, the bird should be placed in an ambient temperature of 29° to 30°C as soon as possible, as a warm environment is crucial to oil-contaminated birds. Clean the bird's eyes, nose and mouth, treat the eyes with ophthalmic antibiotic ointment if available, and smear cream over its legs and feet.

Correcting dehydration and starvation is the next step. Fluids administered by a vet are the most effective; otherwise, give an electrolyte mixture orally in small amounts every hour until the bird is responding, and offer food as soon as possible.

If the oil is non-toxic, cleaning may be delayed for one to four days until the bird is eating and stronger. Several products are used by the professionals when cleaning these birds. These include a 1% solution of liquid dish-washing detergent in the ratio of 100 mL to 10 litres of water; the oil solubiliser Polycomplex A-11 in the ratio of 30 mL to 4 litres of water; and the Amway product LOC. Stubborn oil may need to be dissolved first in mineral or vegetable oils before applying the detergent.

Once the washing process has begun, repeated gentle washing and rinsing in 40°C water will be necessary until the bird's feathers repel water and become fluffy again. The bird should be dried quickly—pet grooming dryers are useful and take about 30 minutes to completely dry a bird. Stop the washing or drying procedures if the bird appears stressed.

When the bird is strong and eating, rehabilitation can begin in a small, warm aviary with a shallow area of water. Gradually expose the bird to normal weather and a larger pool, bearing in mind that water is essential for seabirds for grooming and waterproofing. Release should wait until a bird is totally fit.

NUTRITION

The initial and most important task when contemplating feeding injured or captive wild birds is to correctly identify the species so that a suitable diet can be fed.

Strict hygiene is essential; treat food preparation as you would for your own family and prepare food freshly daily. Captive wild birds are susceptible to infection and must have clean food and water bowls. For most species, small frequent meals will be needed until birds are eating voluntarily and maintaining their weight.

To weigh a bird, place it in a plastic or paper bag with its head exposed through a small hole and then weigh it on a set of kitchen scales. Palpating the sternum or keel bone is also a good indicator of weight.

To be acceptable to birds, food must look good, as senses of taste and smell are not as important as sight. Most wild birds will not readily accept unfamiliar food, so patience and perseverence is essential, and the food must resemble as closely as possible a bird's natural diet.

The best way to stimulate eating in birds other than seed eaters is to offer birds live food. This may mean small mice for kookaburras and owls, or insects and earthworms for magpies. (Seed eaters are much easier!) Once taking food voluntarily, most birds will eat a variety of foods, which is necessary if they are to receive a balanced diet. Unless birds are getting a large proportion of their diet as natural food, vitamin and mineral supplementation is essential. (Ornithon is a good supplement; many others are available from vets and pet shops, and all come with suggested dosages and methods of administration.) Bear in mind that the problems referred to in 'Backyard Wild Bird Feeding' (page 183) also apply to captive wild birds.

Seed eaters

Seed eaters include rosellas, galahs, cockatoos and other parrots, finches, pigeons and doves, and are the easiest birds to feed as most will readily accept commercial seed mixes. They may prefer the seed scattered on the floor of the cage at first, and small parrots will appreciate a mixture of budgie and parrot seed mix. Supplement the seed daily with chopped and sliced fruit (apples are good), green vegetables, seeding grasses and thistles, and branches containing native flowers and nuts. The Wombaroo company produces a granivore bird mix for these species.

Finches need a finch seed mix, supplemented with egg and biscuit (make your own by mixing hard-boiled egg yolk with crumbled arrowroot biscuit, to which you can add water or milk and vitamins and minerals). Fruit, grass heads and greens should

also be offered.

Doves and pigeons are basically seed eaters, but should also have commercial pigeon mixes that contain the correct balance of vitamins and minerals. They like dried peas and grains such as corn, wheat and milo. Some species will eat fruit and vegetables.

All of these birds should have fresh water, grit, and a cuttlefish for calcium.

Nectar eaters

Nectar eaters, which include lorikeets, lowries and honeyeaters, derive their protein from nectar and insects, and their carbohydrate from the sugars in nectar and from fruit and seed.

A complete diet can be achieved by feeding a combination of the Wombaroo lorikeet and honeyeater food and the granivore mix. Otherwise, any other diet for a nectar eater should include varying mixtures of the following: wholemeal bread or cereals soaked in a mixture of glucose with vitamins and minerals, milk powder and water (one teaspoon of glucose to 100 mL of water); small amounts of commercial pollen; baby foods such as Heinz cereals; ripe fruit; and seed mixes.

Provide natural foods by offering branches of flowering native shrubs such as grevillea and bottlebrush, and catch and feed live insects to the bird. Fresh water should always be available.

Carnivorous birds

Carnivorous birds include all raptors, or birds of prey such as owls, hawks, kites, kookaburras and frogmouths. **The natural diet of these birds is based on whole animals—they must not be fed an all-meat diet in captivity** but must be given the opportunity to feed on feathers and fur as well as meat (refer to 'Backyard Wild Bird feeding' on page 183). Depending on the size of the bird, prey includes mice, rats, small birds, small lizards and insects.

Carnivorous birds can be difficult and stubborn to feed and most species will require initial feeding with live food to stimulate eating. Live food is also essential to maintain a bird's ability to recognise and catch its natural prey. Dig earthworms, culture your own mealworms, or catch live insects around outside lights at night. You may also need to find a source of laboratory mice, or day old chicks for larger species of carnivorous birds.

Really obstinate birds will require force feeding; frogmouths, for example, may never learn to eat voluntarily in captivity. To force feed these birds, obtain some blunt forceps (tweezers) from a chemist, cut the food into bite-size pieces (about 2 to 3 cm square depending on the size of the bird) and gently place the food at the very back of the bird's throat. This usually stimulates the swallow reflex. The bird may need to be wrapped in a towel and the mouth gently prised open at first, but most birds will quickly learn to gape and accept the food offered, even if they refuse to pick it up voluntarily. It is best to offer frequent, small feeds and to avoid overfeeding (it is often possible to feel if the crop is full).

Once a bird is eating voluntarily, it may then accept dead baby mice or day old chicks, hard-boiled eggs, pieces of raw rabbit or poultry including skin, feathers and fur (this supplies important roughage and is always eaten in the wild), and softened, dry dog and cat food. Dog food is useful as it contains the correct proportions of nutrients for carnivores, as well as added vitamins and minerals. Wombaroo insectivore food mix is an alternative balanced diet for carnivores. Meat may be fed in small amounts and always with vitamins and minerals. Mix the meat with calcium carbonate powder before feeding, in the ratio of a half teaspoon per 500 g of meat. Fresh water should always be available.

An interesting phenomenon should occur if carnivorous birds in captivity are being fed adequate amounts of roughage: they should regurgitate a neat ball of indigestible material several hours after a meal as they do in the wild.

Omnivores

Omnivores include magpies, currawongs, magpie larks, blackbirds and cuckoo shrikes, and these birds eat both meat and vegetable matter in the wild. Hence their diet is basically as for the carnivores, but should be supplemented with berries, wholemeal bread, cake, egg and biscuit, grated cheese and fruit and oatmeal. Supply vitamins and minerals and fresh water. Baby magpies are well known for having amazing appetites and will easily adapt to a very varied diet.

Insectivorous birds

Insectivorous birds, which include wagtails, swallows and flycatchers, are notoriously difficult to keep in captivity because it is physically impossible to catch enough insects to feed them each day. The Wombaroo insectivore mix is the best way to supplement your insect catch, and offer egg and biscuit as well as small amounts of minced meat with vitamins and minerals. Always supply fresh water.

■ Providing the correct food for native birds can require ingenuity. Here is an idea for collecting live food for insectivorous birds.

Shore birds

Shore birds such as plovers, herons and ibis also respond poorly to captivity. They stress easily and should be kept for short periods only unless they are in expert hands.

Most shore birds are insect eaters. Offer as many live insects as possible and supplement this with the Wombaroo insectivore mix, cooked egg yolk, poultry starter crumbles, minced beef, vitamins and minerals and fresh water.

Herbivores

Herbivores, which include ducks, geese, swans and emus, are eaters of vegetable matter, but many species also like to include live food such as snails and earthworms in their diet. Provide these birds with a varying mixture of duck pellets or crumbles (it is worth seeking these out), grains, cereals, wholemeal bread, chopped greens, seed sprouts and fresh grass and clover. Catch and feed snails and worms to the birds. Unless the duck pellets are the basis of the diet, supplement with vitamins and minerals.

Species of ducks, geese and swans must have copious and constantly replenished supplies of water. They should also have enough water to allow them to fully submerge themselves and bathe. Large-sized grit is also essential.

Emus are largely herbivorous, but also eat insects. Their natural diet consists of fruits, flowers, seeds, lush green grass, herbs, shrubs and insects. Base their diet on balanced poultry (turkey) pellets, lucerne and chopped fresh greens, some bread, grains, grit and water. Supplement the diet with vitamins and minerals.

Seabirds

Seabirds are birds such as seagulls, pelicans, cormorants and penguins (see separate section below). Seagulls are omnivores and are the great scavengers of the seaside; they are therefore easy to satisfy once they are eating voluntarily. Base their diet around a mixture of small whole fish like whitebait, or chopped large fish, canned 'fishy' cat food, softened, dry dog and cat food and tablescraps such as bread. Always supplement the diet with vitamins and minerals, especially vitamin B; many species of fish (particularly if frozen) have an enzyme that destroys the B vitamins.

Pelicans, cormorants and similar birds are more exclusive eaters of fish, so you will need to feed them whole fish. Pelicans may need force feeding until they are eating voluntarily. Two people may be required for this: one to hold the large bird wrapped in a towel if necessary, the other to open the mouth and place the whole small fish at the back of the bird's throat. Always add vitamin B, as well as other vitamins and minerals.

All of these seabirds require enough water in which to submerge and bathe so that they can maintain grooming and water repellency. **Most species must also be fed in the water**, and many will only defaecate in water. Change the water supply frequently.

Penguins

Penguins are seabirds that only come ashore to rest or moult. They require totally unpolluted waters: even the slightest amount of oil will seriously decrease their water repellency.

Penguins found by the general public may be suffering from car accident injuries, oil pollution or feral cat or dog wounds. Depending on the season, some may be starved, and young birds often have very heavy worm burdens.

Injured penguins require urgent professional attention. They are easily stressed, difficult to maintain in captivity and should always be forwarded to a vet or zoo as soon as possible. Make sure you keep them cool when they are being transported as they are vulnerable to heat stress. Injured specimens will usually be weak, hypoglycaemic and dehydrated. If you are unable to get to a vet, administer small amounts of an electrolyte solution every hour (or a mixture of one teaspoon of glucose in 100 mL of water) until the bird is stronger, then you can try feeding.

As penguins will only respond to live food they always initially need force feeding and must be given small, frequent meals. Feed virtually any fish, including squid, scallops and small crustaceans. Young penguins may be force fed a blended mixture of fresh fish, canned fish and vitamins and minerals.

Never attempt to keep an injured penguin permanently—seek expert help as soon as possible.

REARING ORPHANED BIRDS

Rearing orphaned birds is a time-consuming procedure that requires infinite patience and should not be undertaken lightly. If you do find a baby bird, always make sure that it is, in fact, an orphan bird and not one whose parents will be returning—too many birds have been taken from the bush prematurely without any effort to locate a nest. Always make every effort to locate a nest, or leave the bird in low branches and observe it for several hours. Certain species of birds hide their babies and will always return for them.

If you have an older, feathered orphan bird and there are other members of its species in the vicinity, always try placing it outside during the day. Hang the cage in a tree and furnish it with perches that extend on either side of the cage. Species like kookaburras have been known to 'adopt' orphans in cages and feed

them as one of their own.

There are two types of baby bird. Altricial birds remain in the nest and are fed by their parents. They are usually born featherless and require constant warmth and very frequent feeding. Examples are parrots, magpies and owls. Precocial birds are those that are born with a covering of feathers. They can immediately leave the nest and follow their parents, and are capable from the start of feeding themselves. Ducks and plovers have precocial young.

Rearing baby birds is exactly the same as rearing any orphaned animal. The important factors for success are:

■ a warm ambient temperature which is critical; featherless birds must be maintained constantly at 28 to 32°C;

■ Precocial orphans such as ducklings and emus require daily exercise; they will quickly learn to be 'taken for a walk'.

- security in the form of an artificial 'nest'—use a small box thickly padded with tissues then place this inside a larger cage or box; consider a brooder for precocial young like ducklings;

- establishing a regular routine—irregular meals in particular will result in orphans that are vulnerable to disease;

- perfect hygiene of human baby standard; this means that you must clean all feeding apparatus thoroughly between every feed and prepare food daily; keep the nest clean of left-over food and droppings; and clean any excess food from the bird's beak and feathers after each meal as candida (thrush) is common in hand-reared birds;

- weighing the orphan regularly; palpate the sternum to determine the success of your feeding programme.

Precocial young need daily exercise and, once strong and eating well, should be taken for short walks.

As the baby bird grows, gradually decrease the temperature of its surroundings and slowly increase the size of its cage. Add natural branches when perching is mastered and a shallow water bowl only when you are sure the bird is mobile and can drink without assistance. Once the flight feathers have developed, the bird should be placed in a long aviary with sufficient room to fly. From this time the orphan should be prepared for release. If you can, find other, similar orphans of the same species to place in the aviary, or locate the bird where it can see and associate with others of its kind. Refer to 'Rehabilitation and Release' on page 206.

Feeding

Altricial young will need feeding almost constantly at first; it is almost impossible to overfeed these birds. It may be necessary to feed several times an hour for the first few days, then once every hour.

Altricial birds are the species that 'gape' for their parents, and the general rule is to keep feeding until the baby bird stops gaping. Sometimes you will have to find the stimulus for the gape reflex; tap the bird gently around the beak and head until the right movement causes it to open its beak. Be patient as it is safer for the bird to take food voluntarily.

Use an instrument like a pair of blunt forceps to very carefully place the food bolus at the back of the bird's gaping mouth.

Nutrition

The crucial factor when preparing an orphan bird's diet is to vary the foods used, or at least include a wide range of the suggested foodstuffs in your mixture. It is easy to inadvertently feed a diet deficient in certain vitamins and minerals if only a narrow range of foodstuffs are used. Always include vitamins and minerals.

Initially it may be difficult to determine the species of your orphan. Most young birds are fed insects by their parents during the first stage of life, so a diet to provide similar nutrients can be based around mixtures of the following: protein in the form of dog food, hard-boiled eggs, powdered milk, baby cereals and poultry starter mash; carbohydrates in the form of greens like spinach, wheatgerm, oatmeal, raisins and other dried fruit; and vitamins and minerals. The mixture should be blended and mixed to a slurry with water, and fed warm. The general idea is to vary the food mixture to ensure a balanced diet is being fed.

Try to include as many freshly caught insects as possible. These must be killed before being fed to baby birds as parent birds always kill insects for their young.

For seed eaters, the Wombaroo granivore mix is a completely balanced diet. It may also be fed as a supplement or mixed with fruit or hard-boiled eggs. There are numerous other successful rearing diets for seed eaters, and all are based on varying mixtures of the following foodstuffs: fruit, poultry starter mash, powdered milk, hard-boiled egg, baby cereals, wheatgerm, rolled oats, soya meal and ground seed. Blend the mixture with water, vitamins and minerals and add a small amount of glucose every few days.

Seed eaters will feed from a teaspoon; make the mixture runny initially and feed it warm, then make a drier mix as the bird grows. When feeding all birds you should observe the crop, which should be empty before each feed.

The Wombaroo lorikeet and honeyeater food is especially formulated for nectivorous birds. Other foods that are useful include: poultry starter mash, hard-boiled egg yolks, powdered milk, baby fruit and cereals and pureed fruit. Mix any of these with water, a little glucose (one teaspoon per 100 mL of water) and vitamins and minerals. The food should be fed warm as a very wet mixture.

The diet for carnivorous orphans is a minced or blended version of the adult diet. For example, include softened dog food, eggs, minced pieces of rabbit and chicken (not just the flesh) and only small amounts of muscle and flesh. Add vitamins and minerals. The Wombaroo insectivore mix can be used as the basis of the carnivore diet, or can be mixed with any of the above.

The parents of young birds of prey tear apart the youngsters' food in the nest and feed pieces to their babies. These birds may need a similar initial stimulus before they will gape for food, but as they grow, food should be placed into their talons.

Feed omnivorous birds a mushy, minced version of the adult diet. For example, mix grated cheese, egg, oatmeal, dog food, small amounts of meat and add vitamins and minerals. You can also use the Wombaroo insectivore mix.

Herbivorous birds, for example ducks, are usually precocial and are therefore able to feed themselves from a shallow dish, although sometimes a young chicken may be required initially to show ducklings or goslings how to eat. Provide a wet version of the adult diet, and some live food such as chopped earth-worms and snails. It is important that the orphans exercise and learn to scratch in the earth, so allow them access to turf and take them for short walks. Provide fine grit and water in shallow dishes.

Emu eggs are incubated by the father, and he takes care of the precocial young over the subsequent six to eighteen months. Emu chicks retain their striped plumage until three months of age. Bone deformities, which commonly occur in hand-reared emus, are thought to be the result of underexercise and the overfeeding of high protein diets. In the wild, the young travel extensively with their father, and their diet is not particularly high in protein. It is recommended that at least 50% of a chick's diet consist of chopped fresh greens and lucerne (or ad lib), the remainder being based on poultry starter crumbles. Grit, fresh water, and vitamins and minerals are essential, and food must be chopped or the young birds develop impactions. They also eat *anything*, so remove any foreign objects in an emu's yard. Finally, exercise is essential, so you should take orphans for daily walks.

Seabird orphans should be fed a mashed up mixture of the adult diet, which would include chopped fish and canned cat fish food. Add egg yolk and vitamins and minerals (especially vitamin B), and provide water in *shallow* dishes or lightly spray the birds each day. The Wombaroo insectivore mix is also suitable for these birds.

REHABILITATION AND RELEASE

As with all native fauna, the care of injured and orphaned wild birds must always be undertaken with the eventual aim of releasing them into their natural habitat.

All injured wild birds should be assessed by a vet before any treatment is undertaken, then they will need to be totally fit and strong before being released again into their natural habitat. Euthanasia should be considered for any birds with injuries that will obviously prevent their return to full health. This is a difficult decision to follow through but unless a bird can be happily relocated in an aviary, or is a member of a rare species and can be placed in a zoo, it is the correct decision. Many birds will never adapt to captivity and for them the choice is obvious.

Rehabilitation of injured birds can be a prolonged process and birds such as raptors may need expert care and knowledge. Birds that are caged while a fractured bone heals rapidly lose the ability to fly because their flight muscles atrophy. After bones have healed, birds will need to be transferred to long-enough aviaries to allow flight. It will then take a bird at least three weeks before its muscles have regained their full strength—this is assuming the bone has healed perfectly.

As already stated, birds must be very fit and strong before release, and they must be able to recognise and catch food. This applies particularly to orphan birds which, before release, must be taught to recognise their natural diet and be able to find and catch it. Orphans will also have 'imprinted' on their foster parents and must be taught to associate with their own species. Organisations like WIRES can help to locate orphans in aviaries with others of their kind and arrange for their release at the correct time.

Birds should always be released as closely as possible to where they were found, or in an area where their species exists. Always band birds first as this allows for easier follow-up observation.

The proper timing of release is also essential. Birds active during the day should be released early in the morning after a good feed. Nocturnal species should be released with a full stomach at dusk.

If birds are gregarious, like galahs, wait until they can be released into a flock. Similarly, migratory birds will need to be kept in captivity until they can be released into a flock of their

■ The effective release of native birds into their usual environment is very important. Galahs, for example, are gregarious and should preferably be released into a flock of their own kind.

own species. Flock and migratory birds accept newcomers to their flocks readily. However, species like kookaburras and magpies can be extremely difficult as they are aggressively territorial. Birds from their own family group that have been absent for only a week may be refused entry and attacked viciously. These birds *must* be strong and healthy before release.

CHAPTER 5

NATIVE MAMMALS

Australian mammal fauna is typical of an island where the evolution of animal species has occurred in isolation, with very few introductions from neighbouring continents. The resultant fauna collection has been called a 'living museum' of mammals, many of which cannot be found elsewhere in the world.

Australia was once connected to South America and Antarctica, but broke away about fifty-five million years ago and our island continent began to drift in the ocean, carrying with it a collection of primitive mammals, many of them marsupials. These marsupials were able to continue developing in isolation, while on other continents marsupials were becoming extinct. South America does have marsupials, but the opossum of North America is the only marsupial in the entire northern hemisphere.

As the Australian continent drifted it came close to the islands now known as Indonesia and, then, around ten million years ago, Australia's placental mammals arrived: bats and, more recently, rodents. Dingoes are thought to have 'island-hopped' with wandering native people as recently as five to ten thousand years ago.

Mammals are distinguished from reptiles by being warm-blooded, feeding their young on milk and by possessing fur. The three types of mammal—monotreme, marsupial and placental—occur together only in Australia and New Guinea. Monotremes (platypuses and echidnas) lay eggs as well as suckle their young; marsupials (for example, kangaroos) give birth to very immature young and most rear them in pouch-like structures; and the placental mammals (bats, rodents, dogs etc.) have specialised membranes, or placenta, that nourish the growing unborn young in the mother's uterus.

There has been a great surge of interest and corresponding veterinary research into Australian mammals in recent years, and many vets are now involved in treating native fauna. You can help this crucial 'knowledge bank' by becoming a member of a wildlife organisation, and by referring sick and injured native fauna to vets, zoos or your particular organisation. Even dead animals can be useful for research; museums are often interested in receiving freshly dead specimens and details of their location and circumstances.

This section is designed to help those concerned Australians who wish to aid injured or orphaned native animals. The species described herein are those most commonly rescued—if rarer animals are found, the closest zoo or vet will always give advice. Alternatively, there are excellent wildlife organisations (listed on pages 299 to 300), that will take on the task of animal care.

NATIVE ANIMALS, YOU AND THE LAW

There are strict laws protecting our native fauna and governing the involvement that the general public may have with these animals. *All* native animals belong to and always remain the property of the Crown, and only sick, injured and orphaned animals may be held in captivity, and only until they are convalesced. Within three days of taking possession of a native animal you must obtain a licence from the National Parks and Wildlife Service in your state, which lasts only until an animal is fit for release. (Refer to the list of state government wildlife services on pages 299 to 300.)

It is essential that the general public, no matter how well-meaning, understand that native animals in their possession are 'on loan'—to care for them is a temporary privilege. The ultimate aim of rearing native animals, reptiles or birds must be to release them into their natural habitats when they are deemed fit.

REHABILITATION AND RELEASE

The task of preparing hand-reared and injured animals for release can be difficult. For successful rehabilitation, an animal (or bird or reptile) must:

■ be in excellent health;

■ be the correct age;

■ be able to find and catch prey or otherwise recognise its natural diet;

■ be strong enough to protect itself against predators or hostile territorial displays from its own species;

■ be released into the area from which it came or a similar geographical area where members of its species are known to live; and

■ be wary of humans.

It is *not* good enough to merely release animals into a 'nice bit of bush' and to hope for the best.

Injured animals will hopefully retain their fear of humans and their knowledge of survival in the wild. For these animals, being fit and being released into the correct location are essentials for a successful return to the wild. For hand-reared animals, the very strong bond between foster mothers and orphans must be gradually broken and the animals taught to recognise and socialise with their own species.

The ideal situation for orphaned animals occurs when they are reared on farms within their natural habitat in the country, and can be released onto the same property, gradually becoming part of the local community of their species. Unfortunately, this situation is unlikely for most foster parents. If you have an orphan native animal always seek the advice of people skilled in release: WIRES, or similar organisations (see page 299), are practised at rehabilitation and release. They can place orphans with groups of their own species, gradually weaning them from their dependence on humans. The groups of orphans are identified by tagging or banding, transported to ideal areas for release and observed from a distance for several weeks wherever possible.

COMMON PROBLEMS OF CAPTIVE MAMMALS

All injured and captive native animals may have many common disease and stress syndromes. Most of these occur as a result of their forced domestication, no matter how temporary.

STRESS

Stress is the greatest killer of captive fauna. Wild animals are extremely sensitive to their surroundings and most have great difficulty adapting to humans and handling. Signs of stress include depression and lethargy, refusal to eat, possible stomach ulceration and watery diarrhoea.

Stress-induced illness is very difficult to treat, so it is far better to prevent stress by avoiding the following contributing factors:

- Overhandling: newly acquired fauna should be kept in quiet, dark locations and disturbed only for feeding until they become accustomed to their new caretakers. Allow nocturnal animals to sleep undisturbed between feeds during the day or, if adult, feed only at dawn and dusk.

- Failure to treat injuries or illness promptly.

- Lack of safety and security: animals—both adults and orphans—must be housed away from dogs or cats that may possibly harass them.

- Failure to recreate a 'natural' environment for both adults and orphans, for example, room to climb for possums, or to dig for wombats, or the provision of safe, warm and secure pouches.

CAPTURE MYOPATHY

Capture myopathy, a very common and serious stress-related disease of recently captured marsupials in particular, results from the stress and fear of capture, and is exacerbated by excess physical exertion such as a prolonged chase and/or any struggling during capture.

Acutely affected animals become depressed and die suddenly. Others show muscle stiffness, spasm and pain, especially in the muscle groups of the neck, back and hind limbs. The muscle tissues die, becoming hard and fibrotic, breathing becomes laboured, the heart rate increases, there may be brown urine from muscle fibre breakdown and paralysis and convulsions occur. Affected animals may die in several days, or as much as two to four weeks later.

Capture myopathy is difficult to treat. Tranquillisers and intravenous fluids will help if they are administered early enough.

Much is now known about the 'chemical restraint' (administration of tranquillisers, etc) of natives, so in difficult situations allow a vet to use sedation and anaesthesia to effectively reduce the stresses of handling. Once captured, transport animals in dark, cool and quiet surroundings.

HYPERTHERMIA

Hyperthermia is heat stress and it can be rapidly fatal. It usually results from prolonged capture and rough handling techniques, and from incorrect transporting and housing. In orphans it may result from the overzealous use of radiators and hot water bottles. Echidnas and platypuses are especially sensitive to overheating.

Overheated animals must be cooled with fans, or by immersion in cold water baths. Veterinary treatment is essential to prevent irreversible brain damage.

HYPOTHERMIA

Animals suffering from hypothermia have cold stress and they should be warmed using warm water baths, heaters, rugs etc. The condition occurs frequently in orphaned marsupials that are not constantly maintained in sufficiently warm environments, and in recently captured animals that are kept and transported in cold surroundings.

MALNUTRITION

Many caretakers of sick or orphaned mammals are not conscious of the fact that their charges are being underfed. Apart from the problem of imbalanced diets, many orphans are weaned too early and become malnourished young adults.

Orphans in particular must be weighed once a day. Keeping a daily record of weight, treatment, diet, behaviour etc., is the easiest and most efficient method of following closely the progress of native mammals in your care.

THRUSH

Thrush, a yeast infection that is caused by *Candida albicans,* is extremely common in captive marsupials. It can result from unhygienic feeding practices of orphaned or sick fauna, or as a secondary invader of already sick animals, or in animals on oral antibiotics. Stress may play the most important role in the onset of thrush.

The organism mainly affects the gastrointestinal tract, from the mouth to the cloaca. Sometimes greyish-white plaques are seen in the mouth, but often the disease only causes vague symptoms of depression, loss of appetite and diarrhoea. On postmortem examination, some of these animals have thick, cheesy lesions throughout their stomachs and intestines.

The yeast organism can be detected in faecal examinations if thrush is suspected. Nystatin, prescribed by a vet, is effective if used early enough. It must be administered after meals, not mixed with the formula, and may need to be given for up to fourteen days. *Candida* is an organism that spreads readily from animals to humans and back again, so strict hygiene is essential.

COCCIDIOSIS

Coccidia are protozoa (microscopic parasites) that inflame the intestinal tract, and are commonly present in healthy marsupials in the wild. In captivity stress appears to initiate the disease coccidiosis, which occurs in weaned and grazing macropods, wombats and possums. The disease is signalled by black or watery diarrhoea containing blood, and accompanied by severe dehydration, abdominal pain, weakness and collapse. Hand-raised marsupials may die without warning.

As the coccidial oocysts (eggs) must be picked up from ground contaminated by marsupial faeces, the disease does not occur in animals fed only milk formula. Affected animals must have grazed with other marsupials before being orphaned, or since weaning.

The oocysts survive best in warm, humid conditions and can build up rapidly if animals are confined to small areas. Avoid overcrowding, collect droppings at least every second day and place the feed of marsupials above ground level away from their faeces.

Treatment of coccidiosis is difficult. Sulphonamides and intravenous fluids may be successful if used very early in sick animals. Healthy animals that are old enough to have grazed before being orphaned or that have come in contact with known coccidia carriers can be treated with Amprolmix Plus, available from a vet.

OTHER INTERNAL PARASITES

There are numerous worms that affect captive native mammals which, in the wild, rarely cause disease. Problems are seen in overcrowded wildlife parks, or in groups of hand-reared marsupials that are grazing in a restricted area. These situations result in a rapid build-up of worm eggs on the pasture.

Heavy worm burdens cause loss of weight, a rough coat and diarrhoea. Parasites are rarely a problem in isolated, hand-raised orphans until they are grazed with others of their species (marsupials, for example, cannot be infected with sheep and cattle worms). Once weaned and grazing, it is wise to have your vet do faecal checks at least twice a year for any worm eggs.

REARING ORPHANED MAMMALS

The difficulties and problems associated with hand-rearing orphaned mammals cannot be overemphasised and it is not a task for the faint hearted. It requires intelligence, a strong sense of responsibility, a certain amount of spare cash and unflagging dedication and patience, so please place any orphaned native animals into caring and experienced hands if you are in any doubt as to your suitability as a foster parent. Hairless marsupials in particular are extremely difficult to rear, and this task should not be attempted by the inexperienced. Contact the right organisation as soon as possible— don't wait until orphans are sick, or your enthusiasm has waned. Consult the list of organisations on page 299, or ring a vet or the nearest zoo.

The crucial factors affecting the successful rearing of orphaned mammals are:

- initially assessing the age and species of orphans;

- feeding a formula of the correct quality and quantity;

- providing constant and correct ambient temperatures;

- preventing dehydration, diarrhoea and/or hypoglycaemia;

- preventing stress from failure to adjust to new surroundings; and

- preventing infection resulting from poor hygiene.

INITIAL ASSESSMENT

The species of any orphan must be determined as soon as possible; seek advice from wildlife organisations if necessary.

Age assessment must then be done within the first week that you acquire an orphan to rear. Orphaned mammals grow at a slower rate than those reared naturally, so age estimation by weight is not accurate after a few weeks in captivity.

The charts on pages 227, 234, 235, 237 and 240 are a guide to ageing, and the Wombaroo company (see details below) provides very detailed growth charts for all of the commonly orphaned animals. This information enables you to feed the correct diet for an orphan's stage of development and to estimate times for weaning and release.

Most orphaned animals are found stressed, dehydrated and often injured, and should always be taken to a vet for immediate assessment. Correcting dehydration (easily and efficiently done by a vet) gets orphans off to a good start.

RECORDING DAILY PROGRESS

Rearing orphans can never be approached haphazardly. A daily diary of an orphan's weight, diet (the volume taken and the times the animal is fed), behaviour and any illnesses is invaluable. Of these, daily weighing is the most reliable indicator of an orphan's progress: weight will usually drop for the first week of captivity, but weight loss after two weeks indicates problems. Once orphans are progressing well, weighing can be done twice a week.

FEEDING FORMULA

Native mammal milks have a very different composition from cow's milk. Levels of protein, fat and calcium are much higher in the milk of native fauna, and carbohydrates differ mar-

kedly. Lactose, the common sugar in dairy milk, is very poorly tolerated and digested by young marsupials in particular. Native fauna milk also changes quite dramatically over the typically long periods of lactation, providing higher levels of fat, protein and sugars as young animals grow.

Cow's milk is therefore inadequate, and old-fashioned formulas should not be used as they make it extremely difficult to stabilise orphan fauna. Several low-lactose milk formulas now available include:

- Wombaroo milk formulas for all the common species of marsupials, placental mammals and monotremes (and which come with useful age assessment charts); and

- Divetelac, another low-lactose milk formula available from vets. When rearing marsupials (as opposed to puppies and kittens) the concentration of Divetelac should be gradually increased from one scoop per 70 mL of water to one scoop per 50 mL of water.

Using the correct teat is also important and each mammal species requires a teat of a different size and shape that replicates its mothers' nipples. These can then be attached to a glass syringe or a pet nurser bottle with graduated volume markings. (Refer to 'Macropod Orphans' on page 226 for further feeding details.)

Wombaroo products are available from a vet, or from Wombaroo Food Products, PO Box 151, Glen Osmond, SA 5064. (Suppliers of Wombaroo products for each state are listed under

'Useful Societies and Organisations' on page 299).

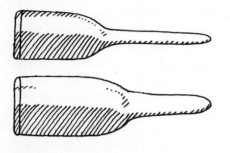

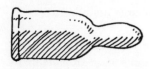

■ Mammal orphans require specific teats for successful rearing: above are two typically long and slender kangaroo teats, and a shorter teat for flying foxes.

AMBIENT TEMPERATURES

Ambient temperature means the surrounding air temperature, hence this measurement should be made within the substitute pouch or nest box near but not touching the animal or the heat source. Don't just guess: use a minimum/maximum thermometer. Accuracy is crucial.

Marsupial young are accustomed to the constantly warm, dark, moist and secure environment of their mother's pouch. Recreating this artificially is extremely difficult, but is one of the most crucial factors for success. Placental mammals also require warmth, but monotremes have a lower body temperature than other mammals and must be maintained in cool environments.

Using hot water bottles and radiators to provide warmth is inefficient and can be dangerous. Heating pads and electric blankets can be used, but they should be placed outside the pouch or nest box (hang the pouch against the electric blanket on a wall, or sit it on the heating pad). Fuel stoves run constantly are ideal, as maintaining a room to the correct temperature is far better than trying to heat a youngster and its immediate surroundings.

STRESS

Stress causes vulnerability to disease and it is as equally important to prevent stress in the orphaned animal as it is in recently captive adults. The following are some of the major sources of stress for orphans:

■ Overhandling of orphaned mammals by family, children and friends is common and stressful, especially if young animals are removed frequently from their pouches to be 'shown off'.

■ Forced removal from the pouch at too young an age can stress orphans who would normally be permanently undisturbed in their mother's pouch or nest. Conversely, some orphans are left in their pouches much longer than they would be in the wild.

■ Many orphans are taken to work with their caretakers—some cope, others become stressed. Orphans are best left quietly at home.

■ A lack of 'bonding' with caretakers causes insecurity

—bonding is best achieved if only one person feeds and handles a youngster.

Other stresses discussed elsewhere include poor diet and incorrect ambient temperatures.

DIARRHOEA AND DEHYDRATION

Diarrhoea is extremely common in hand-reared mammals and can result from a combination of factors, such as a diet too high in lactose, lack of warmth, irregular feeding patterns, psychological stress (see 'Stress' previous page) and from bacterial and yeast infections from poor hygiene.

Diarrhoea and the resultant dehydration must be treated quickly. Intravenous fluids given by a vet are the best and fastest way to overcome life-threatening dehydration. Treatment can then continue at home —the aim is to correct dehydration while still maintaining energy levels. This is done by continuing the formula, but supplying extra fluid in the form of water and electrolytes (such as Lectade or Vytrate from a vet) in between normal feeds. Give orphans as much fluid as they will drink. Keeping sick marsupials warm is equally as essential.

Enteric mixtures such as kaomagma and charcoal have very variable effects—correcting dehydration and body temperature are more important. Many debilitated orphans will also have thrush (see page 213).

An orphan's total environment must be assessed to discover the reasons for the diarrhoea.

HYPOGLYCAEMIA

Hypoglycaemia is the occurrence of low blood sugar levels and is a result of poor feeding and management practices, such as irregular and insufficient feeding of formula, and from the lack of a constantly warm environment. Animals with hypoglycaemia become depressed and lethargic and may have seizures. Low blood sugar often occurs with hypothermia (cold stress), and orphans may be found collapsed in their pouches after a cold night.

If given early enough, glucose and warmth give a rapid response, although intravenous glucose administered by your vet is the fastest way to treat hypoglycaemia.

HYGIENE

Maintaining strict hygiene is essential at all times to minimise the bacterial contamination of an orphan's environment. Feeding implements should be sterilised between every feed by boiling, or in human baby bottle sterilisers. Milk formula can be made up once a day and kept refrigerated, but any left over after each feed must be discarded.

Until an orphan learns to defaecate and urinate, you must stimulate these procedures by gently rubbing the cloaca after each feed, or between feeds if necessary. The aim is to keep the animal's living quarters clean and dry.

Milk formula, urine and faeces must be washed off an orphan whenever necessary, at least after each meal. Use a pure, gentle soap and dry with a hair dryer on WARM. An orphan's bedding should be changed immediately it becomes soiled, as orphaned mammals will quickly succumb to disease if they are left in dirty, wet and cold bedding. Always have available several clean pouch liners and pouches.

INFECTIONS AND OTHER PROBLEMS

Thrush, the yeast infection described on page 213, is very common in macropods, possums and wombats and results from stress and poor hygiene.

Pneumonia is commonly caused by impatient feeding techniques, so you should never force feed orphans. Reluctant orphans must be given small amounts of milk and then time to swallow—forcing milk will result in aspiration onto the lungs and secondary infection. Less than ideal temperatures will also cause respiratory infections. Coughing or heavy breathing should not be ignored; you should seek veterinary advice quickly for these problems.

Cloacal prolapse is not uncommon in baby marsupials and it can result from excessive rubbing of the cloaca (anogenital opening) to stimulate urination and defaecation, from *candida* infection, or from straining following the passage of diarrhoea. The cloaca everts and a pink, swollen mass is visible, and affected orphans may strain continually. If left untreated, the prolapse becomes dry, cracked and inflamed. Veterinary attention is advisable; a purse-string suture may be required to hold the cloaca in place until swelling subsides.

Alopecia, or loss of hair, occurs in some orphans. The cause is not known, but it may be due to incorrect diet and stress. The hair loss begins over the hindquarters and spreads from there, with thickened bands of skin also appearing on the tail. Treatment involves correcting the diet and making sure the orphan is getting some solid foods.

A major problem in lightly furred orphans is **xerosis**, or drying. In the pouch, the immature babies are kept constantly moist. To simulate these conditions and keep the skin supple and moist, frequent application of good quality skin lotions is required. Dimethicone lotions such as Skin Repair are best, or baby oil or Vaseline may be used.

Pathological **bone fractures** are seen in hand-reared orphans that are being fed correctly but lack regular exercise and sunshine for vitamin D absorption. This occurs in macropods especially: so refer to 'Passive Exercise' on page 229.

MARSUPIALS

Marsupials differ from other mammals mainly in their patterns of reproduction. After a very short pregnancy, their young are extremely immature at birth—tiny and hairless, only their mouths, front legs and shoulders are at all developed to assist them in their furry climb to the pouch. (Some marsupials lack a true deep pouch like kangaroos and instead develop a temporary depression during breeding.) Once inside the pouch the chosen teat swells inside the joey's mouth, firmly attaching the newborn to its milk supply. This is followed by a prolonged period of suckling.

Marsupials are the most abundant and varied of all Australian mammals (about 130 species), ranging from tiny marsupial mice to the largest marsupials in the world, red kangaroos. These divergent animals have evolved over many millions of years, each marsupial adapting to a particular Australian habitat from rainforest to desert.

Since European settlement, marsupials have suffered more than any other group of Australian animals. They have been slaughtered for their pelts, killed as predators and forced to compete for food or protect their young against introduced species such as rabbits and cats. Increasingly, they must cope with the destruction of their habitats, and as a result many exist in vastly reduced numbers and some are presumed to be extinct.

MACROPODS

Kangaroos and related members of their family are usually gregarious animals. They are herbivorous (eat vegetable matter) and usually nocturnal, being active at dusk and resting during the heat of the day in order to survive their hot and dry environment. This comprehensive group of mammals are often referred to as macropods, a word of latin derivation meaning 'big foot'.

The macropod digestive tract is similar to that of ruminants (grazing animals such as sheep and cattle) with a large, sacculated stomach that copes

with the bulky herbaceous diet. The lower jaw bones are not fused, resulting in a scissor-like chewing motion in macropods.

Like many mammals, kangaroos groom themselves regularly. Their small second and third hind limb toes sit inside a common skin sheath and the claws are used as combs. Joeys are cleaned meticulously by does every morning.

Life-span records of red and grey kangaroos indicate that although an individual may reach twenty years in the wild, half the young die before reaching two years of age.

The members of the macropodid family most likely to be encountered injured or orphaned fall into three groups: large kangaroos, wallabies, and wallaroos (or euros).

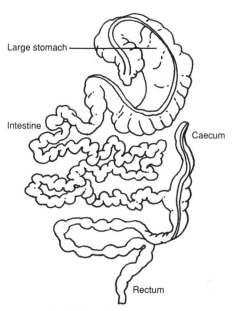

Large stomach

Intestine

Caecum

Rectum

■ The macropod digestive tract is rather like that of the cow or sheep: a large stomach is necessary to cope with the considerable volumes of bulky herbage consumed.

Kangaroos

The three common large kangaroo species are the red kangaroo (*Macropus rufus*), the eastern grey kangaroo (*Macropus giganteus*) and the western grey kangaroo (*Macropus fuliginosus*). Like wallabies and wallaroos, coat colour varies with location—red kangaroo females are often in fact a blue-grey colour.

Red kangaroos have very short, dense and woolly coats, and have distinct black and white markings on their muzzles. This species has the longest hind limbs, and bounds bent over with head down. Red kangaroos inhabit the semi-arid, inland plains and grasslands, and are well-adapted to heat and water deprivation. Red kangaroo males may reach 80 kg and stand 1.8 m tall. Does are always markedly smaller, weighing around 30 kg, but they are faster and more alert. Does take total responsibility for rearing and nurturing the joeys and are almost continually pregnant except in times of prolonged drought, when most kangaroos stop breeding.

The red kangaroo doe gives birth to a tiny, hairless joey that weighs less than 1 g, and is a mere 2 cm long. After making its way to the pouch, the joey remains attached to a teat for about six months (190 days) before leaving the pouch intermittently. About a month later (at 235 days), the joey vacates the pouch permanently, suckling from the outside until it is at least one year old. Total independence from the doe occurs by two years of age.

Meanwhile, a fascinating thing has happened. Immediately after giving

■ The distinctive head of the male red kangaroo, with black and white markings around the muzzle.

■ Distribution of the red kangaroo.

birth, a doe mates again but this pregnancy only develops briefly. The embryo is held 'in limbo' until the resident joey begins to leave the pouch. Within a day of permanent vacation of the pouch the new joey is born (this embryo will also resume development if a pouch joey dies prematurely). Most red kangaroo does are therefore rearing two joeys of different ages for about six months of each year. Each joey has its own teat that produces milk of different composition.

Grey kangaroos are usually slightly smaller than red kangaroos and have a hairy muzzle. They live in woodland and eucalypt forests rather than open plains, and they bound with their heads and bodies upright, like wallaroos. Their fur colour varies from grey to a dark brown.

The floppy eared and lightly furred grey kangaroo joeys first poke their heads out of their pouches at about six months of age. By eight to ten months they are completely furred and are constantly in and out of the

■ Distribution of the Eastern (horizontal lines) and Western (vertical lines) grey kangaroos.

pouch, leaving it permanently at about ten months of age. They remain with the does to suckle from the outside for a further eight months.

The grey kangaroo doe's reproduction differs from that of red kangaroo's. Grey does do not normally mate until their joeys have permanently left the pouch and the next joey is born in a little over a month. They too, suckle two joeys of different sizes for six to seven months.

For macropod 'Handling', 'Nutrition', 'Disease', and 'Macropod Orphans' see sections following 'Wallaroos' overleaf.

Wallabies

Wallabies are virtually identical to kangaroos except for their smaller size; 20 kg is considered a maximum size for wallabies. They are a very diverse group, but all prefer to inhabit forest undergrowth and scrub. The

■ The grey kangaroo has a soft, furred muzzle.

rock wallaby species live amongst boulders, caves and cliffs and have well-padded hind feet with roughened soles to grip rocks as they travel.

For macropod 'Handling', 'Nutrition', 'Disease', and 'Macropod Orphans' see sections following 'Wallaroos' below.

Wallaroos (euros)

The various wallaroo subspecies have a wide distribution. Those that dwell inland are considered to equal the camel in their ability to tolerate dehydration. They have adapted extremely well to drought conditions, living on a diet of spinifex, and often drinking only once every two weeks. They differ from kangaroos by preferring steep, rocky hills (coastal or inland). Of the three groups, wallaroos have the shortest hind limbs and long, thick, shaggy fur. They hold their bodies more upright as they hop and have a stocky appearance. A large area of bare, black skin around their nostrils

■ The red kangaroo bounds with head bent over, while the grey kangaroo and wallaroo bound with their bodies upright.

helps to identify them.

Wallaroos have a similar delayed implantation type of reproduction to red kangaroos.

HANDLING

Manipulating the tail is the best way to control a kangaroo or wallaby, but the tail must be held by the base or it may be injured. Small to medium-sized macropods can be grasped firmly by the tail, then lifted off balance before being placed into a hessian bag, wool bale or other large, strong bag. Always keep the tail stretched back to keep control of the animal. If an injured animal is unable to rise, you should still hold the tail, but put pressure on the shoulders, and hold the back legs

■ Distribution of the wallaroo.

above the hocks to control them before placing the animal in a bag.

Placing a bag over the head often quietens macropods and it is essential to handle them gently. Apart from the dangers of stress myopathy, struggling kangaroos and wallabies can injure themselves if they are not held correctly, as sudden movements can cause fractures or tear ligaments.

Large kangaroos can be very aggressive and dangerous—a vet or wildlife officer may be needed to sedate and catch these animals, and at least two experienced people will be required. The tail is still used to control a large kangaroo, but beware of sharp claws on front and back legs and of the kangaroo biting. Once a large bag is pulled over their heads and bodies, these kangaroos seem to settle down quickly. Unless you are certain you won't stress these animals while handling them wait for professional help.

Legislation may soon require those handling marsupials commercially to use specific tranquillisers to minimise stress.

NUTRITION

The macropods discussed here are all herbivorous, so captive adults should be offered a varying mixture of the following: green grass, grass or lucerne hay, chopped fruit and vegetables (carrots) and grain in the form of sheep, horse or preferably commercial kangaroo pellets, which must be introduced slowly and never given in large quantities. (Kangaroo pellets are available from Doust and Rabbage, 1 Concord Avenue, Concord West, NSW 2138.)

An important component of the diet in the wild is roughage in the form of bark (branches of gum, wattle, casuarina and other native shrubs) and tough, fibrous grass. Supplying bark and other roughage to captive macropods keeps teeth and gums healthy and appears to help prevent 'lumpy jaw' (see below). Always supply fresh water.

Many hand-raised macropods develop a liking for 'human' foods such as bread, or even dog and cat food. These will only cause digestive upsets and should *never* be fed to them. Bread is too soft and is better replaced by roughage.

DISEASE

Macropods in captivity commonly develop certain diseases that relate to their diet, housing and to stress.

'Lumpy jaw'

Lumpy jaw has been recorded in many species of wild and captive macropods. The infection begins in tooth sockets, then spreads to nearby bone and soft tissue such as lips, jaw bones, tongue and neck. Internal organs such as the lungs and liver may become infected.

The organism causes necrosis (death) of the affected tissues and pus formation. Large swellings result that are particularly noticeable on the jaws. Affected animals, usually adults, become weak, refuse to eat, and may discharge from the nose and swellings on the jaw. Death may occur in days or several weeks.

Treatment is very difficult, so prevention is essential. Breaks in the lining of the mouth or of tooth sockets allow the bacteria to become established. Soft diets that include bread but no roughage lead to unhealthy gums and teeth; stress, poor condition and dirty surroundings can also be involved.

As the organism is common in faeces, it is important to remove the droppings of captive macropods every day. Feed animals above ground level to avoid faecal contamination of food, and don't crowd a group of macropods into a small area. Affected premises should be left vacant for eight to twelve months.

Coccidiosis

Coccidiosis is discussed more fully on page 213. Amongst macropods, coccidiosis most severely affects eastern and western grey kangaroos and certain strain of wallaby. Recently weaned captive animals are the most susceptible.

Eastern grey kangaroos have their own strain of coccidia, which is apparently not susceptible to the usual preventative drugs. The disease usually appears in orphaned grey kangaroos between emergence from the pouch and release into the wild and is rapidly fatal.

Toxoplasmosis

Toxoplasma gondii is a protozoan whose widespread contamination of the Australian environment is largely due to feral cats, as the oocysts are passed in cat faeces. Marsupials fed hay can be infected if the hay has been contaminated by farm cats, and carnivorous marsupials can become infected when eating raw meat. Refer to 'Toxoplasmosis' under 'Cats' (page 94) for details of this disease.

Although rarely causing disease in cats, marsupials are very susceptible to toxoplasmosis. The disease is usually fatal and primarily affects the brain and lungs. It is crucial that food for captive marsupials not be contaminated by cat faeces—feed above ground level, and prevent access by cats to food storage areas.

■ One method of spreading toxoplasmosis to hand-reared kangaroos is via hay contaminated by farm cats.

Other internal parasites

For more information on internal parasites see page 214. Have your vet perform faecal examinations on grazing animals about twice a year to check for parasites.

Tetanus

Tetanus is caused by a clostridial bacterium that produces a nerve toxin. Affected animals become stiff and have continual muscle spasms. The disease usually occurs in weaned macropods grazing outside and starts with a wound which the bacteria infect (for example when an animal is teething, or has a skin tear). It is as difficult to treat in marsupials as in other animal species. Once emerging from the pouch, have your vet vaccinate orphans against tetanus. Repeat the vaccination after four weeks and then again before release.

Nutritional myopathy

Capture myopathy is discussed on page 212. The disease occurs in hand-reared macropods that may have been chased or harassed by dogs, causing obvious muscle stiffness and the onset of paralysis within twenty-four hours. Animals are reluctant to move, their urine may be brown with muscle pigment and death usually occurs within a week.

Nutritional myopathy is a different disease that is thought to result from a combination of lack of exercise and deficiency of vitamin E. Adult captive marsupials (including possums) that are kept in small enclosures and are unable to exercise sufficiently are the most susceptible, and the more exercise is restricted, the more vitamin E becomes important. The disease causes the muscles of the hind limbs to shrink and paralysis may occur. Treatment with vitamin E can be helpful in many cases.

Bone fractures

Broken bones most commonly occur after car accidents, or when a kangaroo becomes tangled in a fence. Whenever possible transport these animals to a vet immediately for injury assessment. If you are unable to move the animal a vet or members of a rescue organisation such as WIRES may help.

Joeys taken from the pouches of dead does by the roadside should have all of their limbs and their tails examined carefully. Because of a joey's position in the pouch, often both back legs and the tail are fractured at the same level. Immediate setting is essential and must be done by a vet; homemade splints waste valuable time.

Intestinal obstructions

Joeys love to suck material like hessian and wool, but these fibres can be swallowed causing obstruction and very sick joeys. Make sure a joey's pouch or bedding is of non-fraying material.

Flea infestation

Flea infestation is common in captive marsupials that live in close proximity to the family dog or cat. Only flea powders *safe for cats* should be used; avoid other insecticides unless prescribed by a vet. After applying flea powder, always rub it into the coat well and wipe off any excess with a damp cloth. Macropods groom themselves like cats and could ingest any insecticide left on their coats.

MACROPOD ORPHANS

As joey kangaroos and wallabies are the most common marsupial young to be hand-raised, knowledge of their problems has grown significantly. The following notes which apply to kangaroos and wallabies as well as other orphaned mammals should be read in conjunction with 'Rearing Orphaned Mammals' (page 214).

Initial assessment

The initial assessment of any orphan joey should begin with a veterinary examination and treatment for any injuries or dehydration.

The next task is to determine the species of marsupial (a wildlife service may help) and to assess the joey's age and physiological stage of development by weighing and measuring tail and foot length (refer to the charts on the following pages). Remember to do this within the first week for greatest accuracy. All this information will allow you to estimate the correct times for leaving the pouch and for weaning and release.

Recording daily progress

Always keep a daily diary of your joey's weight, diet, behaviour and any illness.

The ideal growth rate for wild joeys is about 1.5% of body weight per day, but in the hand-reared joey this drops to about 1%. Hand-raised orphans never attain normal weight before weaning, therefore plotting weight gain is crucial.

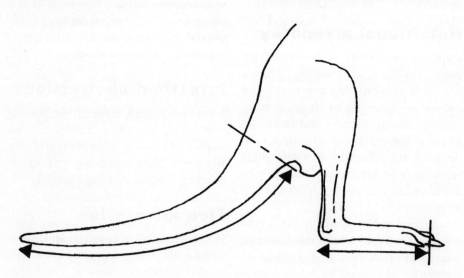

■ Age assessment is crucial for newly acquired orphans. Tail and foot measurements are used to age macropods.

GREY KANGAROO AGE ASSESSMENT

Age (days)	Tail (mm)	Foot (mm)	Stage of development	Ambient temperatures	Comments
90	99	53	permanently in	32–35°C	very hard to rear,
130	152	87	pouch, naked,		oil skin etc.
180	233	142	immature		
210	290	180	will soon leave pouch for short periods	30°C	finely furred, eyes open, needs sun, offer solids
250	376	239	in and out of pouch often, exercising	28°C	thickly furred, exploring, needs sun and solids,
310	526		fully out of pouch	warm room	provide solids, water, safe and warm rest area
365			wean: formula once or twice a day		feed an adult diet, give exercise and sun
540			independence		prepare for release

RED-NECKED WALLABY AGE ASSESSMENT

Age (days)	Tail (mm)	Foot (mm)	Stage of development	Ambient temperatures	Comments
60	46	24	permanently in	32-35°C	very hard
100	90	44	pouch, naked,		to rear, oil
130	132	62	immature		skin etc.
180	220	101	soon leaving pouch for short periods	30°C	finely furred, needs sun, passive exercise and solids
220	307	138	in and out of pouch, exercising	28°C	thickly furred exploring, needs sun and solids
280	463		fully out of pouch, active	warm room	provide solids, water, safe and warm rest area
350			wean: formula once or twice a day		feed an adult diet, give water, sun and exercise
up to 450			independence		prepare for release

Feeding formula

The formula given to orphans must be low in lactose, and it is essential that correct diets such as Wombaroo and Divetelac are used (refer to 'Rearing Orphaned Mammals' on page 214). Wombaroo produces milk formulas that match the age and stage of development of joeys.

Joeys require fixed feeding routines, which means you must feed them at set times each day (and through the night if necessary) at the same concentrations and temperature (30°C) and giving the same volume each feed. As joeys grow and the daily volume of formula increases, this must still be divided into equal volumes for each feed. If you need to change to a different formula, do it slowly. Mix the two formulas at first then gradually increase the proportion of the new one.

The Wombaroo species charts advise on feeding times and volumes. For Divetelac, a good rule of thumb is to feed naked or lightly furred marsupials every three hours, and thickly furred orphans every six hours. Decrease this to every eight to twelve hours by weaning age, but this is very dependent on the progress of the individual. Joeys usually drink 10 to 15% of their body weight daily (this means a 1 kg joey needs 100 to 150 mL per day divided into equal feeds). Feeding joeys over 20% of their body weight will lead to diarrhoea.

Never wean joeys too early—marsupials have very long lactation periods, and early weaning is very stressful. Use the age assessment tables to estimate time of weaning in the wild

and adhere to this strictly.

Use the correct teats for each species, which you can obtain from most vets or Wombaroo. Attach teats to glass syringes or volume-marked pet nurser bottles, as you must know how much joeys are drinking at each feed.

Many joeys refuse to suck for the first few weeks, so be patient: trickle a little milk in and wait until it is swallowed. Don't force feed animals or pneumonia may result from milk reaching the lungs. Sit joeys in their pouches on your lap and be prepared to spend some time each feed until orphans begin to suck.

When it is time to introduce solids (during the last third of pouch life), offer fresh grass and grass roots with a little soil after each feed. Leave the grass close to the pouch; joeys in the wild lean out of their pouches to nibble while does are grazing. As joeys begin to graze, start teaching them how to lap fresh water from a bowl (most will still prefer to suck their formula from a bottle). Grazing times should be early morning and late afternoon, as macropods dislike grazing in the heat of the day. Try to have available a mixture of grasses of mainly native species.

Joey maladjustment syndrome

Unlike many placental mammals, whose young take in protective antibodies in colostrum only in the first twenty-four hours of life, macropod mothers produce antibodies for a considerable part of their lactation period. This means joeys are getting, via the milk, a constant supply of protective immunoglobulins. Hand-raised joeys are therefore 'immune deficient', and are very susceptible to disease and stress.

Maladjusted and stressed joeys frequently develop diarrhoea, which is one of the most common causes of death in hand-reared joeys. The reasons for the diarrhoea are thought to be multiple, but basically relate to a failure to recreate the conditions of the pouch for young orphaned joeys, including the correct temperature, humidity, and volume and composition of the diet. Most joeys with diarrhoea are in poor condition with rough coats, and are depressed and very dehydrated. Any joey that develops diarrhoea must be treated *immediately*. Refer to 'Diarrhoea and Dehydration' on page 217 for details.

■ In the wild, joeys are forced to have exercise in the sunshine by their mothers. Even hand-reared joeys too young to leave the pouch should be given passive exercise and some sunshine daily.

Passive exercise

Some hand-reared joeys emerging from the pouch break their bones when they are exercising, a problem which appears to be due to an overall lack of exercise and sunlight, and is seen particularly in those joeys that have stayed too long in their pouches.

In the doe's pouch a joey wriggles and stretches and, even at a very young age, parts of the body are hang-ing out of the pouch exposed to sunlight. The answer is to perform passive exercises after each feed on orphans, such as alternate stretching and bending of the limbs, and to encourage daily exercise as soon as joeys are old enough to exit from the pouch.

Stress

Sources of stress are discussed on page 216, and include overhandling; lack of bonding with a caretaker; forcing joeys to leave their pouches too early, too frequently, or for long periods before they are physiologically or psychologically ready and, conversely, allowing them to stay in their pouches for too long; early weaning; irregular feeding patterns; and failure to provide a suitable environment.

Ambient temperatures

Methods of achieving the desired temperatures are discussed on page 216. Naked joeys permanently in the pouch cannot regulate their own body temperatures, which must be maintained at 32 to 35°C. You can drop this to 28 to 30°C once joeys are lightly furred and emerging from the pouch. When orphans are thickly furred and completely out of the pouch, a warm room is still needed especially at night.

Monitor all heat sources by using minimum/maximum room thermometers near joeys. *Never* overheat; macropods lick their forearms to cool themselves, so if you notice this behaviour the joey may be too warm.

It is crucial that ambient temperatures be constantly maintained as fluctuations can be as stressful as cold temperatures.

Hygiene

Cleanliness of feeding implements, pouches and joeys is essential: sterilise feeding gear and wash the orphan and its bedding whenever soiled.

You must also take over the role of stimulating a joey to urinate and defaecate. Refer to 'Hygiene' on page 217 for details of all these procedures.

Artificial pouches

Joeys must be kept 'hanging' in homemade pouches, placed so that they just touch the floor. Make up several outside pouches of fairly sturdy material and design them to hang conveniently on a coat-hanger. You should then sew at least six pouch liners to allow for constant changing if it is required. Both the inner and the outer pouches should be made of non-fraying, non-synthetic, easily washed, soft material; flannel is an ideal choice. Avoid the traditional hessian pouches as they do not retain heat well and frayed edges

can be sucked and swallowed. Synthetic materials cause heel ulcers and are also poor insulators.

Behaviour

All mammals groom themselves and macropods are no exception—doe kangaroos groom their joeys at least once a day. The joeys take over this task fastidiously as they age, using their 'double' hind toes as a comb. An unkempt coat in older joeys indicates illness.

You must take the place of the doe by washing (and thoroughly drying) your orphan as required. Small washes may be needed after every feed and the passing of urine and faeces.

Many hand-raised joeys suck themselves or their pouches excessively, and this can lead to inflammation of favourite sucking areas like the toes, tail tip, testicles and cloaca. The problem is difficult to correct and if the area becomes ulcerated it may need to be dressed. Some joeys may do this because they are hungry so offer more frequent feeds. Other joeys may be stressed so always make sure the orphan's surroundings allow it to feel secure and comfortable.

Macropods 'chew their cud' in a fascinating manner: joeys will appear to be heaving and preparing to vomit, then may actually regurgitate a small volume of food, chew energetically and then return to normal.

Aggressive behaviour is a normal part of growing up for young macropods. Young adults may attempt to 'play' with their family by grabbing and kicking, but as their 'family' is now human and not macropod, this

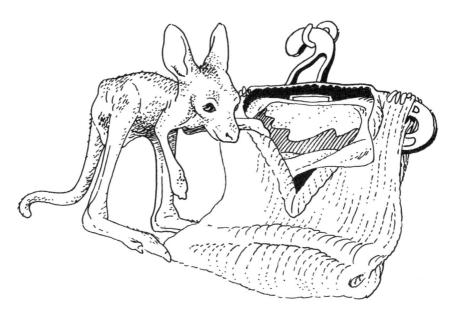

■ The young orphan joey soon learns to get in and out of its pouch, which should be hung near the floor for ease of access. Artificial pouches must be soft and warm with removable liners.

can become a problem with older and larger macropods that should already have been released into the wild.

Release

Before release, joeys should have spent time with others of their species and their attachments to their foster parents should be broken (see page 211: organisations like WIRES can help in these situations). Whenever possible this preparation for release should be organised before joeys have left the pouch permanently, as it is less stressful for them to join others of their kind before being weaned and totally devoted to humans; orphans should in fact be slightly fearful of humans before they are released.

Releasing several animals of the same species is wise as they give each other support while establishing their territories in the wild. The preferred times for release vary with the species, and advice should be sought from experts. As macropods dislike the heat of the day, release them at dawn or dusk.

POSSUMS

Possums have several common characteristics: they are nocturnal, they have long, flexible tails and different dentition to other marsupials and the females have a definite, forward-opening pouch. But apart from these characteristics, they are a very diverse group.

Like many marsupials, the crucial survival time for all possums is during their first year of independence (after weaning), when they are moving out from the family group and trying to establish their own territories. Males in particular suffer heavy mortalities.

HANDLING

Beware of the sharp claws on the front and hind feet of possums, and of their teeth. All possums can scratch and bite, and they move *fast*. Sugar gliders in particular have very long, sharp incisor teeth.

Before approaching an injured possum, have a strong bag (for example hessian) or a cage ready. If the possum is quiet due to its injuries, grasp the tail mid-length and lift, keeping the possum facing away from you and continually swinging the tail. Swing the possum into the bag straight away. Work quickly, as possums are agile and can climb up their own tails. If you are inexperienced at handling these animals, it may be easier to quickly wrap a very thick blanket around the entire possum and place it straight into the bag or cage.

■ The brushtail possum.

■ Distribution of the brushtail possum.

Common brushtail possum

The very abundant common brushtail possums (*Trichosurus vulpecula*) have adapted to European settlement better than most marsupials, living in rooftops, eating rose buds and generally residing happily alongside humans.

Brushtail possums have large ears, prominent pink noses and a fur colour that varies from silver grey to nearly black. The end of the familiar bushy tail is pink and hairless underneath. Like most possums the brushtail is arboreal (tree-dwelling), and has an opposable 'thumb' on the hind foot for gripping branches.

Brushtails are nocturnal, spending their days in hollow trees or logs, or in roofs and their nights foraging for food. They are omnivorous, eating both vegetable and animal matter including eucalypt and other leaves, fruits, buds, bark and insects. They are rather solitary, and the males in particular make much use of the scent glands under their chins, on their chests, and near their anuses to mark territorial boundaries.

Brushtail females give birth to a single young, which remains attached to a teat in the pouch for four to five months. After leaving the pouch the baby possum still suckles for several months, but travels clinging to its mother's back.

NUTRITION

As brushtail possums are omnivorous, they require a diet of mainly vegetable matter with some animal protein. Variety is essential. Offer them mixtures of the following: eucalyptus fronds, lots of different fruits and brown bread with peanut butter. Small amounts of cat food, dog kibble, or minced meat will provide animal protein, and you should supply a balanced vitamin and mineral supplement if the diet is not balanced and varied. Feed possums at dusk.

DISEASE

Brushtail possums adapt well to hospitalisation and generally respond favourably to medication. A vet must prescribe the treatment for the diseases described here.

Brushtails appear to be susceptible to several skin diseases. **Sarcoptic mange mite** can cause itchiness and hair loss, and is treated with insecticidal washes or Ivermectin. **Bacterial**

skin infections cause matted fur and scab formation, usually along the backline. Severe infections cause dehydration, septicaemia and death, but if treated early enough these problems respond well to antibiotics.

Coccidiosis can be a problem in older possums, or any that have started eating solids. Amprolmix Plus is a useful coccidiostat: check with your vet first. Sulphonamides are the best drugs for treatment.

ORPHANS

Orphaned possums, like all hand-reared marsupials, require constant warmth, strict hygiene, regular weighing and alleviation of stress (refer to 'Macropod Orphans' on page 226 for more detail). 'Pouch' orphan possums in small, well-padded and insulated boxes or hanging nests. As they grow and become active, it is wise to place their pouches inside cages at night to prevent mayhem in the household (unsupervised orphan possums have drowned in toilets at night). Place solid food out at dusk.

Refer to the age assessment table overleaf for the correct age of emergence from the pouch and, once possums are out and tolerating cooler temperatures, transfer them to large aviaries equipped with branches and nesting boxes. A red light bulb attracts insects at night so the skills of catching food and climbing can be learnt before release. House several orphan possums together at this stage if possible, and release them together. As they are nocturnal, always release them at dusk after a good feed.

The milk formula for orphan pos-

BRUSHTAIL POSSUM AGE ASSESSMENT

Age (days)	Tail (mm)	Feet (mm)	Stage of development	Ambient temperatures	Comments
60	44	15	always pouched, immature	32–35°C	hairless, oil skin
90	77	26	soon leaving pouch for short periods	30°C	finely furred, eyes open, needs sun, start solids
120	121		in and out of pouch constantly	28–30°C	thick fur, needs sun, exploring, active, on solids
150	174		fully out of pouch, active	warm room	provide solids, and water, keep secure and warm in a nest box
210			wean: formula once or twice a day	aviary	very mobile, adult diet
270			independence		prepare for release

sums must be low in lactose. Wombaroo produces two possum formulas to cover different stages in an orphan's development, or you can use Divetelac at one scoop per 50 mL of water. The age assessment table should help you estimate the approximate age of brushtail orphans.

Common ringtail possum

The much smaller common ringtail possum (*Pseudocheirus peregrinus*), almost as well adapted to living in the suburbs as the brushtail possum, is also nocturnal and arboreal. However, unlike brushtails, dietary preferences are strictly vegetarian and consist of leaves, fruits and flowers.

■ The ringtail possum.

Ringtail possums have soft grey bodies and tails that are white on the lower half. The tail is very prehensile

■ Distribution of the ringtail possum.

Ringtails begin to feed solids to their young like the koala, producing a soft faeces from the caecum thought to 'prime' the weanling possums' intestinal tracts with bacteria for digestion.

NUTRITION

As ringtail possums are more strictly leaf eaters, a wide variety of leaf material should be offered such as eucalypt branches with young growth and leaves and flowers from other native shrubs and trees. Try a mixture of finely minced fruit and vegetables, and brown bread with milk, honey and peanut butter. A varied diet is important.

with a roughened pad for grasping branches and carrying nesting material. Ringtails often build large, spherical nests from shredded vegetation in dense undergrowth.

Females give birth to a litter of two baby possums, which leave the pouch at about four months of age. They then cling to their mother's back, or remain in the nest between suckling.

DISEASE

Ringtail possums are not as robust as brushtail possums, and tend to succumb to infections such as *candida* (thrush) and *salmonella* diarrhoea, making strict hygiene essential. Oral

RINGTAIL POSSUM AGE ASSESSMENT

Age (days)	Tail (mm)	Stage of development	Ambient temperatures	Comments
40	47	always in pouch, naked	32–35°C	immature, oil skin
70	92	in last one third of pouch life, passively exercising	30°C	finely furred, cutting teeth, offer solids
100	138	emerging from pouch frequently	28–30°C	solid foods thick fur, mobile, needs sun
140	198	permanently out of pouch	warm room	adult diet, provide nest box
180		wean: formula once or twice daily	aviary	provide adult diet, need exercise and sun
over 210		independence		prepare for release

antibiotics (tablets) must be avoided in ringtails as they are very poorly tolerated.

ORPHANS

Follow the instructions for all mammal orphans (page 214) and brushtail possums (page 233).

Sugar glider

Sugar gliders (*Petaurus breviceps*) are only 30 cm from nose to tail tip, with relatively very long and fluffy tails. Fur colour varies from blue to brown-grey with a light coloured belly, but all sugar gliders have a central dark stripe from their foreheads to mid-backs. They have a very wide distribution, occurring in forests from the tropics to the alps, and are very active, nocturnal creatures. Sugar gliders are omni-

vorous, living on insects, small birds, mice, nectar and the sap that oozes from eucalypts and acacias.

Like all gliding possums, sugar gliders have flight membranes, which are extensions of the body skin that stretch from the fifth finger of the front foot to the first toe of the hind foot, and that enable them to glide over 50 m. The long tail provides

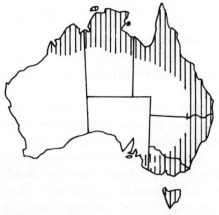

■ Distribution of the sugar glider.

■ Sugar gliders.

balance and is also used to carry nesting material.

Nests are shared by the group and are built from twigs and leaves in tree hollows. After two months in the pouch, the two baby possums remain in this nest for another month before beginning to venture outside. Mortality is high during the first twelve months of life, primarily from predation by kookaburras, owls, goannas and cats.

Sugar gliders live in small communities and use their scent glands to mark their territory as well as all the possums in the group. Within this familiar group they are relatively peaceful, but are extremely aggressive towards intruders. Injured gliders that are returned to the same site within a few weeks will have lost their common scent and are often killed by their previous 'family', making rehabilitation of this species very difficult.

NUTRITION

Being omnivores, sugar gliders need both vegetable and animal matter in their diet, so vary any of the following: eucalypt, wattle and other native shrub fronds, blossoms of these trees if possible, a variety of chopped fruits and brown bread or baby cereals with honey and peanut butter. Small amounts of animal protein should be provided in the form of mince meat, dog food, cheese, high-protein baby foods and boiled eggs. Whenever possible offer insects like crickets and mealworms.

ORPHANS

Follow the instructions for all mammal orphans (page 214) and for brushtail possums (page 233). House orphans in pouches or well-padded nest boxes until they are fully emerged, then transfer them to aviaries furnished with branches for climbing. As sugar gliders are so territorial, housing several together from an early age (before emergence) will produce a compatible group for release. Never release single sugar gliders, as they will be attacked fiercely by others in the same vicinity.

SUGAR GLIDER AGE ASSESSMENT

Age (days)	Head (mm)	Leg (mm)	Stage of development	Ambient temperatures	Comments
40	17	12	fully in pouch	32–35°C	immature, hairless
60	23	20	emerging from pouch	28–30°C	finely furred, offer solids
80	29	29	fully out of pouch	warm room	offer solids, needs water nest box, and sun
100	35		weaning	aviary	provide adult diet, needs sun and exercise

WOMBATS

There are two genera of wombats occurring in Australia: the common wombat and the hairy-nosed wombat. Both are ground dwellers, herbivorous and largely nocturnal, although they can often be seen sunning themselves and nibbling grass on cold winter days.

Wombats are extremely strong, weigh up to 40 kg, and are powerful diggers. Female wombats have well-defined pouches that open backwards, sensible in a burrowing animal. Wombats also have the distinction of having the largest brain (specifically, cerebral hemisphere) of any marsupial. They are relatively long-lived, surviving at least five years in the wild and over twenty years in captivity.

For wombat 'Handling', 'Nutrition', 'Disease' and 'Orphans' see sections following 'Southern Hairy-nosed Wombat' opposite.

Common wombat

Rather solitary animals, common wombats (*Vombatus ursinus*) spend the day resting in one of several burrows in their territory, and the nights grazing on native grasses, roots and tree bark. Although their habitat has decreased, they still have a relatively large distribution over the forested areas of south-eastern Australia.

Each wombat may have and share numerous burrows. Important burrows used for daytime sleeping can be up to 20 m in length and branch into separate resting areas.

These wombats have coarse, thick dark-brown fur, and bare noses. The female common wombat gives birth to a single young only 2.5 cm in length. The young wombat is carried in the pouch for six months, then remains with its mother until it is eighteen months of age.

■ The common wombat.

■ The black areas indicate the distribution of the hairy-nosed wombat; the shaded areas the distribution of the common wombat.

way to pick up a wombat is to approach it from behind, placing both arms around its chest or both hands behind the front legs. To carry the wombat, lift and hold it against your chest to prevent biting.

Hand-reared wombats should always be released if at all possible, as large wombats in domestic situations can be hazardous to humans and gardens—wombats need to have access to a considerable area of soil for burrowing. Adult males may also fight other wombats.

Southern hairy-nosed wombat

Hairy-nosed wombats (*Lasiorhinus latifrons*) have fine, soft and shiny coats, fur-covered snouts, and long, pointed ears. Now scarce, they exist only in the arid, treeless plains of south and western Australia near the Nullarbor. They have adapted to cope with water deprivation for three to four months if necessary, and will cease breeding in very adverse conditions. This species prefers native grasses to leaves and roots, and lives in communal burrows.

■ The bare-nosed head of the common wombat (left) is distinctly different from that of the hairy-nosed wombat (right). The latter has a much finer, furred muzzle and long pointed ears.

HANDLING

Wombats are extremely strong and can be aggressive, so care should be taken even when handling injured animals. Have a strong bag ready and place the wombat head first into it. The safest

NUTRITION

Wombats are herbivores, and although they may eat animal protein it is not well digested and should not be fed. Provide a varying mixture of the following: lucerne hay, fresh grass, chopped carrots and grain in the form of commercial kangaroo, sheep or horse pellets. These pellets must be introduced slowly—never feed them suddenly in large quantities.

DISEASE

Wombats adapt quite well to hospitalisation and treatment, and appear to be relatively free of disease. However, one of the most common and widespread problems in both wild and hand-reared wombats is **sarcoptic mange**, caused by the mite *Sarcoptes scabei*. This mange mite causes intense itchiness, redness, scab formation and loss of hair. In chronic cases, wombats can become almost bald with thick, wrinkled skin. The disease can be diagnosed by veterinary examination of skin scrapings under a microscope (the mites live in burrows in the skin tissues). These mites can cause similar lesions in humans.

Weekly washing in amitraz or a similar insecticidal rinse is helpful to control the mites (these drugs must be prescribed by a vet as young wombats can be susceptible to insecticides), or injectable insecticides are now available. Unless treated early, this mange can be very difficult to cure.

Thrush (*Candida albicans*) also occurs in wombats, and can cause chronic diarrhoea and weight loss for weeks before affected wombats become very sick. Testing their faeces can confirm the disease and treatment with Nystatin can be started. Thrush can be insidious, with very serious lesions developing in the intestinal tract early in the course of the disease.

ORPHANS

Although robust when adults, young wombats are just as vulnerable to stress, cold and poor diet as any young marsupial (refer to 'Macropod Orphans' on page 226 for general rearing instructions).

COMMON WOMBAT AGE ASSESSMENT

Age (days)	Body length (mm)	Stage of development	Ambient temperature	Comments
60	107	permanently in pouch	32–35°C	hairless, immature
120	169	still in pouch	32–35°C	immature
180	208	preparing to emerge	30°C	finely furred eyes open, starts solids, needs sun
240	247	in and out of pouch constantly	28–30°C	well furred exploring solids, needs sun
290	280	fully out of pouch	warm room	solids, water 'nest box'

Pouch orphan wombats in well insulated boxes that feel secure and are well padded. The boxes may need to be placed inside cages at night once orphans assume nocturnal activity. Once fully emerged from the pouch, house orphan wombats in outside runs with provision for digging so that they can practise these skills before release. Adult wombats are difficult to keep in captivity, requiring plenty of room for the digging of burrows. Always aim for release, and try to rear and house several youngsters together.

Wild wombats may not be weaned until eighteen months of age, the time of independence. After twelve months of age (360 days) start weaning slowly, increasing the adult component of the diet.

■ The female koala, with young on her back.

KOALAS

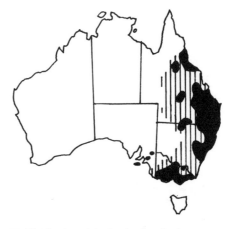

The distribution of the koala (*Phascolarctos cinereus*) has seriously diminished since the times when the Aborigine and dingo were its main predators. Massive slaughter to support a pelt industry almost resulted in the koala's extinction by the 1920s; today, habitat destruction and disease are causing their numbers to dwindle rapidly again. Their present status is classed as 'very vulnerable'.

Koalas are the only living members of their family and, despite their being arboreal and wombats being terrestrial, koalas are most closely related anatomically to wombats. Common features between the two include cheek pouches, a backward-facing breeding pouch and a vestigial tail,

■ Distribution of the koala: the shading indicates the koala's original distribution, while the solid areas show the much-reduced distribution of this native mammal today.

suggesting a common ancestor millions of years ago. These creatures are nocturnal and almost exclusively tree-dwelling, returning to the ground only to move to another feeding area.

They sleep propped between branches and they have opposing, sharply clawed digits to grasp branches as they climb.

Koalas are quite solitary—males have scent glands on their chests which are rubbed onto tree trunks to mark territory, especially during mating. A mature male can weigh 12 kg in Victoria (northern koalas are usually smaller, as are the females).

The tiny, naked newborn is a mere 19 mm long and weighs less than half a gram. It remains in the backward-facing pouch for six months, then rides on its mother's back until fully weaned at twelve months of age. Several months before leaving the pouch, the immature koala is fed a greenish fluid produced from the mother's caecum, as well as milk. This caecal faeces is thought to prime a young koala's digestive tract with bacteria ready for an adult diet of leaves.

Like most marsupials, the period of time following weaning appears to be the koala's most vulnerable. Koalas that survive to breeding age (two to four years) have the best chance of longevity, and koalas have lived for over fifteen years in captivity.

HANDLING

Although tame koalas can be very gentle, those in the wild are agile, aggressive and dangerous, biting and scratching with very sharp claws even if injured. Always approach injured koalas with care.

Be prepared with a strong bag and if possible, place it over the koala's head and body while it is clinging to a tree trunk. A koala may then be lifted

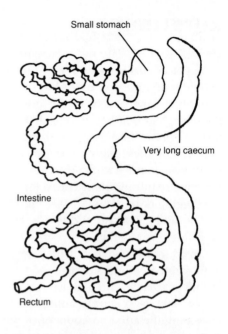

Small stomach

Very long caecum

Intestine

Rectum

■ The koala's digestive tract has an extremely long caecum (appendix) where much digestion of its bulky, leafy diet occurs.

off by grasping the upper front legs above the elbows from behind. Another method is to grasp the loose skin on the neck scruff and the rump and, holding the koala at arm's length facing *away* from you, place it in the bag. If an injured koala can climb, a rag tied to a long pole can be waved above its head to persuade it to climb down. Koalas are extremely sensitive to rough handling, so it may be quicker and less stressful for injured animals if you contact your state's wildlife service for help.

Caring for koalas is a specialist's task, so never be tempted to keep them at home. You must take injured koalas to the appropriate authorities as soon as possible. Every koala saved is important.

NUTRITION

Despite extending over a wide climatic range, koalas eat only the leaves from a small number of eucalypts (less than fifty species). This highly specialised diet makes their conservation difficult. In Victoria, the preferred gums are the manna gum (*Eucalyptus viminalis*), the messmate (*E. obliqua*), the swamp gum (*E. ovata*), the peppermint gum (*E. radiata*), and the mahogany (*E. botryoides*). In New South Wales, preferred eucalypts include the forest red gum (*E. tereticornis*), the Sydney blue gum (*E. saligna*) and the brush box (*Tristania conferta*).

Koalas can eat 1.5 kg of leaves daily, with a digestive tract designed to accommodate this bulky diet. Cheek pouches assist with the chewing of leaves and koalas have very long caeca (appendixes) of 2 m, the site of much bacterial digestion. They rarely drink, as adequate fluid is provided by their food.

If you are unable to take a captive koala immediately to a vet, zoo or wildlife service, pick a large variety of eucalypt fronds from the tree or area in which you found the koala. Don't just pick leaves as koalas prefer to nibble leaves off branches. Keep the koala in a quiet, dark place.

DISEASE

The adrenal glands produce hormones that help an animal in stressful situations. Koalas have smaller adrenals than most mammals and a very poor ability to cope with stress. They are also very difficult to treat, responding poorly to medication such as antibiotics and often refusing to eat.

Chlamydia psittaci

Habitat destruction, probably the most crucial factor affecting the koala's future, leads to stress and disease such as we now see in the much publicised disease chlamydiosis. Epidemics of what now appear to be *Chlamydia psittaci* were reported in the 1880s, and today chlamydiosis is still widespread amongst the koala population.

Chlamydia pstittaci is a contagious organism that affects the eyes, respiratory tract and urogenital tract of male and female koalas. The eyes develop a severe conjunctivitis with profuse discharge, pain and possible ulceration of the cornea. The infection in the urogenital tract is thought to be sexually transmitted and reproductive tract infections may cause scarring and irreversible changes in the cervix, uterus and fallopian tubes with resultant infertility. Infections occur in the urinary bladder causing incontinence ('dirty tail'), straining and loss of weight.

Research is proceeding into the many unanswered questions that remain concerning the spread and treatment of this disease. It is crucial that the general public become involved by forwarding any sick or injured koalas to the appropriate authorities. The future of the koala may hinge on this research.

MONOTREMES

Only three species of monotremes exist in the world today: the platypus and echidna of Australia and the long-beaked echidna of New Guinea. Marooned on the drifting Australian island continent like the marsupials, monotremes were able to evolve and thrive. They are the sole representatives of an ancient type of mammal.

All mammals evolved from reptiles, but monotremes have retained an intriguing mix of mammalian and reptilian characteristics. They lay eggs like reptiles, then suckle the newborn like mammals; parts of their eye and skeletal structure echo the reptile, as does their widely fluctuating body temperature range. Normal mammalian temperatures approximate 37° to 38°C, whereas monotreme body temperatures vary from 22° to 35.5°C (with an average around 32°). This makes the platypus and echidna vulnerable to heat stress, especially in captivity.

Like mammals, monotremes are furred, have a four-chambered heart, mammary glands and a larger brain than reptiles. *Monotremata* is the latin for 'one hole', relating to the cloaca, a single opening through which passes urine, faeces, sperm and eggs, and is a characteristic shared with marsupials.

ECHIDNAS

Echidnas, or spiny anteaters. (*Tachyglossus aculaetus*) have adapted to an extremely wide climatic range, extending over semi-desert regions to rainforests to the Snowy Mountains. Their ability to alter body temperature means they can adapt to changing activities and environments. In very

■ The distribution of the echidna.

cold climates they may enter a state of 'torpor' (similar to hibernation), where body temperature and metabolic rate falls.

Adult echidnas weigh about 4 to 5 kg and grow to 45 cm in length. They are thought to live for over twenty years in the wild (one zoo specimen lived for forty-nine years). Their spines, which are actually modified hairs, are surrounded by normal fur (in the Tasmanian subspecies, the fur is longer than the spines). These sharp appendages are an obviously successful means of defence. When disturbed, echidnas rapidly dig down vertically until their spines are just visible, or roll quickly into a ball, protecting their spineless abdomens.

In hot climates echidnas are mainly nocturnal; in colder areas they often feed during the day. They have no teeth and their long beak is necessary for finding and apprehending the diet—only ants and termites are eaten by these mammals, and a 3 kg echidna can eat 200 termites in ten minutes! Inside the long nose is a tongue which

■ The echidna has a very long, ridged and sticky tongue. This traps the large numbers of ants and termites that comprise this monotreme's diet.

is equipped with horny ridges and a covering of sticky saliva that traps ants, and which can stretch out for 18 cm. Soil is eaten along with the ants, producing the typical cylindrical echidna faeces. The long beak, a bony extension of the jaw, is also important for respiration and smell, and crucial for finding ants and termites. The mouth and nostrils are located at the end of this beak.

Male echidnas have long spurs on their hind limbs; however, unlike platypuses, these spurs do not connect to poison glands.

Female echidnas lay a single, soft-shelled egg that is rolled into the temporary pouch that develops during breeding; this pouch is merely a deep, muscular depression. The egg hatches in seven to ten days, and the minute, hairless newborn remains in the pouch for three months. The female echidna has no nipples, rather the

milk is exuded onto the skin through a series of pores from the mammary glands. Once its spines have developed, a baby echidna is placed in a burrow until it is weaned. Echidna milk is very concentrated, and once in its burrow the baby echidna is only fed every few days.

HANDLING

Echidnas are gentle, inoffensive creatures that cannot bite or scratch. The difficulty when catching injured echidnas is to avoid their protective spines. Use thick gloves if available and, as the echidna attempts to dig in, quickly grasp one hind leg and pull, lifting the animal, then grab the other hind leg. To find a hind leg, touch the echidna's forehead—this causes the hind leg to flick backwards quickly.

Never use a spade to dig out an echidna, as this usually results in injuries to the legs and snout.

Once caught, transport an echidna in a solid box. Keep it cool— they are very vulnerable to heat stress. A temperature of around 22°C is best, as echidnas can die if exposed to temperatures of 35°C or above.

NUTRITION

Recently captive echidnas may need the stimulation of natural food to begin eating, so offer them ants or termites, preferably in some soil. Once they are eating, provide a varying mixture of the following: raw mince meat, milk (milk powders for orphan echidnas can be used), eggs, grain breads, cereals such as bran, Farex, wheatgerm, canned dog food and water. Mixing the meal to a custard consistency may make it more attractive and easier to ingest. Keep offering ants and termites whenever possible. The Wombaroo company's small-carnivore food supplement is suitable for echidnas and provides necessary vitamins and minerals.

DISEASE

There are few reports of disease in wild echidnas, and sick captive echidnas respond well to medication and treatment. **Heat stress** must be avoided when in captivity; ambient temperatures of less than 25°C are ideal for sick echidnas.

Injuries to the long snout are common after car accidents; unfortunately, because the beak is necessary for eating, breathing and smelling, even minor injuries to the beak can be fatal.

ORPHANS

Orphan echidnas can be difficult to rear; any unquilled orphans *must* go to experienced caretakers. Their long snouts make feeding difficult, and they seem prone to diarrhoea and digestive disturbances. It is also difficult to assess their age.

In nest burrows the ambient temperature varies from 14° to 23°C; the young are only suckled once every two to three days; and they consume large quantities (10 to 20% of body weight) at each feed. Orphans should be maintained in an environment and on a feeding routine that recreates as closely as possible this natural rearing pattern.

Make nests in padded boxes (a small esky is excellent as it also insulates) and sit the pre-pared box on a heating pad. Use minimum/maximum thermometers as for marsupial young, but maintain orphan echidnas at around 23°C. Below 14°C, orphans may enter a state of torpor. Once orphans are well prickled, an external heat source is not necessary.

Offer a volume of milk formula equivalent to 10 to 20% of the echidna's body weight once only every twenty-four to forty-eight hours (diarrhoea may result from feeding too much too frequently).

Gentle and careful force feeding may be required for the first few days until the orphan sucks and accepts its new 'teat'. Orphans are fed with a human infant feeding tube attached to a glass syringe, and this tube may need to be placed into the echidna's snout at first. Be patient and allow time for swallowing after delivering each small amount of milk. Orphan echidnas will readily learn to drink from a bowl once they have adjusted.

Wombaroo produce an excellent milk formula for orphaned echidnas. Another formula can be made up using 15 g of Divetelac, 100 mL of water and one 50 g egg. Mix these together and then heat to a custard consistency, cooling before feeding.

Orphaned echidnas may be released when they are weaned and eating an adult diet, and weighing at least 1 kg. Before release it is essential that orphans have been taken out regularly to ant's nests. Break these open and ensure the echidnas can forage successfully for ants.

pellent, trapping air to keep the animal warm and dry even under water. There are no external ear openings; the ears and eyes are located in a deep groove that is closed when diving. The broad bill of the platypus is not horny like a bird's, but is soft and pliable, with a covering of skin over a bony framework. The bill is enormously sensitive and highly innervated, with receptors that can locate prey under water without actually touching it.

Food for the platypus consists of freshwater crustaceans, worms, tadpoles and insect larvae. Captured food is held in large cheek pouches until the animals can surface to breathe and

PLATYPUSES

The unique platypus (*Ornithorhynchus anatinus*) has adapted to an amphibian way of life: feet are webbed, the tail is flattened like a paddle and the dense, brown fur is water re-

■ Distribution of the platypus.

■ The platypus.

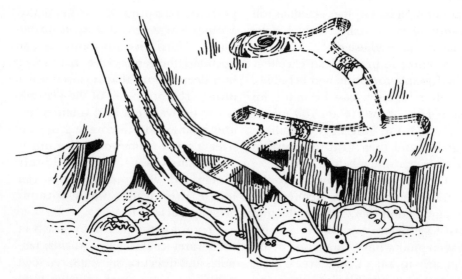

■ The platypus burrow: the female always builds a very long nesting burrow above water level.

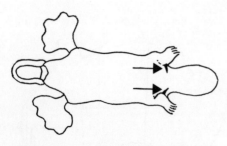

■ The male platypus has a very sharp and poisonous spur attached to each hind limb.

chew. Lacking teeth, the prey is ground between a series of horny ridges and plates. Feeding occurs when platypuses are most active, at dawn and dusk. Much time is also spent grooming their dense fur, and resting time is spent in one of several short, residential burrows. The female platypus constructs very long nesting burrows that may reach 20 m in length, with the entrances to these above the water line. Platypuses are well equipped with strong nails for digging.

Males are larger than females and more aggressive. They average over 1.5 kg and grow to 50 cm. The male platypus is the only venomous mammal in Australia, having a large hollow spur on each hind limb connected to a venom gland in the groin which can cause extremely painful swellings in humans. These spurs are useful in ageing a platypus.

The female lacks any sort of pouch, and once she has laid her soft and sticky eggs in the nesting burrow (between one and three are laid), she curls her tail and abdomen around them during incubation. The suckling newborn are left in the burrow nest of grass and gum leaves for about four months. Like the echidna, the female platypus has no nipples and milk is secreted from pores in the mammary glands.

Platypuses live in freshwater streams and lakes in eastern Australia and Tasmania and, although not considered endangered, these special mammals are extremely vulnerable to habitat destruction by pollution, irrigation and dam building, and to injury from fish netting and dogs.

HANDLING

Female platypuses won't cause injury, but approach males with great care (the large spur on the inner hind limbs indicates the male). Handle these animals by the tail, grasping it at the **base** and lifting. Always hold a platypus away from your body and place it in a cloth bag or smooth-sided box.

Keep platypuses cool; like echidnas they are very vulnerable to heat stress and must be maintained in ambient temperatures less than 25°C. Temperatures over 30°C can cause collapse.

These mammals must be handled gently, as stress is thought to be the greatest killer of captive platypuses. Never try to care for a platypus at home; instead contact a vet, zoo or wildlife service as soon as you can. Until you can place a platypus in their hands, keep it undisturbed in a quiet, cool and dark place.

EUTHERIANS

While Australia has a variety of marsupial and monotreme mammals, only a limited number of indigenous placental mammals (eutherians) exist. These are bats, rodents and seals.

Dingoes, although referred to as Australia's native dog, are thought to have arrived here less than 10,000 years ago. Other placental mammals (eutherians) now established in Australia have all been introduced since European settlement. Many of them, rabbits, cats, mice, donkeys and pigs for example, have adapted too well to their new environment and are creating many problems.

Eutherian mammals have a relatively prolonged pregnancy and nurture their unborn young in the uterus by means of a placenta. The young are then born at an advanced stage, requiring a minimum period of lactation before independent status is reached. Most placental mammals have a larger brain than other types of mammals.

BATS

The bat order of nocturnal placental mammals, consists of insectivorous bats, carnivorous ghost bats and larger fruit bats (or flying foxes). These mammals entered Australia only 10 million to 15 million years ago. Of the fifty or so species here, many are also found in New Guinea and Asia. Bats are the only mammals that can fly, possessing membranous skin extensions that stretch from their front fingers to their toes and tails.

Bats hang upside down by the claws of one or both hind feet to sleep during the day. They can do this with little effort because of a particular arrangement of ligaments in their feet (this is why dead bats can remain hanging until they are disturbed). Flying foxes wrap their wings around themselves when sleeping; smaller bats fold their wings alongside their bodies.

Bats are thought to have evolved in the tropics. Some bats migrate for warmth, while others that now live in cooler climates have adapted by entering a state of torpor, allowing their body temperatures to drop to as low as a few degrees above zero (Celsius). Female bats can store sperm during hibernation, delaying fertilisation until warmer weather and normal activity is resumed. Unlike most hibernating mammals, torpid bats survive on a minimal fat reserve. If a hibernating colony is disturbed and woken, the remaining energy supply may be quickly used up, leading to the death of many bats before warm weather returns.

■ The grey-headed flying fox.

Flying foxes

Flying foxes are the larger, fruit-eating species of bat. They have good eyesight, and have not developed echolocation or the complex ears and noses of smaller bats. Flying foxes have furred, rather fox-like faces with long snouts. They are gregarious creatures, living in huge camps or colonies with up to 10,000 to 20,000 bats in less than half a hectare. They always roost in vegetation, usually mangroves and other swamp trees and rainforest.

The diet of flying foxes includes the blossom and nectar of eucalypts, the fruit of figs such as the Moreton Bay fig, and other fruit such as lilly pillies. They will fly 100 km round trips for food and, although considered a

■ Distribution of the grey-headed flying fox.

scourge of orchards, they eat commercial fruit only when their preferred diet is scarce. Only the juice, nectar, pollen and seeds of fruit are swallowed and the fruit pulp rejected. Consequently these bats have short and simple digestive tracts, and contents pass from mouth to anus in less than thirty minutes! 'Runny' droppings are normal.

The female flying fox usually gives birth to a single young, which is suckled for three months, from nipples in her axillae (armpits). Until the baby is too heavy and is left at the camp, it is carried nightly to the feeding grounds.

HANDLING

Flying foxes are often injured by gunshot, poisoning (from pollution and orchardists) and by becoming entangled in fruit nets and fracturing bones or tearing wing membranes. If a mother bat is electrocuted, her baby may remain alive and clinging to her for several days. Enlist the help of your local county council to retrieve babies in this situation. Bats are very gregarious, so a lone bat seen during the day indicates problems.

Gentle if tamed, wild flying foxes can inflict injuries with their claws and large canine teeth, so always use heavy gloves or thick towels to handle them. Injured flying foxes that are still hanging should be quickly wrapped in a thick towel enclosing head and body. Only then should the hind limbs be unhooked from their perches, and allowed to grasp the towel (bats feel more comfortable if their hind-limb claws are attached to something). The bat should then be kept wrapped firmly inside a towel until placed inside a box.

NUTRITION

Adult fruit bats, which weigh 750 to 1200 g, prefer ripe to over-ripe fruit, and apples have proven to be one of the best foods for captives. Other acceptable fruits include pears, stone fruits and grapes (avoid citrus fruits as these are not eaten in the wild). You could base the diet on apples (about 330 g of apple per 850 g of bat per day) then provide as large a variety of the above fruits as possible. Offer the fruit chopped rather than pureed so the bat can spit out the fibrous portion of the fruit as it does in the wild. As with other captive mammals, it is important to monitor the weight of your specimen.

Wombaroo produces a flying fox food supplement for adults. Added to the fruit at the rate of at least 10 g per day it provides extra protein and the required vitamins and minerals. If the Wombaroo supplement is not available, sprinkle milk powder and calcium powder on to the fruit (one teaspoon to 2 kg of fruit). Water should always be available.

DISEASE

Always take injured bats to a vet for evaluation; broken bones may be able to be pinned and torn wing membranes will often heal.

Many injured bats become **dehydrated**—fluids administered by a vet will give fast results or, if the bat is bright and alert, you can try non-citrus fruit juice mixed with electrolytes such as Vytrate (available from a vet).

Internal parasites are quite common, and a faecal test would be advisable to detect any worm eggs. Orphans tend to pass worms naturally when they begin to eat solids, but heavy burdens can affect growth rate. **External parasites** such as fleas can be treated safely with cat flea powders (carbaryl). As bats groom themselves as assiduously as cats, take care to remove all excess powder.

Whitish-grey areas can appear under the wings of captive bats; these are **fungal** and/or **bacterial infections** resulting from urine scald in orphans that are not washed and dried regularly. They can also occur in adults that are unable to stretch their wings regularly in sunlight as they do in the wild. These lesions require topical ointments from a vet but, more importantly, the bats need access to sunshine.

As in all hand-raised orphans, **pneumonia** resulting from inhalation of milk is common. Don't force feed orphans or use a teat with too large a hole. Other respiratory problems may be seen in debilitated and injured adults. If antibiotics are used, Nystatin may be required to prevent secondary thrush.

REHABILITATION

Once they are over the critical illness, convalescing bats should be housed in large and sunny aviaries measuring at least 4 m by 2 m to allow for proper exercise and the stretching and drying of wings. Bats with prolonged recoveries should be housed with other bats as isolation is very stressful for these social and companionable animals (refer to the organisations listed on pages 299 to 300 for companion bats).

ORPHANS

The following applies specifically to the grey-headed flying fox (*Pteropus poliocephalus*), which is the common fruit bat orphaned. The little red fly-ing fox (*Pteropus scapulatus*) is also seen and both species can be housed together in captivity.

Initial assessment

Always assess as soon as possible the age and species of any bat in your care; *The Australian Museum Complete Book of Australian Mammals* (ed. Ronald Strahan, Angus and Robertson Publishers 1983) is an excellent reference for all native fauna identification and is particularly good for bats.

Most grey-headed flying foxes are born in October and November in New South Wales—refer to the age assessment table below or obtain a Wombaroo age assessment chart.

Baby fruit bats are born weighing on average 75 g. As with all orphans, regular weighing is the best indicator of progress.

Formula feeding

Like marsupials the milk of bats is low in lactose, and products made from cow's milk are inadequate for rearing orphans. Wombaroo produces a completely balanced milk formula for flying foxes or Divetelac (from a vet) may be fed at the rate of one scoop to 50 mL of water, with added vitamins and minerals.

Orphan flying foxes must be fed lying on their sides with their **heads lower than their feet.** Signs of lethargy and low body temperature may indicate that the bat is torpid; **never feed a bat in this state**. Warm the baby bat up slowly until it is active and alert before feeding, or inhalation pneumonia may result.

GREY-HEADED FLYING FOX AGE ASSESSMENT

Age (days)	Forearm mm	Head/body mm	Stage of development	Feeding formula	Ambient temperatures	Comments
7	66	116	immature	feed 3–4 hourly	28°C	furred, with naked belly
28	93	145	can hang unaided	feed 4–6 hourly	28°C	well furred
56	114	165	exploring, active	feed 6–8 hourly	warm room	started on solids
84	129	192	socialises with other bats	feed 8 hourly	house in aviary	adult diet, lives with other bats
140	148	231	weaning	feed 12 hourly		adult diet, glossy fur
180			body weight over 450 g			prepare for release

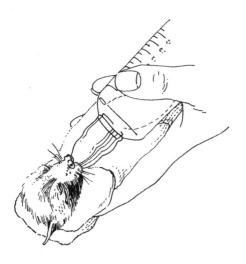

■ Young orphan flying foxes need constant warmth, and must be fed with their heads down.

Very young bats will need three to four hourly feeding which can be decreased to six hourly feeds by four to six weeks of age. Flying fox teats are available, or use small possum or dog teats. Introduce solid foods at about seven weeks of age using, for example, baby food (pureed fruit), and offer this between formula feeds.

By twelve weeks of age orphans can be weaned from the teat and on to finely chopped fruit. Continue the formula, but mix it with the fruit, and don't wean orphans completely too early. Even though they have been eating solids since ten weeks of age, baby bats are not weaned in the wild until about six months of age and, as for joeys, early weaning is very stressful.

By five months of age an adult diet should be being fed, preferably with the Wombaroo flying fox food supplement.

Ambient temperatures

Environmental temperatures of 28°C are critical for a bat's first four weeks of life, or approximately the time its abdomen remains naked. In the wild, baby bats are usually wrapped inside their mothers' wings for this period. To recreate this environment, orphans must be kept wrapped in soft pieces of cotton cloth, ideally man-sized handkerchiefs (see previous page). Once wrapped, baby bats should be placed securely with their heads down amid other warm bedding. Pet heating pads are one of the best ways to maintain the 28°C surroundings, but be careful not to overheat; use a room thermometer to monitor the ambient temperature.

Hygiene

Orphaned bats must be reared in a hygienic manner; sterilise all feeding implements after every feed, and wash and dry bats daily if necessary. Bats groom themselves constantly, so regular cleaning after meals and toileting is essential. Baby oil may be wiped over the fur and membranes of young bats once a day to keep them moist.

Urination and defaecation must be stimulated after each feed by rubbing the genital area gently; always sit baby bats up to do this (adult bats invert themselves from the hanging position for their toilet routines).

Growth and housing

Baby bats become active at an early age, stretching their wings within the first week of life. Allow more activity after each feed as bats grow out of their 'wrapping'. By four weeks, housing is required that will enable a baby bat's wings to be stretched and flapped without danger of fractures.

Constant warmth is also still required. Provide thin, plastic-covered wire, or make sure cages have mesh roofs for the bats to hang on.

Outside aviaries are ideal housing once bats are over twelve weeks of age, but they must be secure, well sheltered and safe from predators such as cats and large birds. They should also allow both shade and sunshine.

Socialising is extremely important for these gregarious animals; so try to house several orphan bats together in an aviary. This also helps to prevent over-dependence on caretakers.

Once orphan bats weigh over 450 g they can be prepared for release into the wild.

Release

The rearing of orphan bats should always be geared to eventual release into the wild. There are several wildlife groups experienced in preparing hand-raised bats for release, two of them being WIRES (NSW Wildlife Information and Rescue Service), PO Box 260, Forestville NSW 2087 and Kuring-gai Bat Colony Committee Inc., 45 Highfield Road, Lindfield NSW 2070.

The two groups mentioned above tag all orphans and adults, which are placed in cages within a bat colony and fed for a period of time before release. These organisations can also arrange for groups of bats to be housed together in aviaries before release. Young or rehabilitated bats should *never* be released singly.

Insectivorous bats

The smaller insect-eating bats have poorly developed eyes and use a system of echo guidance to fly and catch food accurately; they are virtually 'flying blind'. Their external ear anatomy is enlarged to detect high frequency sounds, and many have elaborate skin folds on their noses to help direct these sounds in narrow beams. They all have obvious tails. Voracious eaters, they can devour the equivalent of one-third of their body weight in insects in one hour. Although they are largely unseen, they are obviously important controllers of insect populations.

During the day these small bats live in colonies in caves, abandoned mines, tree hollows and buildings.

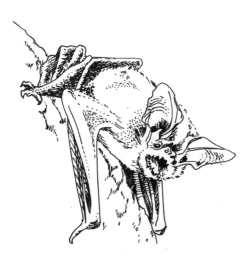

■ The lesser long-eared bat, one of the most widely distributed of the small, insectivorous bats.

Maternity colonies can house enormous numbers of bats.

HANDLING

Gentle handling is essential for these tiny insect eaters. Hold them in the palm of your hand with their heads between your thumb and first finger. Although small, they have sharp teeth and can bite.

Housing should consist of a box lined with soft material capable of providing warmth, as these small bats lose enormous amounts of heat from their relatively large body surfaces.

NUTRITION

Insectivorous bats are much more difficult to convalesce in captivity than the larger fruit bats. Many will only eat live food, and each bat needs to eat a very large proportion of body weight daily. Offer moths, cockroaches, flies and crickets. Mealworms, which are available from pet shops, can also be offered, although they must be supplemented with vitamins and minerals. Larger species may need thirty mealworms a day.

Some bats will eat blended mixtures of the following: cottage cheese, liver, dog food, hard-boiled eggs and chicken. Force feeding may be required for some, while others will learn to eat mealworms left in a cage overnight. Always supply captive bats with fresh water.

Because these bats are so difficult to keep in captivity while rehabilitating, they should be taken to a vet or wildlife organisation.

CHAPTER 6

RODENTS
& RABBITS

Domesticated rodents and rabbits are friendly, intelligent and affectionate pets that tame readily with gentle handling. Their small size makes them a practical pet for those unable to keep larger animals. However, their relatively high intelligence demands that they receive adequate affection and exercise, both mental and physical, to be happy and healthy. Like all the pets discussed in this book, even the humble mouse must have a suitable home in which to live.

GUINEA PIGS

Guinea pigs, or cavies, originated in South America. These gregarious, tailless rodents were first domesticated and kept as pets by the Incas of Peru centuries ago, then introduced to Europe by the Spaniards, from where they have become popular pets worldwide. They are available in numerous colours and hair lengths—but remember the long-haired species requires daily grooming.

Guinea pigs are sociable: they enjoy company, exploring and playing. It is important that you always start keeping guinea pigs in twos, preferably two females, so your pets will never become lonely. A pair will still respond with great affection to their human owners. Healthy guinea pigs have a life span of five to eight years.

Despite having sharp teeth, guinea pigs rarely bite. When being handled they always feel more secure if their bodies are supported by the palm of your hand. Pick them up by sliding your hand around and underneath their bodies, not by grasping their neck scruffs.

HOUSING

Guinea pigs can be housed in cages similar to rabbit hutches, consisting of strong wooden frames and floors with wire mesh sides and tops, and opening at the top to allow for easy cleaning and handling. A space of at least 1 m square for each pair will be needed for adequate exercise.

Like all rodents guinea pigs seem to need and appreciate nest boxes, or a little room or hollow log inside their hutch for security and comfort. For bedding, use hay, wood shavings or torn up newspaper, which should be changed daily and the hutch cleaned totally once a week.

Coming from a relatively warm climate, guinea pigs should not be left outdoors during cold winters; they are most comfortable at temperatures between 16 and 20°C. An ideal arrangement would provide an inside hutch for sleeping and an outdoor cage minus the bottom that can be moved daily around the lawn, making sure that this has a sheltered part for relief from sun and rain. Once guinea pigs are tame they can enjoy some freedom in the garden, but always

■ An ideal outside guinea pig hutch with room for exercise and a covered section for privacy and shelter. This hutch can be moved onto fresh grass daily.

constantly observe them to protect them against predators such as the neighbour's cat.

NUTRITION

Guinea pigs are herbivores, living on vegetable matter, and like all rodents they are constant eaters with teeth that grow continually throughout their lives. This means that food and water should always be available, and their diet must contain some hard matter for chewing exercise.

Commercial guinea pig pellets are the best basis for their diet, as they are completely balanced with all the necessary nutrients. If these are unavailable, use the more readily obtainable rabbit pellets—most pet shops stock these foodstuffs. Supplement the diet with fresh greens daily (such as grass, dandelions and clover), oats, grains and hay, and a variety of vegetables such as cabbage and carrot, and fruit like apples. Small amounts of wholemeal bread are a good treat.

Water is best supplied by a gravity-operated inverted bottle that prevents constant soiling of the water supply. Make sure it has a metal, rather than glass, spout.

Scurvy and vitamin C deficiency

Guinea pigs, like humans, are unable to produce their own vitamin C, so they are very prone to developing scurvy. It is essential that fresh greens be supplied every day, and if these are in short supply then add a balanced vitamin supplement to the diet daily. Foods rich in vitamin C include citrus fruits, juices and cabbage.

Symptoms of scurvy include lethargy, weight loss, rough coat, stiffness, enlarged joints and a reluctance to move. The condition can be treated with 5 mg of ascorbic acid (vitamin C) once a day for two weeks, or dissolve a 100 mg tablet in 500 mL of water once a day. Change and improve the affected guinea pig's usual nutrient intake.

SEXING

To sex a guinea pig, lie it on its back in the palm of your hand. Place gentle pressure near the genital opening: if the guinea pig is a male, a penis will easily become visible. Males also have a greater distance between their genital opening and the anal opening than females.

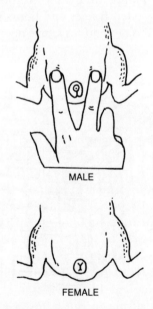

MALE

FEMALE

■ Sexing guinea pigs: gentle pressure on either side of the urogenital opening will cause the penis to protrude in male guinea pigs.

BREEDING

Only breed from your guinea pigs if you have definite homes waiting for the babies. It is far better to have two female guinea pigs than to be overrun with a male and female's unwanted offspring. Guinea pigs are ready to breed by three to four months of age. The length of pregnancy is quite long, sixty-two to seventy-two days, so the young are born very well developed. They have their ears and eyes open, are mobile and have full, thick coats of fur. Within several days they are nibbling solid food, and can be weaned at two to three weeks of age. Two to four babies are born each litter. The female should be separated from the male several days before birth commences, as she will soon be ready to mate again (most rodents have a post-partum oestrus, meaning that females will come into season very soon after giving birth).

MICE

Mice, when domesticated, are clean, smart and friendly and should live for three to five years. Like most rodents they are nocturnal, but appear to adapt to daytime activity when kept as pets. Two females make ideal pets; females have no odour, unlike males, and males may fight.

Frequent, gentle handling will tame mice easily and they will be happiest sitting in the palm of your hand. Don't hold them up by the tips of their tails. Until your pets are totally tame, pick them up by the base of their tails and place them on a table top. Keep very gentle tension on the tail bases while grasping mice behind their necks to pick them up.

HOUSING

Mouse houses should be made of metal, glass, or strong plastic, as wood soon disappears under the onslaught of rodent teeth. Like guinea pigs, the teeth of mice and rats grow continually throughout their lives and chewing on solid objects is essential for keeping teeth healthy and the correct length.

Mouse cages are readily available from pet shops. Choose one that is spacious, easily cleaned and has an exercise wheel and room for a nest box in the corner. Allow about 40 cm square per adult mouse, and make sure the cage is safe from any cats and dogs in the household.

Bedding can consist of sawdust, strips of newspaper or wood shavings, which should be cleaned once a day of faeces and uneaten food.

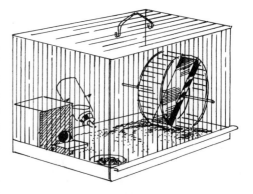

■ A good mouse cage is constructed of metal or similar hard material, has a cosy box for privacy and warmth, and a wheel or similar toy to provide exercise and entertainment.

Exercise equipment is essential for the mental and physical wellbeing of mice; wheels are available from pet shops, or you can add ladders or other toys. A small box in one corner satisfies a mouse's need to have a cosy nest for sleeping. Exercise outside the cage can be a problem unless your mouse is very tame. All mice love to explore and can be hard to find.

NUTRITION

Commercial mouse pellets are the best basis for a healthy diet, supplemented with oats, other grains, birdseed, wholemeal bread, fruits and vegetables. Green twigs are good for essential chewing exercise, as are carrots and hard dog biscuits.

Mice do like cheese, but only give them small pieces as weight problems can occur in mice overfed on household scraps.

To the side of the cage attach an inverted water bottle with a metal spout; mice will inevitably break glass spouts with their strong, sharp teeth.

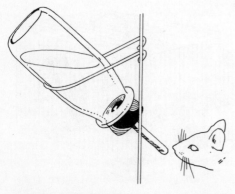

■ Safe and proper drinking bottles for rodents and guinea pigs are available from pet shops. They must have a metal spout to withstand the strong teeth of these small animals.

Food and water should always be available for these constant nibblers in very clean dishes, and each day you should remove any uneaten food.

SEXING

Sexing mice is difficult when they are young. A male mouse has a greater distance between his anal and genital openings than the female, and his scrotum is retracted inside the abdomen. The female has obvious nipples.

BREEDING

One pair of mice is capable of producing over one hundred and thirty young in one year, so breed them only if you have homes for all of these offspring.

Mice are ready to start breeding at less than two months of age and have an average of ten babies per litter. After a pregnancy of only nineteen to twenty-one days, the young are born naked and helpless, with ears and eyes closed. These open after about twelve days, and the babies are weaned at twenty-one days. Female mice, incidentally, will mate again the day after they have given birth so separate males and females before birth to prevent continual pregnancy.

RATS

Rats are amongst the most intelligent of all animals and can make very affectionate and entertaining companions. They have a life span of three to six years.

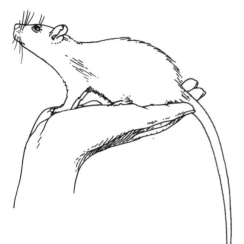

■ Rats can become loyal and gentle pets. Like all rodents, they feel most secure when the body is properly supported.

Like all rodents, rats feel most secure with their bodies fully supported by the palm of your hand. Before they are this tame they will bite if they are frightened, so always handle them quietly and gently. Don't pick rats up by the tips of their tails or you may damage the tail's protective sheath. Rats can also turn around and climb up their own tails. If you need to protect your fingers, grasp and hold rats behind their heads with your thumb and first finger.

Rats need housing similar to mice, but larger. Allow at least 60 cm square for each adult, and inside the cage include exercise equipment and a nest box.

Diet is also similar to that of mice, and should be based on commercial pellets with supplements as per mice. Rats often enjoy eating parrot mix, and their diet should always include hard dog biscuits, or carrots for chewing and teeth care.

SEXING

Rats can be sexed at birth, as a male's testicles are obvious even at this age. There is also a greater distance between the male's anal and genital openings than the female's.

BREEDING

Rats breed from two to three months of age, and have eight to ten babies each litter after a pregnancy lasting twenty-one days. The young are born hairless and with their eyes closed; the eyes open at about two weeks of age, and the young are weaned from three weeks of age.

RABBITS

In Australia the introduced wild rabbit is classified as a noxious pest and does enormous damage to pasture and farming land. Domesticated rabbits, on the other hand, are available from pet shops in beautiful colour combinations and make quiet and friendly companions. Never release pet rabbits because they have not been bred for life in the wild, and if they survive they only add to the nation's huge wild rabbit population.

Rabbits have sharp teeth and powerful hind limbs for scratching, but they are rarely aggressive when handled properly. *Never* pick rabbits up by their ears, as the ears are very sensitive and easily damaged. Until your rabbit is amenable to handling, pick it up by grasping the loose skin behind its neck and support its rump and hind limbs in your other hand. Like rodents, rabbits feel much more secure when their bodies are well supported.

Rabbits are lagomorphs, not rodents. A properly cared-for pet will have a life span of five to eight years.

■ This is the way to hold a rabbit securely and comfortably. Never use their sensitive ears.

HOUSING

Rabbits are best housed in a hutch consisting of a strong wooden frame and floor with wire mesh sides and top (rabbits also like to chew). Include a small house for sleeping, shelter and privacy. Rabbits, like guinea pigs, appreciate a temporary outdoor hutch without a floor that can be moved around the lawn daily. Once tamed, they also enjoy a romp on the grass, as long as they are constantly observed and protected from neighbouring cats and dogs. Use a floor covering of wood shavings or hay, and change this every day.

Allowing at least 80 cm by 130 cm for each adult rabbit will provide room for exercise, and remember that rabbits are burrowers: make sure that the sides of their permanent hutches are buried well below ground level.

NUTRITION

Rabbits are herbivores, so base their diet on commercial rabbit pellets supplemented with daily fresh greens, vegetables such as carrots (good for chewing), oats, hay and wholemeal bread as a treat. Rabbits eat continuously, so food should be available at all times.

Rabbits are abnormally heavy consumers of water, so it is *essential* that large supplies of fresh water are always available.

SEXING

In the male rabbit, the penis is easily protruded with gentle pressure on either side of the genital opening.

BREEDING

Rabbits are prodigious breeders, so you should keep two females unless you have homes for numerous bunnies. Rabbits begin breeding between six to eight months of age, have a gestation period of twenty-eight to thirty-six days (depending on the breed) and an average of six bunnies are born each litter. Separate males from females before the female gives birth and keep them separated during lactation to prevent mating soon after a litter is born. Bunnies' eyes open at about ten days of age, and they are weaned from six weeks.

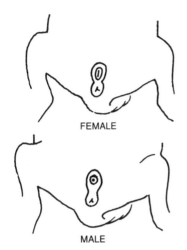

FEMALE

MALE

■ Sexing rabbits: the male urogenital opening is round and a longer distance from the anus than the slit-like opening of the female. The male penis is easily extruded with gentle pressure.

RODENT AND RABBIT DISEASE

Antibiotics are useful and commonly used drugs in most animal, bird and fish species. In rodents, rabbits and guinea pigs in particular, antibiotics must be used with great care and preferably should be administered by injection and by a vet. Antibiotics given orally (tablets) can seriously and sometimes fatally disturb organisms in the intestinal tracts.

Teeth

Rodents and rabbits all have teeth that grow continually throughout their lives. The propensity of these animals for chewing is therefore not a bad habit, but necessary exercise to maintain healthy teeth. Without hard matter on which to chew, the teeth of rodents and rabbits become too long and don't meet properly. Animals with overgrown teeth have difficulty eating and closing their mouths normally, and may salivate excessively.

Your vet can trim any long teeth to the correct level, but it is best to prevent this condition by providing carrots, dog biscuits (for rats and mice), twigs and even lumps of wood for chewing.

Skin disease

All the pets in this section can develop **sarcoptic mange**, a very itchy dermatitis caused by microscopic parasites. These parasites burrow into the skin, lay eggs and live off the skin tissues. Insecticidal washes are very effective treatments but you *must* obtain these from your vet; these pets are very sensitive to many drugs, including insecticides. The relatively safe carbamate and pyrethrin powders may be used on mice and rats, or dichlorvos pest strips can be hung near (but not in) a cage for periods of three days only.

Ear mites are common, causing ears to become itchy and a crusty discharge to build up in and around the ears. Affected animals will shake their heads and scratch their ears to afford relief from these irritating parasites. Insecticidal ear drops from your vet will cure mite infestations.

Ringworm is caused by similar fungi to those that occur in dogs and cats. The disease causes bare areas with scab formation to develop on the head and ears especially, or a severe infection may spread over the body. Obtain anti-fungal creams and rinses from your vet to treat ringworm.

Sometimes older female rabbits will **pull their hair out** in lumps from the chest area. Unless there are signs of inflammation or itchiness, this is most likely normal nesting procedure, as rabbits often use their own hair to line their nests.

Guinea pigs have a disease called **'lumps'**, a bacterial infection causing the lymph nodes to enlarge and become abscessed. Your vet may need to open and drain these swellings and prescribe antibiotics.

Internal parasites

Worms and the protozoan parasites coccidia occur in rodents and rabbits, but are usually only a problem in crowded situations. Diarrhoea can be the result of an excess of fresh greens, but if it persists or contains blood then take your pet and some fresh droppings to your vet, who will look for parasite eggs under a microscope.

Myxomatosis

Myxomatosis is a rural disease of rabbits and was introduced into the wild rabbit population in an endeavour to control their huge numbers. Unfortunately, as the virus is spread mainly by mosquitoes, it is possible for

pet rabbits to become infected and the disease is almost always fatal.

Rabbits of all ages can be affected, but young bunnies are the most vulnerable. The first symptom is a severe conjunctivitis: the eyes become inflamed and swollen and develop a profuse milky white discharge. Affected rabbits become listless, won't eat and have very high temperatures. Death may occur at this stage, or swelling of the head region may develop; the nose, lips and ears swell and the ears droop. The anal opening and the scrotum become very red and inflamed, with most rabbits dying in one to two weeks.

Vaccination is illegal due to the rabbit's status as a noxious pest. In country areas, keep pet rabbits indoors at dawn and dusk (the worst times of the day for mosquitoes) or house them in mosquito-proof hutches.

Snuffles

Snuffles, which is caused by the bacterium *Pasteurella multicida* and is the most important cause of illness and death in captive rabbits, is particularly common if large numbers of rabbits are kept together. The bacteria mainly infect the respiratory tract, causing conjunctivitis, nasal discharge and sometimes a pneumonia. Abscesses, ear infections and septicaemia (serious infection throughout the body) can also occur. The disease appears to be more serious in older rabbits, many of whom develop chronic and persistent infections, and antibiotic medication given early by a vet is the only effective treatment.

Other bacterial infections

Rodents can develop infections similar to the rabbit disease snuffles, causing nasal discharge and pneumonia. Other bacteria can cause infection in other organs, or even septicaemia, and a high death rate usually results. However, these bacteria are usually only a problem in dirty and over-crowded situations; pets kept in clean, dry and warm surroundings will rarely be affected by these organisms.

In some species (mice in particular), adult males will fight aggressively in the prescence of females, then develop abscesses from fight wounds. These should be cleaned and treated with antibiotics. To prevent fighting, house all adult males separately.

Tumours

Tumours occur quite frequently in mice, and appear as swellings under the skin anywhere on the body. They can be removed surgically, but many will regrow.

CHAPTER 7

REPTILES

Herpetology, the study of reptiles and amphibians, holds great fascination for a surprisingly large number of people. Reptiles are amongst the most ancient of animal orders, considerably pre-dating birds and mammals. They retain some unique features. As ecto-therms, reptiles are unable to inter-nally control their body temperature, so they must utilise the environment to thermoregulate; they bask in the sun for warmth and cool by retreating to the shade of rocks or burrows. Apart from crocodiles, all reptiles have a three-chambered heart (unlike the mammalian four-chambered heart), resulting in some mixing of arterial and venous blood. The body tissues are therefore less oxygenated, so that reptiles can move fast but only in short bursts.

Many reptiles have a well-developed sense of smell. The flicking tongue of snakes and many lizards carries particles from the external environment to be analysed by Jacob-son's organ in the roof of the mouth, after which messages are relayed to the brain. Prey must 'smell good' to snakes in particular, or they will not eat.

Most reptiles have keen eyesight and moveable eyelids. Snakes' eyes are lidless, unblinking and covered by a transparent lining of tissue, the 'spec-tacle' or optical scale, which is shed when snakes shed their skins. Lizards and tortoises have visible outer ears that are lacking in snakes, and which

Reptiles are either viviparous (meaning they give birth to live young), or oviparous (meaning they lay eggs). Inactive sperm can be stored in a female's reproductive tract, retaining its ability to fertilise eggs months or years later; female tortoises can lay their brittle eggs four years after being separated from the male. Breeding in captivity is difficult and will only occur under ideal conditions.

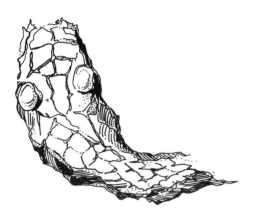

■ A properly shed snake skin should include the optical scales, or spectacles.

'hear' instead by detecting and analysing vibrations from their surroundings.

Non-venomous reptiles have some interesting defence mechanisms, changing colour to blend with their surroundings, or mounting great displays of bluff with brightly coloured gaping mouths or puffed-up bodies. Many lizards can drop their tails to confuse their enemies—their tails 'break' at one of the inbuilt weak spots along the vertebrae and, although most tails will regrow, they may look different.

Ecdysis is the term for the slough-ing or shedding of reptile skin. Snakes begin to shed at the mouth, literally 'walking' out of their old skin leaving it inside out. Lizards tend to peel their skins off in large patches, and tortoises shed their old scales one by one.

Many reptiles hibernate in cooler climates, allowing them to overcome difficult periods when food is scarce. Hibernating reptiles must be in very good condition to survive; if lacking in body fat, death may occur during hibernation.

REPTILES, YOU AND THE LAW

Reptiles, as part of Australian native fauna, legally belong to the Crown and as such are protected by law. The legalities of keeping reptiles, however, varies from state to state, each having a specific list of reptiles that may be kept in captivity by hobbyists. It is essential that you apply to your particular state's wildlife service for the relevant information and licence before you keep any reptiles in captivity (refer to the list of state government services on pages 299 to 300). These laws also apply to the temporary captivity of injured wild species.

This chapter is aimed at both the concerned individual who may rescue an injured reptile and wish to care for it during its return to health, and to the person who wishes to keep reptiles in captivity on a more permanent basis. As reptiles are so acutely sensitive to their surroundings, it is important that all keepers of reptiles are aware of the correct management procedures and common disease problems relating to these creatures.

RELEASE

If you are caring for an injured reptile always aim to release it after it has recovered from its injuries, and try to do this in the area in which it was found. If this is not possible, you should research an animal's normal habitat and geographical location, seeking help from wildlife organisations if you are unsure of the procedure (refer to the list of wildlife organisations on pages 299 to 300).

HANDLING

Obviously, self-protection is essential, so venomous snakes should *never* be handled by inexperienced people. For any other species, the general rule is to support a reptile's body evenly to give it a feeling of security and to restrict the animal as little as possible; reptiles struggle when they are held tightly. Gently hold an aggressive reptile's head behind the neck (refer to the handling sections for individual species).

Injured reptiles should be transported in a soft bag inside a box. They must be kept in a cool and dark place, with water, and assessed as soon as possible by a vet. You can then prepare a suitable environment for rehabilitation and treatment.

HOUSING AND ENVIRONMENTAL CONTROL

Reptiles, like native mammals, are extremely sensitive to their environment. Less than ideal conditions will initiate stress, which is the greatest killer of captive and injured specimens. It is therefore crucial for anyone contemplating keeping reptiles to understand the physiological requirements of these distinctive and interesting creatures. It is highly recommended that reptile keepers become members of one of the herpetological societies listed on pages 299 to 300.

CREATING NATURAL SETTINGS AND PRIVACY

Aim to provide reptiles with an environment that mimics their natural surroundings, using branches, rocks, water and foliage to suit the species. Within this 'natural' setting, hiding places should be constructed to enable reptiles to find seclusion, security and privacy. This applies particularly to recently captured specimens, which are easily stressed by exposure to humans or other reptiles.

AMBIENT TEMPERATURES

Ectotherms are totally reliant on external sources of heat. In the wild they can seek shade or sun to thermoregulate; in captivity, this responsibility

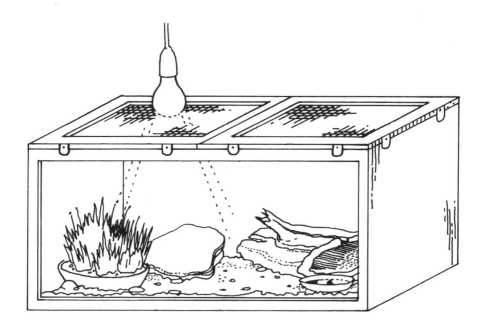

■ An excellent reptile cage: note the natural materials such as logs and herbage that provide privacy, the rock for basking, the flat water bowl and the heat source over one end of the cage.

lies totally with the keeper. Creating a constantly correct environmental temperature for captive reptiles is one of the most important and difficult tasks for keepers.

Housing for reptiles should be maintained within a 5° to 6°C range, the optimal temperature for each species lying in the middle. Heat sources must be placed to one side and sufficient space provided to allow reptiles to have a choice of temperatures. Reptiles must *never* be kept continually under the optimal temperature range.

The best heat source is an infrared or incandescent spotlight (or a 60 to 100 watt blue or red light globe) suspended outside and above one end of the cage. Coloured lights provide constant heating, while allowing darkness at night time when other lighting is switched off. Other means of heating include enclosing lights in small wooden boxes under or in cages; placing heating pads or coils under part of a cage; and for temporary heat only, placing cages near hot water pipes or central heating. Heat indoor ponds for tortoises with aquarium heaters.

Always monitor temperatures with a minimum-maximum thermometer; very high or very low temperatures can be fatal. Light bulbs used as heat sources can be connected to thermostats. Adult reptiles kept within their own geographical range may be kept outside in pits without any heating. If hibernation is not desired, they may be kept inside under heat during winter.

LIGHTING

Light, along with ambient temperature, plays a vital part in the control of a reptile's physiology. Captive reptiles should be maintained under lighting conditions that mimic normal daily patterns. *Never* provide constant lighting.

The best light sources are full spectrum fluorescent lamps such as True-lite, Gro-lux and Vita-lite. There is much controversy about the use of ultraviolet lamps to mimic sunlight; most herpatologists avoid their use as they can cause damage to skin and eyes. If possible, provide at least one hour a day of natural sunshine.

HYGIENE

Cages must be easy to clean as unsanitary housing leads rapidly to diseased reptiles. Uneaten food, faeces and shed skin must be removed every day, and cages should be constructed of materials that allow you to disinfect them when needed.

HUMIDITY

Most reptiles must be kept as dry as possible. A range of 33 to 70% humidity should be maintained, adjusted to each species' needs; rainforest reptiles for instance need abundant foliage in their housing and this should be with water sprayed twice daily.

Excess humidity produces infections of first the skin, and then internal organs. Too dry an atmosphere causes dehydration, kidney disease, incomplete skin shedding and gout.

As water needs to be present at all times, the ideal cage should contain a dry floor area (under the heat source) and a water source for drinking and sloughing. Water is best provided in shallow dishes or ponds large enough for each species to comfortably and totally submerge.

NOISE

Reptiles should be housed in a quiet location as inexplicable external noises, even machinery vibrations, can be very stressful and prevent adaptation to captive environments.

CAGE FITTINGS

Cages should be as natural as possible, but simple and easily cleaned. Floors

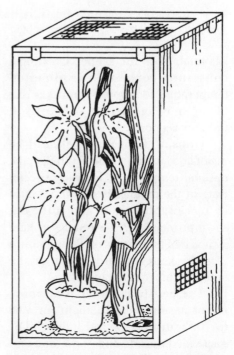

■ Tree snakes require tall cages with natural branches to mimic their normal environment.

must be dry and consist of pebbles, coarse sand or gravel. Provide branches and flat rocks under the heat source for basking, leaf litter for burrowing and hollow logs for hiding places. Always have water available in a wide, shallow dish, away from the heat source. Potted plants can be interchanged (sterilise the soil used for any plantings in a 200°C oven for two hours).

TYPES OF CAGES

Lidded glass aquariums are useful for all small species or juveniles, although heat control may be difficult to main-tain. Boxes that are combinations of glass, wood and metal are better alternatives, although the wood must be smooth, and sealed to make it waterproof. Hinged, top-opening lids are safest for cleaning and handling.

For large reptiles, and any kept within their climatic range, external pits are the best form of housing. These should be at least 1.5 m high with an inner overhang of 30 cm. The sides should be smooth and extend underground for at least 50 cm, and a drain should be included to allow easy cleaning. Furnish external pits naturally as outlined previously under 'Cage Fittings'.

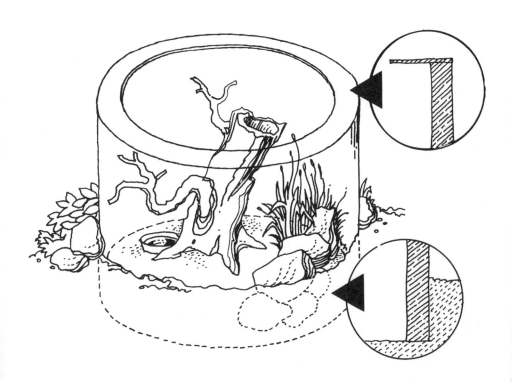

■ Larger reptiles are best kept in outdoor pits when in their natural climatic range. These pits must be extended underground and have a good overhang to prevent escape by burying or climbing. Branches, rocks and herbage mimic nature.

HIBERNATION

Hibernation is mainly important for breeding reptiles. Specimens housed outside can be allowed to hibernate if this is normal, or brought into a heated environment for the winter. In cold climates even indoor specimens will hibernate if the heating is lowered, so keep the temperature above 10°C.

Never allow reptiles in poor physical condition to hibernate— they need good fat reserves to see them through this period; and never disturb hibernating reptiles, as once awake they may use up their fat reserves prematurely. It is essential that all hibernating reptiles inside or out, should have deep dry leaf litter in which to bury themselves.

COMMON HEALTH PROBLEMS

Almost every disease seen in captive reptiles is a result of poor care, mismanagement and lack of environmental control. As such, these diseases are largely preventable. However, once a health problem exists it is wise to always consult a veterinarian. As many more Australians become interested in reptiles, more vets are becoming experienced in their treatment and care. A herpetological society will usually be able to refer you to a veterinarian interested in reptiles.

Sick reptiles should be isolated and kept in simple caging on frequently changed absorbent paper. Ideal conditions of temperature and humidity are essential, as is freedom from stress. The reptile's usual cage must be cleaned with safe disinfectants such as Hibitane (phenols are toxic to reptiles) and the gravel sterilised by placing it in a hot oven for several hours.

Newly arrived specimens should be quarantined for at least two to four weeks. Treat them for mites, and have their faeces examined by a vet for worm eggs and other parasites. The vet will also be able to advise on the use of any restricted drugs that may be necessary.

Chronic stress syndrome

Like all wildlife, reptiles are vulnerable to stress and are very sensitive to their surroundings. Reptiles that are maladjusted to captivity become debilitated, refuse to eat, lose weight, heal poorly and succumb to parasites and infections. The surroundings of stressed reptiles should be assessed critically and altered if necessary, and warmth is an essential provision. Force feeding may be necessary, and supplementation with vitamins and minerals. It is best to seek professional help.

Nutritional problems

As with mammals, an 'all-meat' diet commonly causes calcium deficiencies and calcium/phosphorus imbalance in reptiles (refer to 'Nutritional Secondary Hyperparathyroidism' under 'Dogs' on page 54). The result is shell deformities in growing tortoises, and swollen limbs and tails and weak and fractured bones in all reptiles. Whole animal diets must be fed rather than meat alone, as this mimics the diet in the wild. For amphibious species, cuttlefish or a piece of limestone in the water provides some calcium. Wombaroo produces a reptile food supplement that supplies carnivorous requirements.

Vitamin D deficiency occurs in those animals deprived of daily natural sunlight, and bone deformities result. Vitamin A deficiency is also very common, causing bulging and swollen eyes, conjunctivitis, blindness and pneumonia. It occurs especially in growing tortoises that are fed mainly meat. Unable to see, many of these tortoises refuse to go into water to eat and can starve. All reptiles in captivity should receive a total mineral and vitamin supplement (available from pet shops and vets) as well as a varied and balanced diet (refer to the nutrition sections for individual species).

Problems associated with feeding

The correct ambient temperature is essential when feeding reptiles, as their digestive enzymes will not function at low temperatures (less than 21°C), and ingested prey rots rather than digests.

Reptiles should also not be handled after feeding as they will regurgitate their food; snakes in particular should not be handled less than one week after feeding. Many reptiles will not feed unless they feel secure, so provide plenty of 'hides'. Scent is very important, especially to snakes, and live food may be necessary to stimulate eating.

Constipation usually occurs in reptiles that are being fed whole animals, including feathers and fur, but are deprived of the necessary space for proper exercise. Constipated reptiles may also be dehydrated, and small amounts of paraffin, gentle massage or enemas are required for those which are uncomfortable, can't coil and won't eat.

Obesity is common in captives that are overfed and underexercised, so provide these reptiles with larger cages, and control their diets.

Reptiles will eat their young if they are not removed promptly after birth. Mixing incompatible species, or large and small specimens in the same cage, will also often result in cannibalism.

Internal parasites

Worms appear to cause few problems in the wild, but can increase to significant numbers in reptiles in captivity. Affected reptiles become thin, lethargic, may develop intestinal obstructions and adult worms may be passed in their droppings. You should have your vet perform faecal examinations twice a year to identify any worm eggs.

'Skin worms' are immature forms of a tapeworm that harmlessly encyst under the scales of reptiles such as the common green tree snake. They may be removed through a small incision.

Traumatic injuries

Traumatic injuries commonly occurring in captivity include cracked shells, abrasions from rough cages, wounds from other reptiles in overcrowded situations, rough handling and bites from live food animals. Use killed prey wherever possible, as live mice and rats can inflict serious injury on reptiles that are lethargic and have low body temperatures. Always observe live animal feeding and remove uneaten prey within one to two hours.

All wounds should be treated promptly with weak iodine or hydrogen peroxide, and antibiotics should be administered if injuries are severe.

Hyperthermia

The use of inadequate heat sources can cause hyperthermia (heat stress) or burns. Bulbs or heating pads may have been placed where escape from their heat was difficult, or snakes may coil around naked bulbs placed inside their cage. Cage temperatures must always be constantly monitored.

Reptiles appear not to move away from excess heat and serious burns often result. Rapid treatment with cool water baths will reduce the damage, which should be followed by topical treatment and antibiotics but in the case of burns consult a vet.

Disecdysis

Shedding is a variable process that can occur several times a year to accommodate the life-long growth of all reptiles. Disecdysis, or incomplete shedding, results from low humidity, dehydration and skin damage. A build-up of scales may occur on the body, the toes and tail tip, or where the limbs meet the body, restricting blood supply to these extremities. Soak affected reptiles in water with weak

disinfectant for several hours, then gently remove the old skin. Snakes may retain only their spectacles; soften these membranes with wet cotton balls, then carefully remove with tweezers.

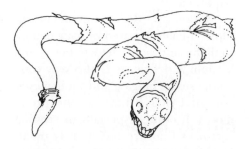

■ Reptiles kept in inadequate conditions may not shed their skins normally. The obvious tags of the old skin will need to be moistened and gently removed.

Necrotic stomatitis

Necrotic stomatitis (canker or mouth rot) a bacterial infection common to all captive reptiles, is secondary to such traumas as teething, oral wounds (caused by striking at cages when aggravated) and general debilitation and stress. Beginning as yellow-red patches of haemorrhage and swelling of the gums, the disease progresses to a build-up of thick, cheesy material in the mouth. If not treated quickly, the infection then invades the jaw bones, and spreads to the lungs and gut.

Antibiotics are usually required for this infection, so you should contact your vet as soon as you notice these symptoms. Isolate the affected animal, carefully remove the cheesy material and swab the lesions with weak iodine or disinfectant solutions every day, and continue the course of antibiotics.

Necrotic dermatitis

A similar infection to canker, necrotic dermatitis (or skin rot) is caused by dirty cages, excess humidity and low temperatures. The disease causes visible, expanding dark areas to develop under the scales, especially on the belly, which quickly become severely ulcerated. Treatment involves antibiotics, vitamins, improved housing and daily cleansing of the wounds.

Blister disease

Blister disease is another problem resulting from excess humidity, in particular from wet flooring. Raised areas filled with clear fluid appear on the affected reptile's belly. This clear fluid is then replaced by thick pus. Your vet will open and drain the lesions and the reptile may be treated with antibiotics. Daily flushing with a solution such as weak iodine will aid healing.

External parasites

Ticks are usually located at the junction of the limbs with the body or in the ears. They should be removed by grasping them close to where they attach to the skin with forceps (tweezers) and pulling firmly.

Mites are common inhabitants of reptiles, causing debilitation, anaemia and irritation when present in large numbers, and infected reptiles will twitch and rub against objects in their cages. The tiny white droppings of mites are often easier to see than the small brown mites themselves. Mites live around the mouth, eyes, ears and anus; to see them, lift the scales slightly, or brush reptiles over a white sheet. To treat adults, hang a dichlorvos pest strip above the cage (not over the water bowl) for one to three weeks. Juvenile reptiles are more susceptible to insecticides and should be washed in a weak disinfectant. Cages should be scrubbed and all of the contents destroyed.

Eyes

Snakes develop infections behind their spectacles that can be fatal. Their normally transparent eyes become opaque and bulging as pus builds up behind the membranes. The first signs of infection must be treated promptly, or the whole eye may become infected. Treatment requires the membrane to be opened and drained, and antibiotics to be administered by your vet. Be careful not to confuse this infection with the opacity of spectacles that are being shed normally.

Respiratory tract disease

Pneumonia and related diseases are common in reptiles exposed to low temperatures, overcrowding, stress and poor nutrition, and can be secondary to the infections described above such as stomatitis, necrotic dermatitis, etc.

Affected reptiles breathe with their mouths open and heads held up. They often wheeze, and bubbles of discharge appear at the nostrils and mouth. Tortoises may swim tilted to one side. Antibiotics from a vet are necessary to treat these diseases.

Kidney disease and gout

Kidney disease and chronic dehydration from high temperatures, water deprivation or low humidity results in the deposition of uric acid crystals in joints and various organs, especially the kidneys. Treatment is ineffective; affected reptiles usually become lame with painful joints, or the condition is diagnosed post-mortem.

High-protein diets can also cause gout, and this is seen commonly in obese and overfed lizards such as blue tongues and goannas.

Egg laying

Eggs can become retained, or 'bound', especially in snakes. The reptile will become lethargic and weak and you should contact your vet as injections of calcium and a hormone that stimulates the uterus may be required, or careful manipulation if the egg is near the cloaca may help. If these treatments are not successful, surgery will be required.

Egg yolk may also rupture or escape into the abdominal cavity causing severe and often fatal infections. Once this occurs, the reptile will become very lethargic and sick, and intensive treatment will be needed.

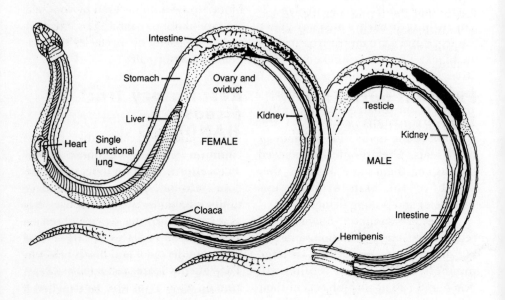

■ Simplified anatomy of female (left) and male (right) snake.

CHELONIANS

Strictly speaking, tortoises are totally terrestrial, or land-dwelling, and are herbivorous. Any chelonian that is totally or partly aquatic is a turtle; this includes sea turtles and the common Australian turtle of freshwater rivers and swamps. In Australia the latter are commonly called tortoises and are usually carnivorous or omnivorous.

Chelonians have an upper shell called the carapace, and a lower shell, the plastron, which are fused at the sides by bridges. They have a horny beak instead of teeth and are oviparous, or egg laying. The common species lay up to twelve hard eggs, which are buried in sand or laid in a simple hole. These eggs hatch in seven to ten weeks.

The common long-necked tortoise (*Chelodina longicollis*) grows to about 25 cm in length with a browny-green carapace and a cream plastron marked in black. The short-necked Murray River variety (*Emydura macquarii*) is longer (to 40 cm in length), and has a plain cream plastron and a yellow stripe on either side of the head.

■ Distribution of the long-necked tortoise.

■ Distribution of the Murray tortoise.

HANDLING

Male tortoises are the most aggressive—they will bite hard and all tortoises have sharp claws. To hold large angry specimens, grasp both back legs and lift, or hold the carapace between the back legs only. Younger and quieter tortoises may be carried by holding the carapace at each side. A foul-smelling fluid may be expelled if tortoises are handled roughly.

Tortoises should be transported in wet bags or in boxes. Soak the reptile

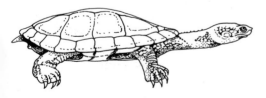

■ The long-necked tortoise.

■ Large, aggressive tortoises should be handled by their hind limbs, or by holding their rear carapaces.

before transporting and again on arrival to prevent dehydration. Allow plenty of space and ventilation to avoid overheating.

COMMON DISEASES

Chelonians are susceptible to many of the diseases affecting other captive reptiles (see 'Common Health Problems' on page 272). They also have more specific problems.

'Shell rot' is a bacterial infection resulting from poor water hygiene. It causes ulceration of the carapace and plastron and appears as multiple, discoloured, pitting lesions. These should be cleaned and painted once a day with weak iodine or similar solutions, and affected tortoises must be kept dry except when feeding. A course of antibiotics from a vet may be required in serious infections.

Egg yolk peritonitis occurs when yolk escapes from the oviduct, causing widespread infection in the abdomen. The sick female tortoise will strain without producing any eggs. This infection is very serious, and prompt antibiotic therapy is essential to save the tortoise.

Car accidents often cause serious shell injuries, so take injured tortoises to a vet immediately. Their wounds must be flushed and cleaned, antibiotic injections given and damaged shells repaired with fibreglass or any of the super glues—glueing agents must be applied only to the outer shell. Small cracks can be treated with daily cleansing and antibiotic creams.

SEXING

Young tortoises are very difficult to sex and it is only after four to five years of age that most male tortoises develop a longer and thicker tail than their female counterparts. The male long-necked tortoise will sometimes (but not always) have a slightly concave plastron.

HOUSING

Young chelonians up to 10 cm in diameter will live happily in a large glass aquarium; they require a water area large enough and deep enough to totally submerge, and a land area large enough to completely dry their shells. Coarse sand or pebbles make good flooring, and a large flat rock is necessary for basking and drying. Take your tortoise outside as frequently as possible into direct sunlight (always providing shade as well); vitamin D is essential for growing shells.

Water should be changed frequently (and/or filtered), keeping the

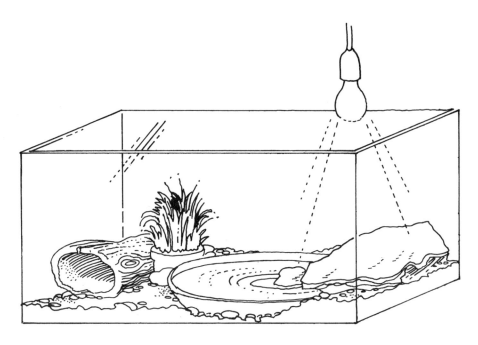

■ Glass aquariums for young tortoises should contain flat water bowls large enough for them to totally submerge in and rocks under the heat source for basking and drying.

old and new water the same temperature. Heat ponds in winter with aquarium heaters to 22° to 25°C and use suspended heat sources over basking areas to provide added heat. The optimal ambient temperature, which should never go over 30°C, is 26°C.

Mature chelonians should be housed outdoors. Their pits should have ponds that are gently sloping, large and at least 30 cm deep, and built for easy draining and cleaning. A space of at least 6 m square is needed for two mature tortoises, and the sides of their enclosure should be smooth and 60 cm high. Always provide some large, flat rocks for basking in the sun.

Unless in poor condition or from warmer climate zones (when they should be heated and housed indoors in winter), outdoor chelonians will hibernate. Provide them with plenty of deep, dry leaf litter and soil for burying, and don't disturb them. Only adults should hibernate.

NUTRITION

Tortoises are largely carnivorous. In the wild they eat small fish, crustaceans, insects and some aquatic plants, so in captivity they should be fed as many whole animals as possible, including small fish, shrimps, yabbies and insects. Supplement these with soaked and softened, dry dog food, pieces of raw fish, dandelions, grass, fruit and lettuce, small amounts only of raw meat and Wombaroo reptile supplement.

Chelonians must be fed in the water or they may not eat. Always remove uneaten food promptly to keep the water free of bacteria. Juveniles should be fed once a day, and adults three times per week, depending on the ambient temperature.

Vitamin D and calcium deficiencies are common in captive juveniles especially, and cause the growth of soft and distorted shells. Vitamin A deficiency causes blindness and pneumonia. Sunlight is required for vitamin D absorption, and vitamin A and calcium deficiency result from 'all-meat diets'. Cuttlefish or limestone placed in the water will provide some calcium, but unless whole animals are fed, supplement with vitamins and minerals.

LIZARDS

Lizards commonly kept in captivity in Australia include skinks, monitors or goannas and dragons.

HANDLING

There are no venomous lizards in Australia, but many can deliver painful bites and scratches. Never catch lizards by the tail, as many species can conveniently 'drop' their tails. Control the head of an aggressive or large specimen by approaching it from behind (use thick gloves, a soft broom, or a towel if handling an injured lizard); grasp the head behind the neck and lift the body with a hand under the belly. It is essential that a reptile's body and tail is well supported at all

times—it will feel more secure and may lie on an open palm quietly.

The tails of large goannas can be used as whips and must be controlled - only experienced people should

■ Aggressive smaller lizards can be controlled by placing one hand just behind the head and by holding hind limbs and tail together.

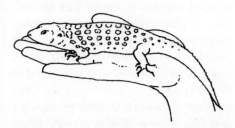

■ Quiet and tame lizards will sit comfortably in the palm of a hand. All reptiles feel secure when their bodies are supported along most of their length.

handle these large lizards. The head, tail and hind limbs must be all controlled.

Transport lizards inside soft bags (not hessian—pillow cases are ideal for smaller specimens). Carry one lizard per bag and place inside a strong, padded box. If possible, provide water before and after the trip, and avoid temperatures that are too hot or cold.

HOUSING

Only the smallest and youngest lizards can be kept in glass aquariums, and indoor cages must provide adequate space. Two skinks or small dragons need a space of 1.5 m square. Large and mature lizards are best kept in outside pits, and three large monitors will require a 9 m square area. Furnish cages and pits as described under 'Cage Fittings' on page 270, providing water and basking and hiding areas. Branches in pits will increase the area available for exercise and activity.

Lizards from warm climates should be kept in heated indoor cages in winter if they are out of their usual geographical location.

Any lizards kept together must be of similar size and of compatible species. Incorrect mixing of species and overcrowding leads to stress, cannibalism, fights over territory and food. Space should be adequate enough for less dominant individuals to eat in safety.

A coloured light bulb suspended high in an outdoor cage will draw insects that the lizards can catch. This provides exercise as well as a complete diet and applies to all lizards housed outdoors.

REPRODUCTION

Apart from several skinks that give birth to live young, all Australian lizards lay eggs. To incubate, bury eggs in damp and sterile soil, sand or vermiculite in covered plastic containers, then leave them alone—they don't need turning. Humidity of 74 to 80% and temperatures between 25 to 30°C are required for hatching to be successful. Incubation takes up to eight weeks, depending on the species. Young born in cages must be separated from adults immediately or they will be eaten. Feed the young an adult diet.

Skinks

Skinks comprise the largest family of Australian lizards, existing from desert to rainforest. They are glossy and smooth-scaled lizards with armour-like plates on their heads. Most of these lizards can 'drop' their tails.

Bluetongue skinks (*Tiliqua* sp.) grow to about 30 cm in length with rounded bodies of varying colours and relatively small legs and heads. When attacked, bluetongues will hiss and open their mouths, flickering their broad, dark blue tongues. They can bite, but are generally harmless. Blue tongues produce up to twenty-five live young each litter.

Optimal temperature for indoor housing is 28° to 30°C, but these skinks are best left outside and allowed to hibernate. Bluetongues are omnivorous, and can be fed soaked and softened dog biscuits, raw or boiled

■ The blue tongue lizard.

eggs, small amounts of meat, chopped fruit and vegetables. Provide them with whole food like insects and snails, and use the Wombaroo reptile mix to supplement the carnivorous part of the diet.

Shingleback or stumpy-tail skinks (*Trachydosaurus rugosus*) are slow moving and sluggish with fat, short tails. Growing to 30 cm in length, they have large, rough and raised scales and broad, blue tongues. Shinglebacks give birth to two large, live young each litter.

■ The shingleback lizard.

Unless kept where they are indigenous, shinglebacks can be difficult to maintain in captivity. They should only be kept west of the Dividing Range in New South Wales, away from coastal humidity, in their preferred hot and dry climate. Optimal temperature is around 33°C. House them inside during winter if you live in a cold area.

A shingleback's natural diet includes seedlings, flowers, fruit and some snails and insects. In captivity, feed them as for bluetongues above, but include flowers such as dandelions.

■ Distribution of the shingleback.

Cunningham's skink (*Egernia cunninghami*) lives in rocky country, growing to 30 cm in length, with rough scales that end in a keel on its spine. These skinks may be housed like bluetongues above. Being insectivorous, the diet should include whole insects where possible (such as grasshoppers, earthworms and fly larvae), supplemented with mealworms, small amounts of meat and the Wombaroo reptile food (or add vitamins and minerals).

■ Distribution of Cunningham's skink.

require a water bowl to lie in. Many male dragons have coloured chests, which become very bright during the breeding season and, as they are very territorial, they need adequate space to prevent stress.

Eastern water dragons (*Physignathus lesueurii*) can remain underwater for long periods. They live in the creeks and swamps of eastern Australia and can be fed raw fish, whole baby mice, softened, dry dog food and fruit.

Dragons

Dragons have rough, dull, often spiny scales, very long tails and gaping mouths that display a bright yellow interior. Unless kept in their natural area, they must be housed indoors during winter with an optimal temperature of 33°C. They all like basking under a heat source, but also

■ Distribution of the eastern water dragon.

■ The eastern water dragon.

Frilled lizards (*Chlamydosaurus kingii*) are very fast, running on their hind limbs, then turning and expanding their neck frill. They have smoother bodies than other dragons. Feed frilled lizards on whole baby mice, and insects, dog food, mealworms and flowers.

■ Distribution of the frilled lizard.

Bearded dragons (*Amphibolurus barbatus*) can change colour to blend with their surroundings and, when threatened, stand with raised body, gaping mouth and expanded throat.

They can grow to 60 cm in length and have rough, spiny scales.

Feed bearded dragons as for the other dragons, including for all three a vitamin and mineral supplement; lizards are as vulnerable to deficiencies as other reptiles (see 'Nutritional Problems' on page 272).

Monitors

The fast and agile monitors, or goannas, vary in size from 15 cm to over 2 m in length and have long bodies and tails, and forked tongues. Large specimens have powerful limbs and all have sharp claws and teeth. The most commonly kept varieties are lace monitors (*Varanus varius*) and Gould's or sand monitors (*Varanus gouldii*).

The optimal temperature for indoor housing is 35°C, but only juveniles or the very smallest goannas may be kept inside. Goannas require the usual hollow logs for security, branches, a shallow pool and plenty of

■ Distribution of the bearded dragon.

■ Distribution of the lace monitor.

■ Gould's monitor.

■ Distribution of Gould's monitor.

space—a group of three monitors only 1 m in length require an area over 3 m square.

Large goannas are all carnivorous, their natural diet consisting of snakes, small mammals (such as mice, rats and rabbits), birds, insects and carrion. A captive diet of whole animals is perfectly balanced; so try to feed goannas baby mice and day-old chicks supplemented with the Wombaroo reptile food, meat and eggs. Goannas

easily become obese in captivity so feed them only once or twice a week according to weight (this is less frequently than most lizard species).

SNAKES

This section refers only to non-venomous snakes as venomous species *must* be handled only by experienced herpetologists.

Snakes lack limbs, outer ears and eyelids. When healthy they slough their skin in one piece, which may occur several times each year. In the week or so before ecdysis (the slough-ing off of skin), snakes become irritable and stop eating, their scales become dull and their optical scales become milky. The eyes then clear a few days before shedding occurs. Rocks, branches and other rough surfaces must be provided as snakes rub themselves when shedding. (Refer to'Disecdysis'on page 274).

Some snakes such as pythons lay eggs, while others produce live young. Eggs are incubated for eight to twelve weeks as for lizards.

HANDLING

All snakes can bite, but not all are venomous. Unless a snake is tame and used to handling, pin the head with a snake stick (jigger), then quickly grasp the snake behind the head and along the body, always approaching from above and behind. As with other reptiles, the body must be evenly and well supported or the snake will feel insecure; two people will be needed to handle and support large snakes.

Transport snakes in soft cloth bags placed in padded boxes. Always let the head go last when releasing.

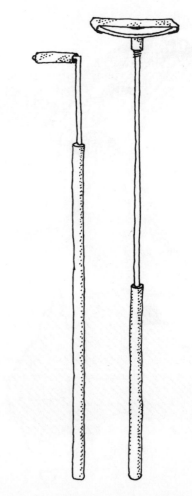

■ Experienced snake handlers use various types of 'jiggers' to control the snake's head.

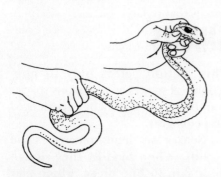

■ Snakes are handled by controlling their heads and supporting their bodies. Snakes should *never* be handled by inexperienced people.

FEEDING

All snakes are carnivores and are extremely sensitive about feeding; the correct scent is essential and most will require live food initially to stimulate voluntary eating. Whole animals must be fed—snakes have no chewing teeth, and their jaws can distend to accommodate large prey. It is possible to wean snakes on to freshly dead or frozen animals that have been thawed and warmed. Apart from being more acceptable to us, this prevents injury to snakes from live prey.

Usually only one animal is fed to the snake at a time, but large snakes

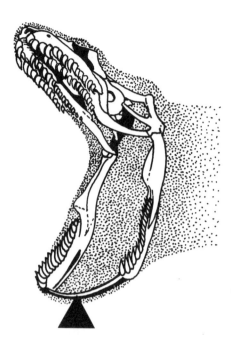

■ To enable them to swallow their prey whole, snakes' jaws are articulated to achieve a huge gape, and the lower jaws are fused by an elastic, stretching ligament rather than by fixed bone.

for example will eat several mice at each feed. Frequency of feeding varies with the season and the individual; feed once or twice a week in summer and less in winter, or not at all if the snake is hibernating.

Snakes must be warm enough and the ambient temperature must be correct (above 21°C) or digestion will not occur. Any transporting or excessive handling of snakes should not be done within one to two weeks of the last feed as many snakes will then regurgitate this meal. Any form of stress will also cause regurgitation. Overcrowding may mean a dominant snake gets all the food, or fatal fights may ensue over food.

Refusal to eat may mean sloughing of skin, insecurity, poor environmental conditions or, in healthy snakes, winter hibernation. Force feeding may be required if a snake continues to refuse food. Consult an expert if this occurs as this is a task for experienced handlers.

Pythons

Pythons are non-venomous snakes that kill their prey by constriction before swallowing them whole. Most are several metres in length, except the children's python which reaches 1.5 m, and they have smaller and more numerous scales than venomous species. All are nocturnal and have pupils that enlarge for night vision. As all pythons climb, branches are essential in their housing.

Carpet pythons (*Morelia variegata*) are very widespread snakes with beautiful markings. They are a beneficial species, preying on rabbits and mice in

■ Distribution of the carpet python.

■ Distribution of the children's python.

the wild; their captive diet therefore should consist of small mammals and day-old chicks. Optimal temperature under a heat source for indoor housing lies between 29° and 33°C.

Children's pythons (*Liasis childreni*) are small snakes, growing to 1.5 m in length. Chocolate brown with the usual cream belly, they have placid natures and make good pets. Optimal temperature is similar to carpet snakes, and both species like branches and a pond large enough for submerging. Feed children's pythons on small mammals and birds.

Tree snakes

Common green tree snakes (*Dendrelaphis punctulatus*) are non-venomous, slim bodied and very agile snakes that grow to a metre in length. They have blue-green bodies with yellow bellies. Being arboreal, tree snakes require tall cages at least 80 cm high, furnished with branches and a variety of foliage. Optimal ambient temperature is 32°C. Feed them whole animals such as small frogs, chicks, tadpoles and small lizards. All snakes can be supplemented with the Wombaroo reptile mix stuffed inside dead, whole prey.

■ Distribution of the common green tree snake.

CHAPTER 8

FISH

Comet

Lionhead

Veiltail

Shubunkin

COLDWATER AQUARIUM FISH

Goldfish are amongst the most ancient of pets, with Chinese literature containing many accounts of the breeding and selling of goldfish as long ago as 1000 AD. Since then, the Chinese and Japanese have developed numerous beautiful strains from a fish that was once a simple member of the carp family.

Goldfish are also one of the world's most undervalued pets. All too often regarded as easily replaceable and cheap, countless goldfish have succumbed to less than desirable surroundings. Providing the correct

environment is not difficult and, armed with a little knowledge, healthy and long-lived goldfish can be everyone's pets.

Always purchase the largest aquarium you can possibly afford; surprisingly, it will be far easier to care for. The first mistake made by most beginners is to buy the traditional goldfish bowl, which is not suitable for several reasons. A good oxygen supply is essential for healthy fish and, as oxygen is absorbed through the water surface, a large surface area is important whereas depth of water is not. Goldfish bowls with their narrow necks have a very small water surface area compared to rectangular aquariums. Small bowls and tanks also become polluted faster, their temperatures are less stable and they are not as attractive as larger, well-planted aquariums.

Try to buy a proper aquarium stand, or at least ensure you have a strong table—water is heavy, and a relatively small tank 60 cm x 30 cm x 30 cm deep would weigh over 60 kg when filled with water. The tank should always sit on a cushioning pad to prevent cracking.

The location of your aquarium is also important. If you can't provide the correct lighting described below, try to place your aquarium in a bright area that receives a maximum of one hour's direct sunlight daily, as excess sunlight results in the thick growth of green algae, which requires constant cleaning. Conversely, lack of light means poor plant growth and an excess of brown algae. The ideal situation is to supply controlled artificial lighting for about ten hours a day. Never leave lights on continually over an aquarium, as fish require normal hours of darkness like any animal or bird. The most satisfactory lights are fluorescent tubes built into a reflector as supplied by fish dealers; otherwise horticultural tubes such as Gro-lux are often recommended as they encourage plant growth. Don't use normal incandescent light globes directly over the tank as they can become too hot.

An aquarium should always have a glass cover that sits on top of the tank above water, with a small space for air exchange (several centimetres is sufficient). The cover keeps the fish in, and cats and children out, cuts down on evaporation and supports the lighting.

WATER

Fish will survive only in unpolluted waters with a neutral ph range between 6.8 and 7.2. Tap water is usually satisfactory, although added chlorine in tap water can be a problem. To ensure it is safe and free of chlorine before being added to the aquarium, tap water can be stood in a bucket for three to four days, or 'water ager' tablets, which dechlorinate immediately, can be used. Rain water from tanks and water from copper pipes can be dangerous, so use a test kit (available from fish dealers) on this water which will enable easy and regular ph testing. Refer to problems with gravel and rocks under 'Furnishing the Aquarium' below.

Aquariums that are unfiltered will require partial or complete water changes several times a week. Filtered tanks will only require top-ups after syphoning off debris, or a partial water change (about 25%) monthly. Any water added should be 'aged' and dechlorinated, and must be the same temperature as the water already in the aquarium. The sudden addition of warmer or colder water, or water from a different source, will weaken fish.

FURNISHING THE AQUARIUM

A bare aquarium with fish and little else is neither attractive to onlookers nor to fish. Fish require privacy and a sense of security that only a well-planned and planted aquarium can give.

Maintaining healthy water is crucial for fish. Rocks picked up from the bush or pebbles and seashells from

■ Hardy plants for coldwater aquarium: (left to right) *vallisneria*, *cabomba*, and *ludwigia*.

the beach will often contain various chemicals and metals that dissolve in water, rendering it unsafe for the fish—one seashell can kill a tankful of freshwater fish. Therefore, always use aquarium furnishings from a reputable dealer, as these will be safer for your fish. This means gravel, plants and any rocks and ornaments.

In furnishing your tank you should aim to achieve as natural an appearance as possible. Gravel, preferably of one colour, is necessary for the rooting of plants, covers any undergravel filter and prevents shiny reflection on the bottom of the tank. Rocks add interest and provide hiding places for fish, and look best buried in the gravel and placed in natural clumps.

Live plants are important for maintaining a healthy balance in an aquarium and are necessary if a soft and natural effect is to be achieved. Plants, like rocks, create hiding places for fish and improve the appearance of the tank. A well-planted tank will have a lower rate of algae growth, and the fish will enjoy nibbling on different plant varieties, while also gaining extra nutrients. Gravel is sufficient for plants to take root, and fish waste products conveniently provide the necessary fertilisation, so soil is not required. Always buy plants from a dealer and, for goldfish, choose acclimatised plants from a coldwater tank.

FILTRATION

Lack of filtration is one of the major reasons for unhealthy goldfish. Filtration keeps the water circulating so that fresh oxygen is continually absorbed, the debris and waste products of the fish are removed, and the water is always crystal clear. This means cleaning is reduced to a minimum and the fish remain healthy. Many beginners assume that filtration will be too complicated and expensive, but neither is true. There are numerous types of filters available for even the smallest of tanks.

The most efficient and natural filters are undergravel or biological filters. These have a plastic grid which is placed under the gravel and water is drawn through the gravel bed. Useful bacteria colonise the grid and break down the harmful waste products from fish into chemicals that are utilised by

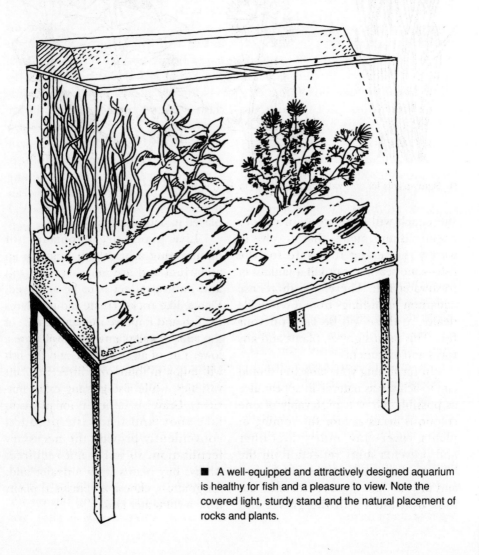

■ A well-equipped and attractively designed aquarium is healthy for fish and a pleasure to view. Note the covered light, sturdy stand and the natural placement of rocks and plants.

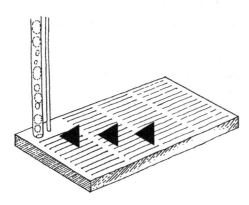

■ Undergravel filters are very efficient, easy to install and simple to maintain.

aquarium plants as fertiliser. Mechanical filters include box filters that use a nylon 'floss' to filter out the debris; this must be washed or changed at least once a week. Unlike biological filtration, mechanical filters keep the water clear but without the useful side effects of breaking down the waste products. All filters must be run continually.

SETTING UP

Everything you purchase for your aquarium must be washed before use, and to do this effectively you should use clean running water without soaps, detergents or disinfectants; even traces of these substances are toxic to fish.

Rinse out the tank well, wipe dry and then clean the gravel by placing it in a bucket and washing continually under running water until it is entirely free of dust and debris. You will need about 7 kg of gravel for every 15 cm square of aquarium; the gravel should cover the bottom of the tank to a depth of about 5 cm.

Put the undergravel filter in place then cover it with gravel, which should be sloped from the back of the tank to the front. This enables any solid debris to sink to the front where it can be easily syphoned out. Next, position the rocks in natural clumps and cover the gravel with newspaper (this is to stop the gravel being disturbed by the water), then pour in the water to half fill the aquarium. Remove the newspaper, add the plants and finish filling the tank.

Have a general plan in mind or, better still, plan your aquarium on paper before you purchase the plants. The usual mistake of beginners is to buy too few plants; most expert aquariasts recommend a beautiful, thickly planted aquarium as a backdrop for a few specially chosen fish rather than the reverse. Examine all plants carefully for signs of snails—many people like to add snails, but they can multiply very quickly, carry disease and eat all the plants. Rinse plants well before putting them in the tank.

Now be patient! Tanks should sit for at least three to four days without fish while the water ages and de-chlorinates.

BRINGING FISH HOME

Never overcrowd your aquarium with fish; the more lightly tanks are stocked, the easier they will be to manage and the healthier the fish. The general rule is to have 2.5 cm of fish per 15 cm square of water surface. Choose fish from reputable dealers and look for specimens that are alert, strong and fast, avoiding those with torn fins. Purchase fish that are roughly the same size and ask the dealer if they will mix amicably.

Fish are transported in plastic bags, which should *not* be emptied straight into the aquarium. Float the bags on top of the tank for about 20 minutes to equalise both water temperatures.

FEEDING

One of the greatest killers of captive fish is overfeeding. You should only feed fish what they will eat within five minutes. Fish can only eat small amounts, and leftover food quickly rots and decays. This in turn multiplies the level of harmful bacteria, decreases oxygen levels, increases ammonium levels, and quickly causes fish to become sick.

The average goldfish should be fed once a day, but if you feel your fish are hungry then feed smaller and more frequent meals, making sure all the food is eaten at each meal. Don't feed fish just before turning off the lights, as they won't eat in the dark and the food will rot.

Commercial foods available from pet shops provide complete, balanced diets; purchase several different varieties and use them alternatively. This will give fish variety and ensure that they are receiving the correct diet. Freeze-dried treats are available from pet shops for even more variety.

During holidays of short duration (two weeks or less), it is safest to leave fish unfed with the lights off. Kindly neighbours have killed more fish by overfeeding them than they have by starvation.

HANDLING

A fish's scales and skin are extremely sensitive and any rough handling will disturb their outer 'slimy' covering and leave small blemishes to become infected. Always handle fish using a proper fine net.

CLEANING TANKS

Other equipment required for aquarium care should include an algae scraper and a simple syphon. All sides of the tank should be scraped free of algae once a week, and obvious debris that has sunk to the front of the tank can be syphoned off. Replace any lost water with aged water of the same temperature and source.

OUTDOOR POOL FISH

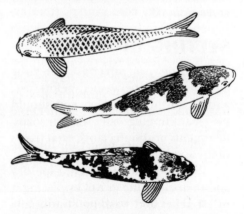

■ Japanese koi are beautifully marked, hardy fish ideal for larger outdoor pools.

Koi, spectacularly coloured and patterned fish that have been bred from common carp, originated in Japan, where their development and breeding has become almost an art form. Their superb colours can take up to five years to fully develop, so when choosing young fish observe them closely, for even the palest of markings will often become richly coloured. These fish will also tame easily and will learn to take food from your fingers.

Koi grow far too large for aquariums and for full growth require sizeable outdoor pools. As in aquariums, the eventual size of the fish is governed by the available oxygen and therefore the size and fish population of the pool.

Although koi are the best outdoor fish, certain varieties of goldfish will also thrive in outdoor pools. Comets and shubunkins are hardy, but lionheads will need to winter indoors.

Many types of outdoor ponds are now available. Basically, they should be wider than they are deep, although in areas with very cold winters (that experience sharp frosts or snow) a depth of at least 45 cm is required. The best ponds are located where they can get some sun and shade each day, as fish can actually become sunburnt if kept in shallow, unplanted and unsheltered ponds.

The principles of caring for outdoor fish are similar to those for aquarium fish:

■ Don't overcrowd ponds with fish.

■ Consider filtration. Filtration is desirable but not essential—the water will remain clearer, but some plants like water lilies prefer still water.

■ Fill and allow new ponds to 'sit' for two to three weeks before being stocked with fish—the best time to stock and plant is early spring.

■ Use plants. Outdoor fish also like privacy and hiding places, preferably provided by plants, which also greatly improve a pond's appearance. There are nurseries that specialise in water plants.

■ Clean ponds annually. If you have an algae problem, then the pond may be getting too much sun or it is not planted thickly enough. Don't keep cleaning pools as algae thrives in new water.

■ Don't overfeed fish. Commercial flake or pellet foods are available specifically for outdoor fish, and freeze-dried live food treats add variety.

Fish can adapt to eating a wide variety of food, including bread, finely chopped liver, canned dog and cat food, small pieces of cooked egg and earthworms, but make sure their diet is based on a commercial completely balanced product.

Fish outside will enter a state like hibernation during cold winters and will not require any feeding. The warmer the weather, the more they will eat, so feed a little every day in summer, less as the weather cools. As the weather cools, the fish will become less active and less inclined to come to the surface to be fed. Their behaviour will be an obvious guide for your feeding routine. Thickly planted pools will also provide fish with natural foodstuffs such as insect larvae, so during short holidays it is safer to leave fish unfed.

COMMON DISEASES

Apart from parasites that are carried by introduced fish, many aquarium diseases occur in fish that are stressed by poor management: lack of filtration, incorrect water ph, overcrowding, rough handling and dirty water from overfeeding. The quarantine of new fish for at least one month in a separate tank with its own equipment is an excellent practice, and is highly recommended for those with one or more aquariums and many fish.

Sick fish are obvious: they will sit on the bottom of the tank, their fins and tails drooping, and they may swim abnormally, tipping sideways or even floating upside down. Fins may be ragged and scales sticking out. Apart from salt water treatment, almost all the chemicals mentioned under 'Fungus', 'Fin Rot', and 'White Spot' below are contained in commercial preparations available from dealers.

Poisonings

Fish are extremely sensitive to changes in their environment and to the slightest pollution. They are affected by most aerosol sprays, including insecticides and room fresheners. The odour of fresh paint is toxic, as is nicotine; a room heavy with smoke can be rapidly fatal to fish. Detergents, soaps, bleaches and disinfectants, and heavy metals like copper and zinc from pipes and galvanised tanks can all be harmful.

Fungus

One of the most common diseases of cold freshwater fish, the spores of *Saprolegnia* fungi are normally present in most water sources, attacking fish that are weak with injuries such as torn fins. The fungus grows into greyish-white lesions like tufts of cotton wool, and is fatal unless treated quickly.

Commercial treatments are available from fish dealers, or you can make a 3% salt water bath. Using rock or cooking salt (table salt has additives), add 30 g of salt to a litre of water in a clean bowl and leave the affected fish in this bath for no more than ten minutes. Repeat this treatment daily until the fish are cured. Malachite green is another useful treatment.

Fin rot

Fin rot is a bacterial infection of torn and damaged fins that is often complicated by a secondary fungal infection. Affected fins become progressively torn and ragged, and fish with

■ (Top) This fish has the obviously moth-eaten and ragged fins of fin rot. (Bottom) Fungal infections result in the development of white, cottonwool-like growths on the scales and fins.

this disease will die unless treated. First always investigate any possible underlying problems with aquarium management; improving the fish's environment will help correct the disease. Other treatments include salt water baths and malachite green. If you have serious problems with large numbers of fish, obtain antibiotics from your vet to treat the entire tank.

White spot

White spot often occurs following the introduction of new fish or plants, or it can flare with the stress of sudden changes in water temperature. It is caused by *Ichthyophthirius multifilis*, an extremely contagious protozoan parasite that can spread rapidly through an entire aquarium of fish. The developing parasite buries under the fish's skin and encysts, creating a lesion like a tiny white pimple. Severely affected fish can be covered by a multitude of these white dots, hence the common names of white spot, and salt and pepper disease.

As the parasites are very irritating, the first symptoms are noticed when fish make mad dashes and rub themselves, often quite violently, against any object in the tank (this is known as 'flashing'). The encysted stage eventually drops off, multiplying into many hundreds of immature parasites that are released into the aquarium when the cyst bursts. Here they swim freely before attaching to another fish.

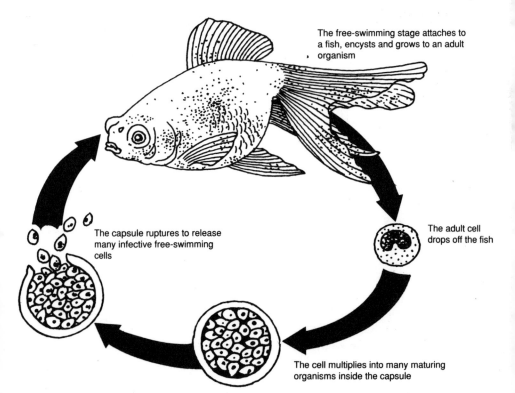

The free-swimming stage attaches to a fish, encysts and grows to an adult organism

The adult cell drops off the fish

The cell multiplies into many maturing organisms inside the capsule

The capsule ruptures to release many infective free-swimming cells

■ The white spot life cycle.

In the free swimming stages the parasites cannot survive for more than fifty-five hours without a host fish, and they are also then most susceptible to treatment (the encysted stage is virtually unaffected by most medications). Numerous commercial medications are available: malachite green is useful, as is quinine sulphate. Give these medications several times at three-day intervals to ensure complete eradication of the parasites.

Dropsy

Dropsy describes the filling of body cavities with fluid, causing fish to become bloated with raised scales. Dropsy is not usually contagious and is a symptom of an underlying disease, sometimes due to bacterial infection, but often of a cause unknown. The condition is difficult to cure, but antibiotics obtained from a vet are the most successful treatment.

Fish lice

The *Argulus* species are a lice of fish. They attach to fish, causing irritation and ulceration and, by feeding on body fluids, they also cause weakness. These round, flat parasites are 5 to 10 mm long and can be seen with the naked eye. In small infestations they can be removed manually, or treated with Neguvon (from a vet) or potassium permanganate.

Euthanasia

Never flush sick fish down the loo; this is cruel as fish can survive in toilets for hours. If you are totally squeamish, have your vet euthanase any sick fish. Otherwise, for a fast, painless death, place the fish on a hard surface and hit it firmly and squarely with a brick or similar solid object.

USEFUL SOCIETIES AND ORGANISATIONS

AUSTRALIAN CAPITAL TERRITORY

Australian National Parks and Wildlife Service
PO Box 636
Canberra City ACT 2601
(062) 46 6211

RSPCA
12 Kirkpatrick Street
Weston ACT 2611
(062) 88 4433

ACT Herpetological Group
c/o ACT Parks and Conservation
PO Box 158
Canberra City ACT 2601

NEW SOUTH WALES

National Parks and Wildlife Service
PO Box 1967
Hurstville NSW 2220

Taronga Zoo
Bradley's Head Road
Mosman NSW 2088
(02) 969 2777

Western Plains Zoo
Obley Road
Dubbo NSW 2830
(068) 82 5888

WIRES (Wildlife Information and Rescue Service Incorporated)
PO Box 260
Forestville NSW 2087
(02) 975 1633 (head office)

Native Animal Trust Fund Hunter Region
8 Conway Street
Toronto NSW 2287
(049) 59 5748 (24-hour rescue service)

Koala Preservation Society of NSW Inc.
PO Box 236
Port Macquarie NSW 2444
(065) 82 1213

RSPCA
201 Rookwood Road
Yagoona NSW 2199
(02) 709 5433 (head office)

Wombaroo agent: Helen George
(044) 65 1328

The NSW Animal Welfare League
65 Herley Avenue
West Hoxton NSW 2171
(02) 606 9333

Australian Herpetological Society
PO Box R-79 Royal Exchange
Sydney NSW 2000

Reptile Keepers Association
PO Box 98
Gosford NSW 2250

VICTORIA

Department of Conservation, Forests and Lands
240 Victoria Parade
East Melbourne Vic. 3002
(03) 412 4011

Royal Melbourne Zoological Gardens
Elliot Avenue
Parkeville Vic. 3052
(03) 347 1956

Healesville Sanctuary
Badger Creek Road
Healesville Vic. 3777
(059) 62 4022

RSPCA
3 Burwood Highway
Burwood East Vic. 3151
(03) 288 5111

Wombaroo agent: Lyppard Chemicals Pty Ltd
(03) 592 7733

SOUTH AUSTRALIA

National Parks and Wildlife Service
GPO Box 667
Adelaide SA 5001
(08) 216 7777

Adelaide Zoo
Frome Road
Adelaide SA 5000
(08) 267 3255

RSPCA
158 Currie Street
Adelaide SA 5000
(08) 51 6931

Wombaroo agent: Ian Hough
(08) 277 7045

South Australian Herpetological Group
c/o South Australian Museum
North Terrace SA 5000

WESTERN AUSTRALIA

Department of Conservation and Land Management
PO Box 104
Como WA 6152
(09) 367 6333

Perth Zoo
20 Labouchere Road
South Perth WA 6151
(09) 367 7988

RSPCA
99a Albany Road
Victoria Park WA 6100
(09) 362 3711

FRF (Fauna Rehabilitation Foundation)
Lot 65
Camboon Road
Malaga WA 6062
(09) 249 3434

FAWNA
(Fostering and Assistance for Wildlife Needing Aid)
Mrs R. Watts
140 Kent Street
Busselton WA 6280
(09) 752 2258

Wombaroo agent: Andrew Keefe
(09) 295 2349

QUEENSLAND

National Parks and Wildlife Service
PO Box 190
North Quay Qld 4001
(07) 22 7411

RSPCA
301 Fairfield Road
Fairfield Qld 4103
(07) 48 0522

Wombaroo agent: Allan O'Grady
(07) 357 7849

ONARR
(Orphaned Native Animal Rear and Release Programme)
PO Box 15
Darra Qld 4076
(07) 379 8514, or (07) 376 1160

Inala Community Conservation Association
71 Fernlea Avenue
Scarborough Qld 4020
(07) 203 5169

Southeast Queensland Herpetologists
c/o 9 Grey Street
Ipswich Qld 4305

Cape York Herpetological Society
c/o Wild World
PO Box 88
Cairns Qld 4870

TASMANIA

National Parks and Wildlife Service
PO Box 210
Sandy Bay Tas. 7005
(002) 30 2620

RSPCA
PO Box 1024
Launceston Tas. 7250
(003) 31 3044

NORTHERN TERRITORY

Conservation Commission of Northern Territory
PO Box 1046
Alice Springs NT 5750
(089) 50 8211

Territory Wildlife Park
Cox Peninsula Road
Berry Springs NT 0837
(089) 88 6000

RSPCA
PO Box 40034
Casuarina NT 0810
(089) 84 3795

INDEX